The Parenting Map

Step-by-Step Solutions to
Consciously Create the Ultimate
Parent-Child Relationship

DR. SHEFALI

HarperOne
An Imprint of HarperCollinsPublishers

THE PARENTING MAP. Copyright © 2023 by Shefali Tsabary. All rights reserved.
Printed in the United States of America. No part of this book may be used or
reproduced in any manner whatsoever without written permission except in the
case of brief quotations embodied in critical articles and reviews. For information,
address HarperCollins Publishers, 195 Broadway, New York, NY 10007.

HarperCollins books may be purchased for educational, business, or sales
promotional use. For information, please email the Special Markets Department
at SPsales@harpercollins.com.

FIRST HARPERCOLLINS PAPERBACK PUBLISHED IN 2024

Designed by Terry McGrath
Unless otherwise noted, illustrations by Riley Johnston & Andrea Daniel, Andreadaniel.art.
Illustrations on page 130 by M.Style/Shutterstock.com.

Library of Congress Cataloging-in-Publication Data is available upon request.

ISBN 978-0-06-326794-7

24 25 26 27 28 LBC 5 4 3 2 1

May this book serve as a wake-up call to all of us parents,
so we realize that our children are never ours to own,
nor to control, manage, produce, or create.
Their presence is bestowed upon us for one reason only:
to ignite our own inner prophetic and profound revolution.
May we all heed this call
so that we can free them—
to be.

My child . . .

I feel no pain greater than your heartache,
No joy greater than your triumph,
No agitation greater than your tumult,
No despair greater than your desertion.

There is no emotion compared to what you invoke,
No experience that comes near parenting you,
No journey I would rather take than by your side,
No adventure I would rather choose than to watch you grow.

You, my dear child, are my greatest teacher.
Through you I learn how to love without control,
To caretake without possession,
And to raise myself before I raise you.

In the face of your astounding radiance, I realize I am nothing.
Yet the fact that you exist suggests that I am everything—
As expansive as your heart
And as limitless as your potential.

There is nothing I can give you
For you already house the sun within,
Iridescent and prismatic,
Inexhaustible and powerful beyond measure.

I may give you birth and hearth,
But without a doubt, it is you who have given me life
And an awakening I could never have imagined on my own.
And therefore, it is you who are my ultimate soul retriever.

Contents

Preface

"I just don't know what to do! All I know is that whatever I am doing is just not working anymore!" Diane's eyes were swollen with tears of helplessness and frustration. Her body was stooped over, and her hands were shaking uncontrollably. She was talking about the trials she was experiencing with her nine-year-old son, who was becoming increasingly aggressive and withdrawn. She didn't know where to turn. Was it his addiction to social media that had created this change in her son? Or his peer circle? Or school pressures? Or his dominating baseball coach? Or was *she* the cause—and the fact that she was busy with her four-year-old daughter, who had her own challenges? What was the problem? How could she fix the situation? Diane was tired of the daily battles—all that arguing and fighting. How had things come to this? She was at a complete dead end.

Mirrored in her desolation was the desperation of a thousand parents with whom I have worked over the decades. In fact, I could even see myself in her heartache. I could completely relate to her panic and her trembling fears about losing connection with her kid. Her words echoed all the times I have felt myself in a total deadlock with my daughter, Maia. If you are a parent, I bet you, too, can relate to the dejection of feeling you are at an impasse with your kids but just don't know how to turn the situation around. Or that sinking feeling that no matter how hard you try, you just cannot reach them in the ways you wish you could. Diane was at a stalemate, and she was exhausted from banging her head against the wall. She was burned out.

Like Diane, most parents are desperate to improve or "fix" their relationship with their kids. For many of us, this is our most important relationship, bar none. When our relationships with our kids suffer, we suffer. Few things bother us more than the relationship with our kids going awry. We would do anything to help them feel supported and connected to us, but many of us just don't know *how* to achieve this. I truly believe that, no matter their age, race, or income level, every single parent has experienced something like Diane's tribulations. We have all been there, done that. This is the nature of parenting—it often feels as if we are lost at sea without a compass.

As I do with many parents, I helped Diane with a step-by-step plan to recover and renew her relationship with her son. After many breakthroughs, Diane was able to learn new strategies to transform her relationship with her son from chaos to connection. Watching their relationship unfold into a joyful and empowered one was deeply heartwarming. This is the reason I am so passionate about my work in helping parents become more conscious, as it creates metamorphic shifts in their relationships with their kids. Bearing witness to these shifts is truly one of the most rewarding gifts ever.

There were days during my daughter's childhood when I felt utterly clueless and helpless and didn't know where to turn. I felt I was failing miserably at parenting her, which in turn made me feel lonely and terribly guilty. The predictable cycle would go as follows: she did something I didn't like, I got upset, I yelled or was mean, she cried, and I felt guilty. Feeling guilty led me to overcompensate and indulge her, which allowed her to take advantage of my softness, which led to my dropping my boundaries again and her not listening—yet again. The cycles were so predictable that it was tragic. I felt disconnected and hopeless. Even more, I felt enraged and resentful. I knew that this was not a good sign at all. I desperately needed to fix this situation.

It wasn't until I began to develop the approach of conscious parenting that I broke out of my endless negative cycles and began anew. By implementing the tools and strategies of this amazing approach,

I began to find my way back to the path of a joyful and renewed connection with my daughter. By offering me a road map, conscious parenting literally saved my relationship with her. I was no longer floating at sea but instead had a concrete direction forward to build a powerful and deep relationship with her.

I get the pains and joys of parenting. I have been engaged in it for more than twenty years now, both personally and professionally, and have smelled its roses and felt its thorns almost every single day. Our love for our kids can take our breath away—both in its limitless expansiveness and in its heartbreaking anxiety. It is the perfect cocktail of the most piercing adoration and the most excruciating fear. This is what our kids do to our souls: they expand them as never before, but also twist them to a pulp and throw a dagger at them. Then they walk away without even noticing.

I never thought such a cocktail of *love* and *fear* was even possible until I became a mom. I didn't realize that having children could take so much out of us. Kids drain us almost 24-7 not just on a financial and energy level, but also on an emotional and psychological level. Children have a 360-degree impact—all around us, all the time, and potentially for the rest of our lives. The enormity of this burden didn't hit me until I was a mom myself. Before that I was clueless as to what was really involved. I was buying the Hallmark version of motherhood—the "birthday cakes, puppy dogs, and playing in the park" version.

You see, no one tells us about the *other* side of parenthood and what it does to us parents on a psychological level. I don't believe any of us knew about the "dark side" before parenthood. We didn't know about all the times we would be rendered absolutely helpless and clueless about how to handle the myriad of situations that parenting throws at us. Maybe our kids are being bullied, or cannot keep up at school, or don't fit in with their peers, or refuse to go to college, or are being abused by an intimate partner. No one gives us a tool kit for these heartbreaking situations, do they? No, we are left to our own poorly conceived devices. Certainly no one warns us about how devastated we might feel when our kids reject us, our influence, or our authority, or how immaturely we might react in response to this rejection. Nope, we are thrown into the high seas of this emotional relationship—perhaps the *most* emotional one of our lives—without a paddle, life jacket, or map.

I have been helping parents for twenty-five years now, holding their hands through their highs and lows. And through it all, I have been humbled by this unique, all-encompassing relationship that never fails to expose the universality of the human experience. As both a professional and a mom myself, I have developed a very specific approach to helping parents and children heal: *conscious parenting*. My first book on this topic, *The Conscious Parent*, was published in 2010. A *New York Times* bestseller, it was prefaced by His Holiness the Dalai Lama, endorsed by Eckhart Tolle, and hailed by Oprah Winfrey as revolutionary. Since then, I have written three other bestselling parenting books. You might be wondering why this one is so different. Here is the reason: My previous parenting books have been instrumental in outlining the *what* and the *why* of conscious parenting. This book is the answer to the *how*. I have been asked over and over again to give parents a *map* so they can follow a step-by-step approach to transform their relationship with their kids. Well, here it is—the map that parents have been waiting for.

I don't know about you, but when it actually came to parenting my own child, I had no clue. Sure, I had helped hundreds of parents by then, but that experience had little bearing on parenting my own child. It's a whole different story when it's our own kid we're dealing with, isn't it? We can all be experts about other people's lives, but when it comes to our own, it isn't as easy, for sure!

I can honestly tell you that if I had not followed the principles of conscious parenting, not only would I have destroyed my child's sense of worth, but I also would have been an extremely unhappy and unfulfilled human. That's why I've written this book, to give you what I wish I had had when I was a young mother—a concrete guide on *how to* parent your kids.

Let me forewarn you: what you are about to read is life-changing. By the time you are done with this book, it is quite likely that your entire perspective on yourself and those you love could be turned on its head. Therefore, this could be a challenging read. You will discover things about yourself that could potentially blow your mind to pieces, so to speak. Nothing might be the same after you read this book. I've been told that all my books are revolutionary in this way. Why? They are paradigm busters, culture shifters, matrix transformers. My books challenge the status quo. They poke at your limiting beliefs and expose your dysfunctions. They shred every false fantasy you have had about yourself, your kids, and your life, forcing you to confront your reality in its naked brutality. My books urge you to wake up and break out of all your life-draining patterns.

This kind of book requires the reader to be brave, daring, and truth-seeking. The fact that you have read this far means that you already have these qualities. Don't give up when the words in this book expose or poke a place of raw pain. Take a moment. Reflect on what is coming up for you. The words are meant to provoke, stir, shift, shake, and spur you to think and act in brand-new ways. Our children deserve parents who are courageous enough to discard old ways of being and doing—and who embrace new ways of connecting to their kids. You can be that parent. The fact that you picked up this book means you already are.

As parents, we are at a critical juncture in time. Never before have we had to compete with the pressures of such a fast-paced technological world. Our parents had fears about our future success, but today's parents have these fears on steroids. We see the world changing so fast around us that we ourselves cannot keep pace. We are filled with a sense of helplessness and dread. What do we do with these fears? We convert them into high expectations and put pressure on our kids to be even more perfect than we were expected to be. Our kids feel that pressure—boy, do they feel it! The proof is in the pudding: mental health disorders are on the rise at never-before-seen levels with no prospect of decline. Our teens are committing self-harm and suicide at alarming rates. Anxiety and depression among our youth have reached untold levels. Our children are in trouble, and we often feel like helpless bystanders.

But here is the truth: we are not helpless, and we don't have to be bystanders. There is a lot we can do; we just need to know how. These pages will help. They will show you how you can clear the debris from your relationship with your kids and start building a new foundation—one where you as a parent feel both empowered and connected. If you begin to follow the steps laid out in this book, you will gradually (and sometimes immediately) begin to witness seismic transformations in your dynamic with your children. The strategies of conscious parenting will be a beacon for you as you leave the dense jungle of confusion you may have been stuck in and move toward a brand-new connection with your children.

Conscious parenting is not for the fainthearted. It is for the brave and valorous. It is for the pattern disruptors and the bubble bursters—for the ones who dare to leave the crowd and begin anew, even if that means being alone for a while. As scary as it is—and I won't lie to you, it is scary—conscious parenting holds the promise of something never offered in parenting before: the embodiment of an authentic connection between yourself and your children that allows you to honor who it is you each are without needing to resort to manipulation or control. Conscious parenting speaks to a connection where you both can stand in your worth with ownership and celebration. If this kind of a connection is something that you have been yearning for, then this book is for you.

Just know that simply by being here, you have taken the first step toward a major transformation in your parenting and your life. Just by showing up, you have declared that your status quo is unacceptable. Remember, not all parents are able to heed the call of conscious parenting. But you are not just heeding the call—you are answering it.

Conscious parenting holds the power to give each one of us what we have always craved: a deep and abiding sense of inner worthiness. Isn't this longing to be truly seen and validated for our intrinsic selves something we all deeply desire? Each and every human yearns to feel free to be who they authentically are without judgment, guilt, or shame. Our children desire this deeply as well, and here is the amazing truth: conscious parenting can teach you how to meet this desire. When your children begin to be seen for who they are—separate from what society expects of them—you can rest assured that there is no greater gift they could ever receive than being allowed to be their authentic selves.

I thank you on their behalf.

Let's begin!

Introduction

The bond with your children is like no other.
It will do both—give you superpowers
And break your heart at the same time.
It will both expand you to an infinite limitlessness
And crush you to a pulp of nothingness at the same time.
It will ignite and inspire your creativity and imagination
And destroy your fantasies and dreams at the same time.
It will be your soul's biggest teacher and transformer
And your ego's ultimate nemesis and detonator at the same time.
It is here to enliven and elevate you to the greatest heights
And to yank and humble you to your lowest levels.
Only this bond has these powers
And it is the only bond for which you will allow
This degree of powerlessness.

Your relationship with your kids is like no other, for two reasons: (1) They are your complete responsibility—from the moment they are born until they are fully grown, and then some. (2) No two children are the same. For these two distinct reasons, this relationship is one of the most challenging, hair-raising, and complicated ones we will ever face. For it to survive and thrive, parents need to tend this relationship using a unique set of skills and tools.

Because they "come from you"—whether biologically or not—your children are your ultimate responsibility. For this reason, the level of your investment in and attachment to their well-being is off the charts. You don't have this kind of connection with any other human in your life, only with your children. This connection has the potential to create euphoric joy when things go well, but also great anxiety, frustration, and pain when they don't.

You can dump and run from other adults in your life. Friendships may be cut or fade away. Relationships end. Divorces happen. But your connection with your kids? Nope. They are yours, for better or worse; you are stuck with them. Your only two choices are to consciously embrace the arduous climb up the mountain—with all its missed turns, steep inclines, and exhaustion—or to fall off the cliff into the sharp abyss of disconnection.

The second reason this relationship is like no other is that they are "children." I put this word in quotes for a reason. Children are a unique category of human. They follow a different set of rules, have a different brain, and require a completely different language. I think we underestimate how great the differences are between us and them. We think, "How hard could it be? They are just smaller versions of us."

Children are *not* smaller versions of us. They are humans like us, sure, but the comparison ends there. On all other levels, there is no comparison. They are completely different. Because we don't equip ourselves with the tools to deal with this difference, we keep botching things up. Most adults aren't equipped to communicate in "Child." Did you ever attend a class in KidSpeak or learn about KidPsychology in high school? Sure, some of you may have taken a course in child psychology, but that does not compare with actually having your own children and learning their ways.

This brings us to the stark and brutal reality of parenting: no matter where we are in the cycle of raising our children, we experience the ginormous pressure of knowing they are our responsibility while also being fully aware that we desperately lack the skills to understand, communicate with, or connect to them with success.

To begin this path of growth and change, we need to acknowledge just how much we don't know. No amount of teaching will impact a student who isn't willing to learn. It all begins with an acceptance of our parental ignorance. A true honest embrace of this ignorance opens our hearts and minds to learning and growing. When we feel the pangs of discomfort, we don't simply walk away. Instead, we lean into the pain and the struggle so that we can transform ourselves.

The fact that we parents pretend that we know—or *should* know—all about how to raise these humans we call our children speaks to our mass parental delusion. So great is our desire to pretend that we are perfect and that everything is going as planned that when things don't go well, we hide our struggles from the world, suffering in silence and shame. We don't reach out for help, we don't share, we don't seek to learn, and we don't find new solutions. The result? Our children are the victims of our unwillingness to own up to our ignorance.

Here is the truth: we are not supposed to intuitively know how to raise children. You are not crazy for feeling crazy as a parent. You are not weird or "bad" for feeling totally inept and helpless. *You are not*. I want these words to sink in. You are not supposed to know.

The step-by-step map that I outline in the following pages is about to reverse all of this. It will teach you, the parent, the *how-to* of conscious parenting in a guided and gentle way. As you implement these steps, you will transform your mindset, your approach, and your communication. Once you've done so, your entire relationship with your kids will change—as will your relationship with yourself.

I have outlined three key stages in this book. Each involves growth within a different aspect of you as a parent. The first stage is called "From Frustration to Clarity." This stage begins with clearing up your mindset and beliefs. We parents are deeply indoctrinated with cultural beliefs about who and how our children should be. These beliefs cause us to impose standards and expectations on our kids that often mar our ability to connect with their authentic selves. It's only when we change at this level that we will be equipped to go deeper.

The second stage is called "From Dysfunctional Patterns to Conscious Choice." Here I expose you to the ways in which your past patterns have conditioned you into lifestyles and decisions without your conscious awareness. You will learn how to disrupt these patterns so that you can begin to make new, empowered, and conscious choices that feel authentic to who you are in the here and now. As this happens, your connection to your children will flourish in direct and powerful ways.

The third stage is called "From Conflict to Connection." This is all about building a more connected relationship with your kids. You'll learn how to understand your kids better so that you can decode their communication and forge a deeper bond with them.

Within each stage, there are steps you can follow to help you reach your goals. Change doesn't happen overnight. It occurs through tiny steps along the way. As you read through the book, it is quite likely that you will feel a nauseating sense of guilt and shame as you remember past moments when you messed things up. Please be aware that these feelings are normal and natural. I strongly urge you to have compassion for yourself when these feelings emerge. As Maya Angelou once wrote, "Do the best you can until you know better. Then when you know better, do better." Have loving kindness toward yourself. And remember, above all, that it is precisely those moments of unconsciousness that have brought you to this moment, when you are reading these pages. The past is the past, but it is this present moment that matters the most. And you are here right now, reading this powerful message—what an act of courage, indeed.

Have patience with yourself as you read these pages, as change often takes time. You are not only trying to change your dynamic with your children, but also altering the dynamics of generations past. For this reason, go easy on yourself. There is no perfect destination that we need to reach, nor any race we need to win. You are displaying tremendous grace just by being here. I am with you all the way, cheering your new awareness and growing transformations. We are in this together.

And just remember this as you go forward: no parent is perfect. There is no such thing. We may project perfection onto others, but as a therapist who has worked with thousands of parents, I can confidently say that not one of us is flawless. On the contrary, each and every one of us is plagued with confusion and doubt. And if you project any sort of perfection onto me, let me dispel this myth immediately and tell you that the very reason I help others is that I desperately seek that help for myself. Therefore, I am one with you. I have had feelings similar to yours—as have all parents, all over the world. Parenting is a ubiquitous dilemma; hence, the profound and pivotal need for the parenting map that this book offers.

On to the first stage of this journey—"From Frustration to Clarity."

STAGE ONE

From Frustration to Clarity

It is with you, my child, that I desired perfection.
Oh, what a fool I was indeed,
For it is you who have exposed to me
That not only is perfection simply impossible
But to yearn for it is my delusion.

TRUTH IS, if you are a parent, you are going to have major f—ups. Colossal ones. There is no escaping this fate. In fact, it is highly probable that in no other relationship will you screw up as much as you do with your children.

Here is the reason: our kids are with us around the clock during their most pivotal years—years when we ourselves are still evolving and coming to understand ourselves. Most of us are still emotionally immature and naive at this stage. So this is the deadly combo: our children need us to be at our best during their formative years, but we are likely still forming ourselves and aren't yet the best versions of ourselves—maybe not even our half-best versions. Right here, in this mismatch, is the major problem. Our children are unformed in all ways, and we as parents are very much works in progress as well. This discrepancy is inevitable and unavoidable. Blame nature.

So the reality is that there isn't a parent I know who hasn't made major mistakes. Not one! So if you are feeling guilt or shame around your own parenting, you can breathe a sigh of relief. This is not about being perfect, or even great. It's about becoming aware and conscious.

Becoming conscious means understanding the core reasons why we struggle. Why, for example, did you lose it and stomp like a three-year-old or yell like a crazy teen? The point is not to *never* have these crazy moments. The point is to understand the *why*. This understanding not only leads to a lot fewer crazy blow-ups, but also—and even better—enables us to grasp why they happen in the first place. Imagine understanding why a six-month-old who's not sleeping brought you to your knees in tears. Or why a five-year-old's meltdown had you saying something you immediately regretted. Or why a snarky retort by your teenager left you having a tantrum as big as the one your seven-year-old had the other day.

So in order to do a better job of parenting, we need to start at the *why*. If we don't understand the why, we won't be able to understand the *how*. If we aren't clear about the reasons *why* we f— things up, then how can we create change? Just as with our physical aches and pains, first we need to understand why we are hurting and then try to medicate the condition. This is what this stage is about: understanding.

The map I have laid out is the one I followed in my own parenting. It took me time to go through the stages and learn the steps. Through trial and error, through endless detours and missteps, I finally began to change my ways. As a result, I managed to shift from being a fear-ridden control freak to being a peaceful and joyful parent. Parenting went from being stressful to being fun. And the greatest prize of all? My daughter increasingly stepped into her own inner worth and power, undeterred from authentically expressing herself, equally joyful in her ordinariness as she was in her excellence. Most of all, the arguments and conflicts dissipated. The less controlling I was, the less she needed to push back. Soon we began to flow with each other with greater ease and confidence.

This approach to parenting takes patience and courage. Each step will bring you closer to your inner truth and healing. With each unfolding, you will not only come home to your own essence but will stop blocking your child from entering theirs. Until you make the journey, both of you will live encumbered and enslaved to old patterns and generational wounds. This method breaks your ingrained ways of being; helps you to step into a new you; and, in turn, sets your children free.

Are you ready? Take a deep breath—let's go!

Step One:
Focus on the Right Problem

I tried to micromanage your moods
And fix your feelings
And dominate your destiny
And control your soul
Until I realized I was all confused.
It wasn't you who needed any solving.
The person with the problem was me!

I am still traumatized by an experience I had with my daughter when she was three years old. It's so clearly imprinted in my mind that it could have happened yesterday. It was only after many encounters with parents that I discovered that my experience was pretty common. Ah, if only I had known that back then; I wouldn't have felt like such a loser!

It was time to leave the park, as I had to prepare dinner. I had given myself plenty of cushion to allow for child-induced delays and protests. I thought I was prepared, but really, nothing could have prepared me for the mayhem that ensued. She absolutely, vehemently refused to leave the park. When it was time to go, my daughter morphed from a sweet, playful little angel into a possessed demon. Ever had that happen to you? Where one moment your kid seems normal and then the next they turn into a stark raving lunatic? Well, this was my first time. To say I was utterly shocked, embarrassed, and mortified would be an understatement.

My daughter literally screamed. No, she screeched, wailed, howled, shrieked, roared, and yowled for the entire twenty-minute walk home. I had to put her in the stroller when she refused to leave the park. The way she protested, you would have thought the stroller was an electric chair. With arms flailing and body stiff, she turned every head on the street. Accusatory eyes bore into me as strangers convicted me of being the worst mother alive. She didn't let up. I thought she would pass out from fatigue. But nope, she got louder and more vociferous. Every second felt like torture.

I tried many desperate tactics. I distracted, yelled, muttered, moaned, groaned, cried, cursed, and panicked. Nothing worked. I paused, sang, soothed, comforted, threatened, and bribed. I used my scary voice, my sweet voice, my angry voice, my kind voice. I teased, joked, and cajoled. I tried logic and reason. Finally, I just let go and surrendered to my fate down the walk of shame back home. It was the longest twenty minutes of my life. I sobbed every long millisecond of it. This was the most humbling moment of my life.

By the time I got home, my daughter had won. She had managed to convert me into a puddle on the floor. I entered the front door and dropped to my knees, howling. I had a ten-minute pity party. "I am the worst mother alive," I thought. "I should be taken to a torture chamber and burned as a witch." When the helplessness and panic I had experienced rose like lava in my body, I let out a blood-curdling scream of rage and frustration. Her father whisked my daughter out of earshot and in a voice of disdain told me to get a grip—inducing even more shame and panic. I left the house and went on a long, long walk.

That was a turning point in my life. On that walk, I finally confronted the sobering reality that I literally had zero idea how to emotionally manage my child's moods, thoughts, and emotions. Zero. It was then that I realized that my child had—and possibly all children have—the capacity to render a parent helpless, and it is this helplessness that invokes rage and insanity in the parent. The problem isn't so much the child's behavior, but what it evokes in the parent.

I felt a shudder of truth reverberate within me. I saw the light. My reactions that day had had *nothing* to do with my child. Nothing. She was just being herself—a child who wanted to play longer. Every single thought, feeling, and behavior I had exhibited had to do with something deep inside me. *It was all me!*

I began to cry. Images of myself as a child entered my mind's eye. I saw myself as a helpless little girl, desperate for control in her world. I saw myself as a little girl seeking validation and worth from her parents and teachers. That little girl was insecure and uncertain, craving attention and power from the adults in her world. She was so lost.

I realized that my three-year-old child had evoked an old wound within me. When she didn't listen to me that day and refused to bend to my will, she ignited a sense of helplessness. I felt ineffective and powerless, just as I had as a child. Old wounds resurfaced and blinded me. I was in a state of panic, trying to rescue the little girl inside me. As a result, I viewed my "real" child as an enemy to be conquered. I lost all semblance of empathy toward her or any awareness of her struggles. The little girl in me had taken over and made things all about her. She just wanted to win, win, win, at all costs.

So strong was the pain from my childhood that it had catapulted me into survival mode. My child's will had clashed with mine, and the clash had invoked terror. I wanted to have control over her, and when she didn't submit to my domination, I lost my mind. I had immediately made her "bad" and an enemy—so much so that I wanted to run away and abandon her. Waves of guilt rose to the surface. I felt so much embarrassment and shame. I couldn't believe that I was capable of such brutal coldness.

Then it hit me like a ton of bricks: It was not "me" per se who had reacted that way. It was something within me that had been buried deep—a part of me that I had had little conscious awareness of. It was my wounded little-girl self. You see, there is an emotional separation that exists between the present and the past that is pivotal to understanding my reaction. I was reacting to the present moment on the basis of wounds from my own childhood. And these old wounds were just that—old. They were from the past. This awareness was like a lightning strike. It jolted me into a state of awakening. Everything became clear in that one moment, and the seeds of conscious parenting were sown.

When I tell clients, "Your kid is not the problem," I'm met with immediate resistance.

They demand, "So who is the problem?"

When I say, "You are!" I observe an immediate shutting down.

Listen, I get it. To be told that you may be the problem in your own parenting is a bitter pill to swallow. However, to realize this truth is the first step in conscious parenting. Until now, because of the traditional parental model we have all been raised with, we have been trained to make the child the focus of parenting. This approach is faulty and toxic. The focus of parenting needs to be the parent, *not the child*. If the focus were supposed to be on the child, parenting would be called "childing."

When I speak before audiences, this message is often met with resistance. People say things such as "That sounds so conceited!" or "What do you mean, parenting is all about me, me, me? Are you trying to say it is our fault?" You may be thinking, "How the heck is it my responsibility that my kid has ADHD or has nonstop tantrums?"

or "What do I have to do with my kid having social anxiety?" We parents detest feeling blamed or judged. We take our identity of "parent" so seriously that any attack feels injurious to our fragile egos, even blasphemous. How dare anyone insinuate that we're contributing to our kids' problems—*no way!*

Like many of you, I also had wrong ideas about being a mom before I became one. I thought that if I just focused on and loved my kid, everything would be all right. I thought focusing on my kid was what it meant to be a "good" parent. The idea of *not* focusing on my daughter felt self-absorbed and selfish. But I am about to show you how topsy-turvy this perspective is and how our focus on our children is actually detrimental.

Culture has totally messed us up, brainwashing us to believe that a good parent is one whose entire focus is on raising the perfect kid. We believe we are supposed to create, curate, and produce the perfect child with the perfect childhood. So much pressure, right? When we fall short, we immediately feel tremendous shame and guilt.

Do you know what a burden both you and your kids feel with these unachievable expectations? We parents feel that we should spawn and grow a kid who is creative, artistic, musical, athletic, intellectual, kind, social, adventurous, and—to top it all off—happy all the time. We have been so deluded by culture and our own massive egos that we actually believe that we are so special that we can pull all this off.

Then reality hits. We realize that we aren't that powerful and our kid is not so super-this or super-that. We realize that they are, dare I say, average. But because culture has told us that average is unacceptable, we feel—and place on our kids—the unreasonable, Herculean burden of being extraordinary. All this pressure arises from a fundamental belief system that is toxic: the belief that *good parenting is about raising a superstar kid.*

As long as you think good parenting is about "fixing" kids, you will micromanage the living daylights out of them. You will try to manipulate and change them. And you know what happens when we try to change anyone other than ourselves, right? We fail, crash, and burn.

If you are a day over forty years old, you have probably realized by now that the only person you can change is yourself. So it is with parenting. But here is the real danger. Because parents have been told that one of their major missions is to *fix the kids*, guess what happens when our kids don't comply? We feel helpless and then enraged. We yell, scream, and punish them—and we feel justified. We believe that it is our sacred duty and obligation to *fix our kids*.

Conscious parenting is the first model to expose the toxicity of this message, and for this reason it's a revolutionary model. Conscious parenting understands that the old model, with its unrealistic and harmful pressure to be perfect, sets up both the parent and the child to fail.

So what do we do instead?

We change the focus of parenting from *creating a kid* to a new focus. Do you know what that focus is?

You!

Your task is *creating a new you*. When you shift your focus, the entire game changes.

Imagine what a difference it would make if every parent knew from the outset that this journey was going to be about raising *themselves* rather than their kids. Parents would turn the spotlight on themselves and start working on becoming their best selves. Instead of trying to fix their kids, parents would try to fix themselves. They would understand that until and unless they re-parented themselves, they wouldn't truly be able to raise their kids.

When we focus on fixing and producing our children's childhood, we are in the mode of managers and tyrants. We are taskmasters and control freaks. We act as our children's bosses. In short, we are nightmares to live with.

Conscious parenting changes this situation. By focusing on you, the parent, conscious parenting forces you to change your entire energy toward your kids. Instead of trying to control them, you work on connecting with them. Instead of trying to teach them, you learn from them. Instead of trying to lead them, you guide them. Instead of being their managers and bosses, you become their allies. Your entire energy and approach are fundamentally different.

This shift in focus embeds in you the new consciousness that parenting is not about what your kid does or doesn't do. It is about what *you* do in response. It's about what *you* feel in reaction. It's about how *you* emotionally cope with it all.

Here is where your past baggage comes into play. If your kid is having a meltdown or being disrespectful, what comes up within *you*? What thoughts pass through *your* mind? Do *you* want to yell or scream? Do *you* take it personally? Do *you* fight, flee, or freeze?

It's all about you.

Your parenting is precisely this—*yours*. It's not about your child's feelings, moods, or reactions. Not about whether they are A students or high school dropouts. Not about whether they are obedient, disrespectful, or happy. It's about you, and only you. You hold the power: it's in how *you* respond.

Here is one of our greatest mental flaws: we believe that the way we respond depends on our kid's behavior. This is where we are drastically erroneous, as most of our responses have nothing to do with our kids or their actions. Most of the time, our responses are completely disconnected from our kids or the situation we are in. They come from our past, and as such, we cannot even call them responses to the present moment—they are reactions to our past. Therefore, much of our disconnection to our kids comes from our level of healing from our past.

Your responses are all contingent on your own inner healing. The more healed you are from your own childhood wounds, the more consciously you will respond. This is the focus, crux, and heart of it all: your inner healing. Conscious parenting is a profoundly transformational process, almost a spiritual one, in which your children are your greatest awakeners. They expose you to your own inner lack and wounds. By mirroring your own inner self, your children reveal how you need to heal and grow.

As we've touched on, every conflict and discord with your kids isn't about them so much as it is about how you need to raise your own consciousness. It is about how much your past traumas and wounds affect your present emotional state of being. The more we have not healed our past baggage, the more our present moment is rife with pain and conflict. So when we look at our parenting issues as a mirror of this state of healing, or lack thereof, we begin to grow and evolve. Instead of fixing our kids, we begin to fix ourselves.

Parenting, then, becomes a precious and powerful vehicle for raising yourself to your next level of emotional integration and well-being.

More than any other beings, our children show us all the ways we are broken. The greater our desire is for them to be something other than who it is they naturally unfold into, the greater is our own inner lack. Wanting our children to be "great" indicates how "lesser-than" we feel within. Once we realize that our desires and expectations for our children emerge from our own internal consciousness, our entire relationship with them shifts.

As we heal from within, we begin to live in a more authentic state. This directly impacts our capacity to connect with our children. The more attuned we are to ourselves, the more attuned we are to them. The more abundant we feel within, the more abundant we see them as being. Our outer connection begins to mirror our internal connection to ourselves. This is the growth of a deep spiritual partnership with our children, in which slowly but surely it becomes clear to us that they raise us much more than we can ever raise them. Herein lies the power of this whole process. Turning the focus to our growth instead of theirs allows us to use every moment with them for our own awakening. Now, it is not about fixing or changing them, but about our own evolution.

Do you feel the power of this potential for your own healing and growth? If you do, you are ready to wake up and become a more conscious parent. Let's try to put the first step into practice.

PUTTING IT INTO PRACTICE

Realizing that your frustrations and conflicts with your kids are more about you and your past emotional wounds and childhood baggage than about them is a big step in shifting your connection with them. From blaming and shaming them, you move toward holding yourself accountable for your own reactions. Once you truly appreciate how your own issues have been playing a significant role in how you parent, you can shift your focus from your children to you yourself.

This exercise helps you to understand just how huge your own fears, wounds, dreams, and expectations from your own past are in this journey and how they have profound impact on your kids.

Complete this sentence: *I became a parent because . . .*

_____

_____

_____

Your answers are probably something like these:

I love kids.
I dreamed of being a mom (or dad).
I wanted a big family.
I wanted to be surrounded with love and acceptance.

What do your sentences begin with? Do they begin with the word "I"? If they do, then the reason you had children had little to do with them and all to do with your own hopes, dreams, and fantasies.

Why is this awareness important? It points to your parental ego, the *I*. It allows you to see that even before your kids were born, you were preloaded with needs, wishes, dreams, and expectations. Without any conscious awareness, you were ready to "dump" these on your kids—without even considering whether your dreams matched with who your kids truly are. Sit with this awareness for a moment, for it is a huge one. It allows you to see how you entered the parenting process with a heavy ego load that then began to color and frame all your consequent decisions about your children: how you praised or shamed them, how you felt disappointed or excited by them, and much more. All your decisions stemmed from how your expectations colored this process way before you became a parent.

Now let's do another exercise. Think about what stresses you about your kids. Complete the following sentence.

I feel stressed with my child because . . .

_____

_____

_____

How did you complete the sentence? What was the first word after "because"? Was it your daughter or son's name or the pronouns "he" or "she"? Or the name of someone else in your life? If so, you are attributing your stress to someone external to you. If it was any word other than "I," we have a problem and need to check whether we have the wrong focus. Let me show you through the example of my client Ellie, who was in constant conflict with her fourteen-year-old daughter, Becca. They argued incessantly. I asked Ellie to complete the sentence "I get stressed because . . ."

She replied, "Because Becca is a nightmare of a child. She is defiant and obstinate. She just doesn't listen to me." She then explained that she had tried all the parenting techniques that she had been raised with. She had tried yelling at her daughter, giving her time-outs, even grounding her. But nothing seemed to work. "She's just the most difficult child in the world. She literally makes my life a living nightmare!"

Do you see what I mean? All of Ellie's focus was on Becca and her behavior. As long as this continued, nothing was going to change. Only when Ellie realized that she was part of the cocreation of this dynamic could the situation change. Until then, she would keep perpetuating the toxic cycle.

I asked Ellie, "Do you want to change this dynamic?"

She almost yelled, "Yes! Why do you think I am so stressed?"

I continued, "To really change this, you are going to have to look at yourself!"

She was stunned. "Me? How is this my fault? Becca doesn't listen, doesn't do her chores, misses schoolwork. How is it my fault that she is lazy and disobedient?"

I replied, "Your connection with her is suffering, not flourishing. This has a huge effect on her mental well-being. You are part of this dynamic. Focus on this part of the problem, your disconnection."

I repeated the exercise with Ellie and asked her to complete the sentence "I am stressed with Becca because . . ." She replied, "I feel like a terrible failure! I expect her to be a particular way, and she always defies this. I feel totally inept around her. It's like I'm a nobody. It's like she hates me!" Finally, Ellie had shifted to the real focus of the dynamic—her own feelings.

As we continued therapy, Ellie was able to trace her feelings back to her own relationship with her mother. "My mom was never around. She was the CEO of her company and was always busy. I never felt I was important enough to get her attention. I tried to be the most obedient and hardworking daughter, but even then I just wasn't important enough for my mom to give me the attention I craved from her. I always felt as if I just wasn't good enough for her and that I was defective in some way." Through our sessions, Ellie was able to understand that she was craving attention and worth from her mother and was displacing these needs onto her daughter. When Becca defied her mother's authority over her or, worse still, ignored her altogether in a way many teenagers do, Ellie took it personally. Just as she had in childhood, she felt unattended, unworthy, and unloved. Instead of just understanding that Becca was going through a developmentally normal phase in her life, Ellie made it all about her own needs for power and significance. She was, in essence, projecting her own needs onto her unsuspecting child. She couldn't see that Becca was just being herself and wasn't responsible for tending to Ellie's unmet inner needs from her own childhood.

Through our work together, Ellie began to understand how she was not parented by her own mother in the way that she needed and this was now blocking her ability to parent her child. Ellie began to realize how her reactions to her daughter were fueled by her rage toward her mother. Once she saw this, she began to soothe that inner rage and shift from within. This inner re-parenting that she began to do for herself transformed not just her but her entire relationship with her daughter.

Now that you have a better understanding of how we can project our inner pain onto our children, let's try this exercise again. Complete the sentence, and see whether you are able to shift away from blaming your kids for your frustrations and instead get to the real feelings inside yourself.

I feel stressed with my child because . . .

When you can own that it is *you* who has feelings about your kid, mainly because your own fantasies and expectations from your past are not being met, you are beginning this path on the right foot. Once we arrive at this new awareness, we can begin to implant a new awareness of the "real" problem: ourselves. Now, instead of blaming our kids or trying to fix them, we can begin to ask questions that are more self-reflective and self-accounting, such as these:

Why am *I* feeling this way around my kid?
What within *me* feels fear and lack around my kid?
How is this moment with my kid reminding *me* of something past?
When have *I* felt similarly in other areas of my life?

When you are firmly planted in the awareness that parenting is about raising yourself, your muscle of self-reflection becomes finely honed. You are quickly able to turn the spotlight within and focus on your internal state of being. With each turn of the spotlight inward, your self-reflection muscle grows stronger. This is how the conscious parenting process helps us raise ourselves to a higher evolution: by using the parenting opportunities we are given to be more self-aware.

For the next few days, I challenge you to notice all the ways you blame your child for your stress and try to replace that blame with inner self-awareness. Ask yourself this pivotal question: "How is my inner emotional state from the past or present affecting my judgments about my kid's behavior?" Becoming aware of our inner projections onto our kids is a huge first step on our journey away from unconsciousness to consciousness.

Step Two:
Destroy the Fantasy

I had the script edited to perfection.
The actors were picked and the director chosen.
The set was ready and the lights were on.
The show was about to start.
Then you came along and stopped the production.
You didn't want to be in my movie.
You rejected the roles I had cast you in.
You tore the costumes and the masks,
You destroyed the stage and the set,
You burned my dreams for awards and glory
By insisting on being yourself.
I was forced to do the unthinkable.
I had to stampede my expectations

And ravage my fantasies.
Instead of writing a perfect script for you
And imagining a perfect future for your life
And dreaming perfect goals for you,
I burned it all into ashes,
And through this something unexpected occurred.
I salvaged something I didn't even know I had lost
. . . my own soul.

We parents are the consummate moviemakers. We are constantly in the preproduction process of writing scripts and choosing endings for our films. Some of these are short films that speak to a singular moment or event, and some are epics that cover the course of years. We don't even realize how many scripts play in our mind at one time. These movies mess up our mindsets big-time. Our scripts keep us stuck in fantasy and block our capacity to interact with our children as they authentically are. These scripts also inevitably lead to shattered expectations, as the films are never made.

There are so many movies that we parents conjure up in our fantasies:

My Exceptionally Gifted Child
Our Perfect Family Goes on Vacation
The Greatest Parent Saves the Day

Trilogies have been scripted, characters have been cast, and our names are painted across the director's chair—all before our child is even born. We have fine-tuned exactly who our children will be, how we will parent, and what our family will look like. Sorry to say, we parents aren't very imaginative. We all basically want the same thing—some version of perfection, unending happiness, and great success. Do you agree?

The child in our movie is nothing short of a genius. Our child "should" be someone who ends world poverty, finds the cure for cancer, fights the war on drugs, fixes the climate problem, or at the very

least becomes the next world leader or superstar—a Nelson Man-
dela, a Martin Luther King Jr., or an Oprah Winfrey—a mini-god.

In our fantasies, we order up the perfect child as if we are or-
dering a gourmet meal. Two scoops of Albert Einstein, a sprinkle of
Mahatma Gandhi, a dollop of Mother Teresa, a heaping spoonful of
Barack Obama, a taste of some celebrity talent—Adele, Tom Brady,
Leonardo DiCaprio, Julia Roberts, or Beyoncé. We are not picky, just
so long as our child incorporates a generous portion of whoever the
richest, smartest, and most successful people in the world are at the
time of our fantasy. Never mind that we were close to none of this
in our own lives; that reality has no bearing on our fantasy children.

Our ideal movie location is some version of a Disneyland theme
park. Here, children are happy all the time, love their parents all the
time, and are always compliant and grateful. They also have nice
manners, write thank-you cards by hand, voluntarily visit the sick,
do the dishes, flush the toilet, make their beds, eat vegetables, get
straight A's, and earn money by the age of thirteen—all without our
begging them.

I know you had fantasies. Each one of us had plenty of these before we were parents. That's why we traipsed into parenthood as
though it were the most glorious sunset, with a million dollars waiting for us at the end. Sometime after hour twenty-two, it hit us like
a ton of bricks that this ain't no picnic! No sunset, no million dollars,
no prize—nothing. This is a life sentence of toil and labor. We now
have a new boss in town, and there is no overtime pay. We are multi-
tasking laborers indentured to these relentless little taskmasters,
who have no mercy.

We were so foolish. We allowed our bubble of fantasy to grow
so monstrously large during those nine months of incubation that
it overtook our rational minds. We actually thought we were "producing" and "creating" angelic children who would be under our supreme control—like pets, or better still, like dolls or puppets. After
all, if we are raising them 24-7, doesn't this mean we own them?

We don't heap one activity after another on kids just because we want to "expose" them to the world's best opportunities. We do so because we want our fantasies to come true in some way. We want to go to at least one damn play where our kid is not just a tree in the background, one concert where we don't need to strain our eyes to catch a glimpse of them in the back row, or one game where they aren't on the bench lollygagging their time away.

No one becomes a parent believing that "I am going to raise a loser kid," or "I am going to spend the next eighteen years of my life begging my kid to take a shower, say thank you, clean up after themselves," or "I am going to suck at this parenting thing." Nah. We all have children because some delusion of grandeur is involved for both ourselves and our children. We are going to be great parents, and we are going to create great children.

Even after our prebirth fantasy films are destroyed by reality, we don't stop making movies in our heads. These projections and expectations continue to shift and evolve all the time. We remain loyal to our fantasies of perfection and greatness. We realize that parenting is hard, but we hold on to our visions that one day in the future—if we just control our kid hard enough—they will win a spelling bee, or some state championship, or even, if all the right ingredients are in place, an Oscar or an Olympic gold medal.

You know what I am saying is true on some level. Your poor kid just has to say that they enjoy banging on tables, and you buy them a drum set and enroll them in a music class. Or your kid likes to count to ten, and you enroll them in a math enrichment class. The fantasy of being a great parent is so strong within us that it comes out of its lurking shadows and overtakes us at the slightest provocation. Before we know it, we are that prototype of the dreaded "stage mom" or "soccer dad," screaming from the sidelines, totally out of control and tragic.

Children who grow up being forced into their parents' movies feel forever misplaced, misunderstood, and claustrophobic. They want to scream, "Hey, I just want to live my own life. Get me out of your movie!" But they cannot do so, because their roles have been cast from infancy and continue to be cast throughout their childhoods—and it is impossible to break free of these roles. Maybe you remember feeling this sort of maddening frustration in your own childhood, when you felt cast in a role you didn't want to play, but the stakes were too high to stop acting, so you just went along. You then grew into adulthood with this gnawing inner sense of inauthenticity and displacement.

It is because we were not fully seen and honored for who we authentically were as kids that we have this gnawing sense of inner lack, a void—so much so that we end up living our lives as foragers, desperately searching for something, someone, some accomplishment, or some possession to fill this unworthy space within us. Although the degree to which each of us experiences this craving and feels compelled to go on this quest differs, there is a common denominator within us all—our desperate desire to fill this inner void. We enter our parenting with this desperation and project it onto our kids. They now become our last salvation, our last-ditch effort to finally feel significant and worthy. This is the hallmark of the unconscious parenting that I am trying to reverse through this radically new approach. Your being here with me on this path demonstrates your own desire to move into a more conscious and self-fulfilled state of being.

The greater our desire for the perfect kid and the perfect life, the greater our sense of inner unworthiness. We don't realize how correlated these two elements of the psyche are, but they are deeply entwined and interrelated. If I read the movie scripts of all the parents I have ever worked with, I would find them to be pretty much the same. They all include this unconscious yearning for a "perfect life." Who doesn't want a great, perfect life? It would be amazing to have such a life. But as we all know, it's an illusion. There is no such thing. We want this outer sense of perfection because we want control. When things fall into place perfectly and predictably, we feel as if we are in control. And why do we want control? It gives us a feeling of comfort and safety. It allows us to feel successful.

This success makes us feel worthy. The less we feel worthy on the inside, the more we seek control and perfection on the outside. We try to control whatever we can on the outside—and of all the people in our lives, who are the ones we feel we can control the most? You guessed right: our little ones. We know we cannot control our partners or most anyone our own age. So we gun for the weak and vulnerable: our children. We begin with fantasies about how they will look, their names, their hobbies, their mannerisms, their qualities, their dreams, whom they will marry. Then we include ourselves. How will our children make us feel? How good, worthy, significant, and successful will we feel around them?

Every single pre-parent has the exact same fantasies. The more the pre-parent experiences a crippling inner lack, the more elaborate the fantasy, and the greater the turmoil when it doesn't come true.

Once our baby is born, everything is mapped out in detail, and the grooming begins. We paint the nursery; buy the toys; and begin to craft, control, and curate. We begin to poke, produce, and perfect our kids into the images of our fantasies. When they oblige us, we applaud them. When they protest or resist, we bristle, burn, and bury their spirits.

Realizing that we are creating movies out of our own inner desperation and lack is an important wake-up call for parents. It's also a bitter pill to swallow. Our ego wraps such a tight grip around our emotions that we lose all awareness of how we are being swept away. A perfect example is the situation of Lauren, one of my clients. She called me urgently one day to discuss her teenage son, Brian. She was ranting and raving on the phone about his inability to make the varsity basketball team. Lauren was horrified—livid, too. "All summer I begged him to practice and stay in shape, but he totally ignored me. He preferred to hang out with his friends and waste his time. And now he didn't get picked for the basketball team. He is going to have no activity after school and is just going to get into trouble. I am so mad at him." I could hear how torn she was and how she was taking everything personally.

Whenever we react to an external trigger with acute emotional intensity, especially when it involves our children, it's a clue that something deeper is going on. It takes bravery and insight to probe deeper. As a therapist, I am clued into this fact and can guide my clients to this reality. They often meet my feedback with resistance.

"Your anger is coming from a place deep within you, Lauren. It is not just about your son and basketball. It is probably about your own fantasy for his life," I explained.

Lauren was so shocked that she was at first speechless. "What do you mean, my fantasy? I didn't have a fantasy for him to be an athlete. It was always his idea. I am only upset with him because he has become a total loser. He could have joined the varsity team and even gotten a scholarship! That's how amazing he used to be at basketball. But now he has thrown it all away. That is why I am angry!"

Parents always have amazing ways of justifying their anger toward their kids, don't they? I know, because I used to be a master justifier myself. I, too, used rationales such as "I only yelled because I was worried"—about my daughter procrastinating at a task, or losing her wallet, or whatever. We never want to look within ourselves to see the real roots of our anger or panic.

I explained to Lauren that of course some disappointment was natural, but her level of anger belied something deeper going on within her. What was it? Why was she so angry at her son for giving up his basketball career? Had she fully bought into it herself? Was it part of her own vision for herself to be a basketball mom with a kid who was an athlete? Was her anger partly due to her fantasies for herself crashing? It took me a while to chip away at Lauren's defense that she was angry only because she cared.

I gently reminded her, "If you care, there are a million other ways to show it. You can empathize and be compassionate, but you are angry." After weeks of therapy, she finally relented and admitted, "I loved seeing him play. It made me so happy. He was so good at it. I was so proud of him. I could see his whole future ahead, and it was bright and successful. This made me feel like I was being a good parent. It made me feel so happy."

Finally, she owned that she was upset because her own feelings had been let down. She acknowledged her own egocentric agenda: "I want my kid to be an athlete because that makes me feel as if I have done a good job." Lauren slowly began to share some history from her childhood that began to put the puzzle together. "I always wanted to be an actor when I grew up, but I was never really good at acting. I was always chosen to be in crappy roles in the school plays, and I yearned to be the star. My parents never encouraged me. They told me that I could never succeed, so I buried my dream and became a pharmacist instead to make them proud. But I never forgot the feeling of rejection and their lack of support in helping me pursue my dreams."

As soon as she said those words, she got it. She saw the connection. Her face changed, and she said, "Oh, my goodness! Do you think I have been so mad at my son because it is reminding me of all my old feelings of rejection and never being given the chance to pursue my dreams? Maybe he isn't even upset by this, but it's reminding me of all that I couldn't do as a kid?"

Lauren was able to see how her old wounds had resurfaced in her parenting. Without her conscious awareness, she had inadvertently placed great stock in her son's high school basketball career. Without realizing, she had become emotionally enmeshed and way more invested in his athletic choices than she realized. When he finally quit, she was unable to separate her own reaction from the situation so that she could be there for him in a conscious and connected manner.

I am sure many of you can relate to Lauren in some way. Perhaps you find yourself becoming inordinately upset by your child's choices and being unable to empathize with their own feelings about their life decisions. I certainly can remember many such moments when attachment to my own fantasies rose front and center and put me on an emotional roller coaster, rendering me unable to stay present and compassionate in the way my child needed me to be. I still remember the time when Maia chose to stop horseback riding after her very first competition, in which she did extremely well. I was devastated. I had so pictured myself as an equestrian mom riding in a trailer with beautiful horses in tow. And now that dream was squashed. She didn't even give me the chance to do it one more time. Darn kid! The only thing that saved me from yelling at her was conscious parenting. I had already written two books on the subject by then, so I knew that it wasn't her at all, but rather my own great expectations at play. But had it not been for all those years of awareness, I would have unleashed my fantasies onto her and made her feel guilty for not fulfilling what were really my own dreams.

When we become aware of the movies in our head, we do our children a great service. We not only stop playing out our self-created fantasies, but we absolve our children of guilt and shame for not making our fantasies come true. We release our children from the roles we cast them in, which are often not their voluntary choices, and instead help them to recast themselves in scripts that match who they truly are. In doing so, we finally free our children from the clutches of our claustrophobic fantasies and allow them, uncaged, to fly into a sky of endless possibilities for their own destiny and authentic essence.

PUTTING IT INTO PRACTICE

The reason for most of our conflicts, especially as parents, is the schism between our expectations and our reality. The greater the schism, the greater the conflicts. The next time you experience any inner turmoil and conflict about your children's decisions, don't blame them. The conflict likely has nothing to do with them but is really between your own fantasy and reality. This is where the schism lies.

So what do you need to do? You need to go within yourself and become honest about your movie and its scripts. The more unconscious expectations you have for your kids, the greater the potential for disappointment when they don't meet these expectations. This is not fair to your kids, is it? They have no idea what your fantasies are, let alone how to meet them. When we unconsciously operate from these movie scripts, we set our children and ourselves up for failure. Take a moment to write down your fantasy movie for your child:

What is the movie called?
Who are the characters?
What are their roles?
How does the movie end?

You can write out your fantasy movie and its script here:

_____

_____

_____

Next, in the spaces that follow, write down all the fantasies you've had for your kids in the left-hand column, and then write your actual reality in the right-hand column. For example, the columns might look like this:

Fantasy	Reality
My kid will be a star athlete	My kid doesn't like sports
My kid will be outgoing and friendly	My kid is shy and introverted
My kid will be a straight-A student	My kid has learning difficulties

Now, fill in your columns here:

Fantasy	Reality
_____	_____
_____	_____
_____	_____

Do you see how a large gap between fantasy and reality can create anxiety and stress within you? Imagine holding these fantasies and having none of them come true—it could feel heartbreaking. You might feel ashamed of your kid or, equally tragically, ashamed of yourself. You might think there is something really wrong with your child or with yourself. If you are unaware of your fantasies, you may live in a chronic state of disappointment and anxiety without even realizing why.

Once you have written down both your fantasies and your reality, ask yourself these questions:

> **Can I let these fantasies go with beautiful release?**
> **Can I accept my child and my reality as they are, without this movie?**
> **What feelings come up for me as I release my expectations?**
> **What about my reality is causing me fear and pain?**
> **Can I find joy and abundance in my children, just as they are?**

Letting go of our fantasy movies can be quite painful. But what we may find, once we accept our reality as it is instead of fighting it, is a greater sense of peace. Instead of blaming our kids for not acting out our fantasy movies, we can shift into finding ways to celebrate what is showing up for our children, without blame or shame.

Our children—just like us—deserve to live in a movie of their own making instead of one crafted by their parents or by the external world. When humans are allowed to carve out their own life experiences, based on their own authentic dreams and visions, they grow resilient and worthy. They see themselves as intrinsically "good enough." So it is with our children. Instead of feeling that they have to live according to our expectations or fantasies, they need to feel anchored in their own authentic relationship with themselves. When we parents drop our fantasies for our kids and allow them to embrace and embody their own life paths, we give them the inestimable gift of self-worth and self-celebration. It all begins with our commitment to becoming attuned to who our kids truly are, instead of molding them into a fantasy version of who we think they should be.

Step Three:
Relinquish Control!

To dance the line of taking care but not taking over
Is a perilous one indeed.
How to be there but not everywhere?
How to love but not smother?
How to walk beside but not overstep?
How to attune but not accost?
Ah, this is the art and heart of parenting.
It is the drama and the magic of it,
The ineffable mystery of it all.
No formula, no prediction, no comfort,
Only an unending tightrope of stepping into the unknown.

We parents are notoriously sanctimonious at claiming that the love we have for our children is of a rare variety and that we are the only ones who love our children the way we do. We often claim that everything we do is for our children's sake and that we are always motivated by the purest of intentions. I am here to burst this bubble. Ouch, this is about to hurt.

First, let me reassure you that you *do* love your kids, immeasurably. Perhaps you even love them more than you have ever loved anyone else. But here is the catch: a large part of your love is fueled by your thirst for—this is where it is going to poke you—control and possession. You think your love is true and unconditional, but it actually isn't. *It is mostly about some sort of control.* Until and unless you are willing to see this truth, your relationship with your kids will suffer. That's guaranteed.

In no other place is our need for control and possession more powerful than with our kids. We hold the subconscious belief that because we are given the charge of raising them 24-7, they are "ours." And, we believe, because they are ours, their thoughts, feelings, and behavior are also ours—in fact, more ours than our kids' own. We subconsciously expect our children to act as we wish them to and to live out their lives according to our agendas. When they don't, we go into control-freak mode and use all sorts of manipulation to get them to follow our ways. The most common tactics? Anger and punishment. When these don't work, then we may use the silent treatment, emotional withdrawal, or even neglect.

Think about it. Do you try to control the adults in your life the way you do your children? With adults, don't you think twice or even a dozen times? Aren't you nicer, more forgiving, and more patient? If a friend was late to a meal, forgot their keys at home, forgot to empty the dishwasher, or didn't spend time with you when you wanted, would you lose your mind? If they lost your favorite book or necklace, would you yell and scream at them? Would you shame and punish them, or take away your love or something they valued? I doubt you would do any of those things so readily with another adult. You would pause and seriously evaluate the consequences.

Why, once we become parents, don't we afford our children the same courtesy? If our child forgot their backpack, why do we yell and scream? If they lost their sweatshirt or phone, why do we punish and shame them? The only reason is that we think we own our children, and so we can. It's all about possession and control. And the tragic irony of it all? We believe that this is the right way to show our children love. We even call it "tough love."

Is love supposed to be "tough"? Does tough love feel good to you? It sure doesn't feel good to me. Do you want to receive "tough love" from your friends or partner? Why should love be about punishment and control? Why can't it be about empathy, compassion, communion, and connection? Love shouldn't come with control, and yet this is precisely what a large chunk of our parenting is about. Parental love traditionally isn't just pure and true love. It is love + possession + control.

This awareness about the controlling nature of our love is profound. Without it, we will remain stuck in manipulative tactics that diminish our children's sense of inner security and worth. You see, our children—no matter how small they are—have an inner knowing that they must be attuned to so that it can grow sturdy and consistent. How do we help this process? We eliminate our desire to control them and replace it with unconditional acceptance and attunement. It's a matter of asking, "Who are my kids truly, and what are their needs?" instead of "Who do I want my kids to be based on *my needs*?"

You may find yourself protesting, "How do I get my kid to do the right thing if I never control them or punish them?" This is a common parental war cry. It's as if the only thing we know how to do is control, or as if we believe that the only alternative to control is complete neglect—that if we chose to give our children the freedom to discover their own voices and destinies, they would throw themselves into an extreme reality show of *drugs, sex, and rock 'n' roll* (a stand-in for any antiestablishment behavior). Do you know why we parents feel this way? It is because we have been indoctrinated in a traditional *fear-blame-shame* model, in which we have been forced to suppress our own *rock 'n' roll* fantasies. Because we haven't integrated these suppressed parts of our own selves, we project this model onto our kids as well. We were raised in control and suppression, and so our greatest fear is to live without this control; hence, we control and suppress our kids.

I am *not* advocating a hands-off, passive approach to parenting. All I am talking about right now is the *mindset of control* and how this impacts our connection with our kids in a toxic way. The conscious parenting approach asks parents to become aware of their internal control mindsets and how they impose these agendas on their children.

Why is this awareness important? When our kids protest, instead of making them feel guilty about doing something contrary to our "love," we can empathize with them because *we* are now aware that we are the ones shoving our agendas down *their* throats. The way we encourage our children to play the piano versus the trombone, the way we push them to become skiers or basketball players when they are young—or to sing, dance, draw, or act—may have less to do with who our children are in their essence and much more to do with the fact that having our children do these things gives *us* a sense of control and significance.

When I got upset with my daughter and yelled at her for dropping horseback-riding classes after I had paid so much for them over the years, was the reason that I loved her or that I felt out of control and angry that my vision of who she needed to be hadn't come true? What about when I got angry at her in the fifth grade for not getting A's? Did I also get angry then because I loved her so much, or was the reason that I was losing control over my agenda of having a superachieving kid? And in every other moment when I got angry with her for not following my expectations, was my anger caused by my love or my need for control?

The truth is this: each and every time I have been upset with my daughter, it has been because of my need for control and power, not because of my love for her. When I expect things to go one way and they go another, I lose my cool. I can pretend it is because I love and care for her and that my anger is out of concern and caring, but this would be a boldfaced lie. The truth is that every expectation we have, every "should" we place on our children, and every need we have for them to be a certain way emerges first out of our own need for control.

Now you may say to me, "What about when my kid makes horrendous choices? When they slap their sibling, or steal from their teacher, or—worse still—take harmful substances?" My answer will be the same: Why are anger and control the solution? These emotions come from our own unmet expectations and crashed fantasies. Our anger and control are not going to fix the problem. The fix lies somewhere else. The fix is not to engender fear within our children so they don't make bad choices again, but to go deeper, to the root of the issue, and to ask, "What is beneath the problem behavior?" There are typically three main reasons for problematic behavior in children: (1) a lack of information, because they haven't had enough life experience to know as much factual data as we do; (2) a lack of skill, because their brains are not yet fully developed enough to allow them to make choices as we would; or (3) a lack of self-worth, because they feel afraid and anxious that we might reject or invalidate them.

All our issues with our kids can be turned around if we move away from anger and control and instead enter into a compassionate and deep inquiry into what is going on within them. Anger and control create separation and disconnection—period. If you are a parent who seeks to inculcate connection, these two toxicities of anger and control need to fade from your emotional repertoire.

Our need for control disguises itself so sneakily that it can be incredibly hard to detect at first. It covers itself up as care, concern, support, and parental protection. As parents, we have been off the hook from looking at ourselves in the mirror for so long that we can literally say that anything is love.

> **I want you to take violin lessons, even if you don't like them,** *because I love you.*
> **I'm only pushing you to become a doctor** *because I love you.*
> **I want you to grow your hair out** *because I love you.*
> **I called you fat the other day** *because I love you.*
> **I yelled at you the other day** *because I love you.*

And guess what? We really believe the things we say. It doesn't occur to us for a moment that our intentions come from anything other than love. After all, what else could they be coming from?

Looking beneath our "love" to the deeper agenda of control and manipulation is a painful process. It asks us to be self-reflective and brutally honest with ourselves. While we can couch anything as love, only the brave among us are willing to confront our subconscious agenda for control and significance. If and when we can see through our "love" to the underlying shadow of control, the quality of our relationships will begin to drastically change, from hierarchy and dominance to connection and reciprocity.

A really ironic thing happens when we are not in touch with our inner control demons. We parents end up feeling victimized by our children when they don't follow our ways. We are left to wonder why we ended up with the short end of the stick. The truth, however, is entirely the inverse. It's actually our kids who are victims of our controlling agendas and ways of being. They are often not doing anything to us or against us per se. They are just being kids. Sure, they can make wrong choices or be immature, but they are rarely doing so to attack us. But because we parents are not in touch with our insatiable inner need for control, we see reality in a topsy-turvy way and think of ourselves as the beleaguered victims!

Letting go of control is the hardest thing for parents to do. Let me make an important distinction here between being in charge and being in control. Letting go of control does *not* mean that you stop being in charge. It just means that you stop imposing control when your ways are violated. This is critical: being in charge and being in control are two different qualities. The former implies being responsible for your children's safety and care, whereas the latter implies holding them responsible for how they make *you* feel about it all. Being in charge involves no conditions, while being in control is riddled with them. This distinction will become clearer as we progress through this book.

PUTTING IT INTO PRACTICE

In order to activate a new consciousness around this idea of control versus love, you need to be clear with yourself. Each time you react negatively toward your children through anger, yelling, screaming, punishment, or emotional withdrawal, you are not acting out of love. No matter how you justify your reaction, this is not love. You may love your kid, but you are not expressing love in that moment. You are expressing a desire for control. So the next time you exhibit any of these behaviors, take a pause and reflect on these questions:

Why do I feel the need to have *my way*? Can I let this go?
Why do I feel the need to be right? Can I let this go?
Why do I feel threatened when my child acts in a way that's different from my agenda? Can I let this go?

When we unleash our control onto our children and silence their voices, we grossly undermine their sense of worthiness. We unwittingly engender disenfranchisement and crippling self-doubt. They begin to wonder, "Maybe I am not good enough or worthy enough to follow my own voice," or "Maybe I am so bad that I deserve to be treated this way." Instead of forging a strong bond, we create dysfunction in our dynamic with them. Remember: anytime fear is involved, there is some sort of disconnection. For true connection to occur, safety and the freedom to express ourselves as we are must be present.

As we reflect on ways in which our interactions with our kids are based on control, we not only stop unilaterally imposing our ways on them, but also begin to have empathy for the ways they have been stifled by this control. As you will learn later in this book, empathy is the cornerstone of connection and the basis of a strong relationship with your kids. Empathy can blossom only when there is no control.

Recognizing the conditional nature of our love is difficult for us as parents, but once we do, we can refrain from unleashing this conditionality onto our children. Here is a powerful exercise to expose the conditional nature of our love:

If my child behaves like _____, *then* I feel proud.

If my child behaves like _____, *then* I feel sad.

If my child behaves like _____, *then* I feel angry.

If my child behaves like _____, *then* I feel disappointed.

Doing this exercise will expose the "*if-then*" nature of your love and its underlying conditionality. In fact, I invite you to examine the many times in a day that you use "*if-then*" statements with your kids. You probably use these statements about a dozen times a day if not more. This kind of conditional control sets up a sense in our kids that their validity is based on pleasing us and being obedient to us. When they behave well, we give them praise and a sense of worth. When they don't, we withdraw our praise.

Don't be hard on yourself if you now see the conditional nature of your love. This doesn't make you a bad parent, just a human one. In fact, I would go so far as to say that most of us reach only conditional love. A rare few among us manage to touch unconditional love.

For most of us, this idea of unconditional love is a foreign concept. The reason is that most of us never received unconditional love from our parents. We were raised on "*if-then*" love and control, the *fear-blame-shame* model, so this is what we pass on to our kids. To change from control to unconditional love takes awareness and clarity. We first need to become aware of all the times we are in control, then make a conscious effort to drop that control. It takes practice and dedication to parent your kids in a way that you may never have experienced in your own childhood. Indeed, you may not have experienced such unconditional love ever in your life.

David and Marcia were struggling with the decision of their twelve-year-old daughter, Sonia, to quit her middle school gymnastics team. Sonia was one of the star performers. She had been engaging in professional gymnastics since she was in elementary school, taking part in all the local competitions. Her room was filled with cups, trophies, and medals. The couple knew all the other parents on her team; they were a big, happy family. Sonia's decision to quit was devastating to her parents. When they came to see me, they had hit a wall with Sonia. Although they had tried every manipulation strategy in the book, nothing seemed to be working. Sonia had completely withdrawn from them, and she had begun picking at her skin.

When they first came to see me, I was shocked at how frail Sonia was. She explained that everyone on the team was on a special diet and exercise regimen. Marcia piped in, "But it is all really healthy food! Sonia is going to thank us later." David then interrupted his wife and said in a frustrated voice, "We don't have time for small talk. Sonia has missed three weeks of practice. If she continues in this way, she will be kicked off the team. I just don't know if she will ever get back on track later. We are losing time here!"

When I asked Sonia why she was quitting, she was surprisingly clear and succinct: "I want to be a normal, regular kid. I don't want to spend six hours a day practicing gymnastics. I enjoyed it when it was fun, but it is not fun anymore. I am stressed out all the time. I don't get to hang out with my friends and do normal stuff like they all do. I am either studying, exercising, or practicing. I hate it. I am done!"

David once again jumped in. "This is not about fun, Sonia! This is about dedication and grit! I thought you understood that! Look how far you have come! If you quit now, then all of this will have gone to waste!"

Clearly the parents were struggling with this decision more than Sonia was. They were so attached to her in the role of gymnast that they were losing sight of who their child was or what she was expressing. I asked her parents just one question: "Why are you not able to listen to your child?" David and Marcia were dumbstruck. They had never asked themselves, "Why? Why couldn't we listen to our child?"

Most of the parents I have worked with share the unconscious belief that they hold the power over their child and should make decisions for them. When Sonia resisted their control, this couple didn't think to ask themselves, "Why are we controlling her?" Instead, they sought to control her more. I said, "Do you see how hard it can be to simply honor and accept your child's decisions? It's not your decision—it's hers! Hasn't she done this enough and succeeded at it enough? Where are you going with all of this? Should she have to do gymnastics for another ten years for you to feel okay with her quitting? When is enough enough?"

I was impassioned with these parents because I could see how blocked they were. Their child was in so much pain, yet they couldn't let go of their own beliefs. It can be challenging for parents to give up old patterns and accept that they need to change. You see, like most of us, David and Marcia saw only the worst ahead. They were gripped by fear that if their child did not continue with gymnastics, then she would end up with fewer options for college. Their movie of having a talented gymnast as a child—one who was exceptional, with medals and accolades—would not get made. They liked Sonia being a star, and they liked being the parents of a star.

David and Marcia believed that controlling their child was the only option they had to "save" their daughter from her "wrong" ways. They thought that if they pushed hard, she would cave in. They thought that control and manipulation were the only ways to engage with their child and correct her. What they failed to appreciate was that, in the present moment, *they* were causing her more pain than anything in the future ever could.

Do you see how our love is heavily tinged with control and fear? It is only when we are willing to look deep within ourselves at our unconscious fears that we may be willing to change our ways. When David and Marcia finally understood how their conditional love was hurting Sonia, they were able to release their control and enter a greater understanding of their child's reasoning and situation.

David and Marcia discovered that Sonia wanted to spend more time with new friends at school and that she also enjoyed drawing—a hobby she'd previously had no time for. Most of all, they discovered that their daughter wasn't just being flighty or irresponsible, but instead was being true to herself. Wasn't this a good thing? Once the parents saw their daughter through the lens of unconditional acceptance, free of power and dominance, they were able to connect with her in a compassionate way. The entire nature of the parenting dynamic began to change.

David and Marcia reframed Sonia's decision from being "wrong" and "fatal" to being a life-blossoming choice that let their daughter stretch her wings and embrace new pursuits. They began to see the value of allowing Sonia the freedom to know her own self and follow her own ways. They saw her lighten from the burden she had been under and finally flower into her more authentic self. Sonia began to have more friends and delve into other art forms. Although she didn't win any awards or trophies, she began to experience more joy, peace, fun, and contentment by just being a "regular" kid. Isn't this what we ultimately want for all our children?

Once we release our conditional approach toward our children, we can discover who they are at an entirely different level—a soul level. Instead of controlling them to suit our own plans, we get to understand who they are in a deeper and more transformational way. This kind of connection can occur only when a parent is willing to let go of the "*if-then*" conditional approach.

Step Four:
End the Chase for Happiness and Success

In my thirst for a feeling,
I ran through humans in graveyards
And shattered many hearts of glass
And smashed through dreams of stone,
All for a feeling . . .
Like an addict rummaging through garbage,
I chased happiness and success like they were drugs,
Until I got to the top of the mountain
And couldn't enjoy it
Because I was out of breath and out of soul
And my view was colored by the blood
Of the pain I had left in my wake.

One of the things that most disrupts our peace and joy as parents is the idea that our kids need to be both happy and successful. Nothing creates more stress and conflict between parent and child than these two notions. For this reason, until you become clear about the potential dangers of this mindset, you will not be able to embrace conscious parenting.

Ask any parent what their greatest wish is for their kid, and they will reflexively say, "I want my kid to be happy and successful." We don't even think through the deeper meaning of our reply. We act as if happiness and success are the holy grails of parenting. I am here to challenge these notions and introduce the idea that chasing these two goals is actually the primary cause of much stress and conflict in parenting.

First, the idea of wanting anything for anyone else is highly problematic. Wishing people well is one thing, but wanting them to be something specific—such as happy or successful—is controlling. Imagine that you are working toward a graduate degree and are struggling with it, and a friend comes up to you and, instead of understanding what you're going through, expresses disappointment about your struggle. She says, "I cannot believe you are not happy! I want you to be happy. Stop being sad." How would that feel? Or what if she said, "Why aren't you getting A's? Why are you doing so badly? This is unacceptable!" How would that feel?

I bet that her attitude would crush and hurt you tremendously. You would surely shut yourself off from her and shut down, wouldn't you? Well, this is precisely how we behave with our kids. So attached are we to wanting them to be happy and successful that we actually make them feel unworthy when they are not.

I can hear you protesting: "What is wrong with wanting our kids to be happy and have choices for success? That is what we want for our partners, our parents, and our friends, isn't it?" Here is the difference that parents need to be aware of: when we wish these things for our children, we aren't simply engaging in the passive well-wishing we offer to other people in our lives. Instead, these are active desires and expectations that we project onto our children. We box them in to our vision of what happiness and success look like, without giving them the freedom to explore, mess up, get sad, get angry, and learn the valuable lesson that the messiness and beauty of life go hand in hand.

Let's deconstruct this idea further. The first thing we need to understand is that, however well-intentioned we are, our desire for our kids to be happy and successful reeks of self-absorption. *We* want them to be happy and successful because then *we* feel happy and successful as parents. *We* feel competent and significant. Our desire is ultimately about how their success and happiness make *us* feel. How do I know this? Well, let a child show contentment with an activity that doesn't meet the parent's approval, and that parent is usually irritated, concerned, and unhappy. Sure, we want our children to be happy—so long as it conforms to our expectations. In truth, we want our children to obey and genuflect in obeisance. Their doing so lets *us* feel happy, believing that we have control and success as parents.

The next thing we need to understand is that the ideas of happiness and success are exactly that—ideas, and nothing more. Ask a hundred people to define either of these two concepts, and you will get a hundred different responses. The reason? These are subjective concepts, not objective phenomena. For this reason, to shove these two objectives into our parenting imposes unrealistic pressures and expectations, setting both us and our kids up for a sense of disappointment, if not failure.

Happiness, as we know, is transient. As life is complex and nuanced, to expect our children—or anyone—to be happy all the time is ludicrous. Success, too, is an esoteric idea determined by many complex qualifiers. For a new mom, success could mean having a sound sleep with her infant. For her best friend, a woman of the same age, success might be kicking her addiction to sugar or alcohol. For her sister, it could be learning a new language, whereas for her niece it could be solving an equation she hadn't been able to figure out the day before.

My point? Happiness and success are ideas we attach ourselves to without realizing that they are devoid of long-lasting meaning. But because of our blind attachment to them, whenever we see our kids unhappy or unsuccessful, we lose our minds. When we see our kids cry, we immediately want to take away their pain—for them, and for ourselves. When we see them failing at school, we want to punish or fix them. Our attachment to these two concepts—happiness and success—trips us up and causes us undue pain and suffering.

Again, these ideas about happiness and success are ingrained within us from childhood and are part of our culture. Our society is geared toward these ideas. We are addicted to them. Unless we realize how empty they are, we will continue to fall into the trap of wanting happiness and success for our kids and will suffer when they aren't embodying these qualities.

I can hear you protest in confusion: "So, are you saying that we shouldn't care when our kids are sad or failing at school? That sounds heartless!" This is the point I need you to gain clarity about. Caring for your kids doesn't mean that they need to turn into happy and successful beings or that it is your fault or responsibility if they aren't.

Caring for your kids means accepting them for who they are. If they are sad, then let them be sad. If they are angry, let them be angry. Or if they are struggling with math, let them struggle. Of course, we inquire about their issues and help them create solutions for their dilemmas—but we don't do so in service to an agenda of getting to a destination called "happiness and success."

Parents, I urge you to get off the train to happiness and success! There is no such destination, and if you don't disembark you will be on a never-ending quest, always searching and never finding. While we all want our kids to feel joyful in their lives, we need to realize that there is simply no human on earth who can feel this way every day. Everyone goes through periods in their lives when they feel fear, frustration, sadness, and failure. And guess what? This is normal. It is human. It is acceptable.

Teaching our kids about the inevitable messiness of life is far more valuable than teaching them to aspire to unattainable realities. When they embrace the notion that life is messy, they will be far more resilient than they would be if attached to the idea that life is supposed to lead to a utopia, replete with nonstop happiness and unabated success. When your kids expect life to be messy, they are not being set up for disappointment when this is precisely how life turns out to be. However, if your kid expects some sort of utopian fantasy to come true, they are going to be grossly upset when that fantasy doesn't pan out.

It is time to replace the idea of happiness and success with something entirely new and different. We need to move away from outcome goals to process goals. Instead, let's focus on something new: *presence and experience*. When we focus on *presence*, we focus on a state of aliveness and connection to the present moment. When we focus on *experience*, we focus on embracing whatever we are going through in the here and now. So whether our children are crying or smiling, our focus is less on judging and more on allowing them to experience an authentic relationship to that state of being. What is their inner connection to their life experiences? What are they learning? What inner transformations are they going through? When we focus on such qualitative moments, life stops being about a fixed outcome and is focused instead on our state of being. There are no "good" or "bad" feelings anymore, just feelings.

Presence and experience are process-oriented; in contrast, happiness and success are outcome-oriented. When we teach our kids to ride the process of life and ignore the outcome, they can release their internal pressures and enter a state of joy and calm. Parents can do so as well.

Focus on presence with your kids. Are they present? If they are, then that's all that matters. It doesn't matter if they are "happy" or "angry." What matters is that they are real and true to their present reality. It's not about the A grade or the bank account, but about the experiences our kids are undergoing. If they are experiencing their own lives in their own ways, it doesn't matter if that looks like X or like Y, so long as they are able to claim their experiences as their own.

Why is this new approach so important for parents to embrace? The reason is that it releases parents, as much as kids, from all the pressure. It allows parents to be more embracing of their kids' natural states of being and self-expression, without forcing them to be eternally cheerful or all-star geniuses. Accepting what is going on for your child—"Hey, my kid is struggling right now" or "My kid is not naturally inclined to math and calculus"—takes the pressure off and eases both parent and child into a flow state of existence rather than a pressure state.

Stacey had the hardest time letting go of her ten-year-old son, Josh, when he went to summer camp. It was his first summer away from her, and she was dreading the three months without him. So enmeshed was she with his emotional well-being that her moods were continually fused with his. On his end, Josh was equally co-dependent on his mother and wanted to be in constant touch with her from camp, reporting how he felt hour by hour and leaving the counselors perplexed about how to manage their relationships with him. When Stacey received an upbeat message from his counselor or saw Josh in an online photo album, she was instantly happier. When she didn't, her mood dipped. She was distracted and preoccupied with her son's mental state, 24-7.

Stacey, like many parents, believed she was responsible for giving her son a wonderful camp experience and childhood. She thought her mission as a parent was to manage his emotions and moods. When he had struggles, she took them on her shoulders and acted as though they were her own burdens. She was fully enmeshed with her son. His happiness meant her happiness. His sadness catapulted her into near depression.

I tried to help Stacey deconstruct the folly of her ways. "Who said kids need to be happy and successful all the time?" I asked her. "Who said it is our job to help them manage their feelings 24-7? Neither of these things is true." I explained to Stacey, "Your son is conditioned by you to be anxious about his moods and feelings. Because you are so focused on his feeling happy, you have made him feel as if anxiety or sadness is anathema. The truth is, these are just passing feelings that come and go if we allow them to. Because you panic every time his mood dips, so does he. You have taught him to be averse to his normal feelings. This aversion causes more agitation and anxiety. It is only when you can embrace all his feelings as just passing states of being that he will, too. Until then, you will both be caught up in a deadly state of fusion."

Stacey was in shock. "I panic every time he is upset. I cannot take it. I feel as if I am failing as a mom—like if he had a good mom, he would only feel good feelings. I remember never seeing my mom genuinely happy, and I was always scared when she would go into her dark room and just lie there. It would seem like years that she would be swallowed in gloom. No matter how hard I tried, I couldn't get her to feel happy. I always dread sad faces, because they trigger my memories of being alone and scared, wondering when the 'happy' mom would emerge from the room." And there we have it—the underlying reason for Stacey's enmeshment with her son. As we all have, Stacey had learned negative associations with big emotions in her childhood. She was raised by a mother who probably didn't know how to manage her own feelings, and this anxiety was passed on to her daughter—who was now passing it on to her son.

Through her work with me, Stacey was able to see how heavily she was relying on Josh to feel happy so that she could feel significant and successful. She was heavily dependent on him. Josh returned the favor by parasitically depending on his mom. He had no choice, really, as the dynamic between them forced him to fuse with her. As a young child, he picked up on her needs. Being the good son he was, he allowed himself to lose his own identity. Her son was now doing the same thing that Stacey had done in her own childhood.

When we believe that our kids should be happy and successful, it means that we think *we* should be happy and successful. It's because of *our* lack of inner happiness and an inner sense of worth that we project these needs onto our kids. When we work on our own inner connection, we stop using our kids to meet our own needs, and we let them have their own life experiences as they unfold without our control or interference.

It took Stacey a long time to learn this lesson, but she was eventually able to unfuse from her son when she saw that her over-dependence on his moods was constraining his freedom to be true to himself. Through much practice, she learned to stop checking up on him so many times a day and asking how he felt. After a few months of painful withdrawal, she began to tolerate the discomfort of not being enmeshed with him 24-7. While Josh still experiences much anxiety, he, too, is learning to rely on other strategies to meet his needs— friends, his therapist, and most important, his own inner guidance.

As much as we all want our children to experience happiness and success, we set ourselves up for failure and disappointment when we focus on that desire. Life is complex and—as I've said before— messy. Happiness comes and goes, and success is an ephemeral concept. Clinging to the desire for either of these is a surefire way to experience sadness when they do not manifest themselves. Let's dump these concepts in the garbage, where they belong. When we do, I can guarantee that we will experience great joy and liberation— and so will our kids.

PUTTING IT INTO PRACTICE

The next time your kid is in an unhappy state or is struggling at school in some way, I want you to watch what comes up for you. I want you to notice how it makes you feel. Are you able to hold space for their feelings of sadness and struggle, or do these feelings trigger you?

Handling our kids' feelings around pain is one of the hardest things to do as a parent. I will be covering this further in Stage Three of this book, but for now, in this stage of creating a clear mindset, I invite you to become aware of how much your kids' moods affect you and how enmeshed you are with them.

It's because our own parents didn't know how to handle our feelings of pain and struggle that we associate those feelings with something unfavorable or "bad." Because our parents never truly knew how to help us handle these difficult feelings, we have a hard time processing them with our own kids. When our kids go through these emotional waves, we immediately try to shun them as we were shunned in our own childhoods for feeling our big feelings. So the next time your kid is going through a struggle, I invite you to say these words to yourself:

> *My child is a human being experiencing human feelings of pain and struggle. These are normal feelings for a human. Every human has these messy feelings. These are not bad feelings. These are worthy feelings that will allow my child to grow into a resilient being who can self-regulate and self-govern. If I wipe away these feelings, my child will lose an opportunity to be authentic. I do not need my child to be happy or successful in order to feel good as a parent. My worth doesn't come from their grades, moods, or experiences; it comes from my own. I will hold space for all that shows up authentically for my child, and through my embrace of the is-ness, I will teach my child to embrace their is-ness as well.*

Let's remove "happiness" and "success" from our vision boards and replace them with "presence" and "experience." In this way, our children can let their lives unfold as they are meant to without any judgment for them to be anything other than they are. Now, this is a beautiful gift to give our children.

We have deeply held beliefs not just about happiness and success, but also about other concepts, such as what it means to be good or bad, beautiful, or loving. All of these beliefs color our perceptions of our kids and influence our behavior toward them. A useful exercise is to uncover your unconscious assumptions around these concepts so that you can be aware when they intrude on your parenting. As you write about these associations, you will begin to understand how your ideas have been shaped by those around you and how your relationship with your own kids has been impacted. In the accompanying chart, I have filled in one row as an example. Try filling in the rest of the rows yourself.

	Mom	Dad	Culture	You
Success	Get A grades	Make a lot of money	Buy a fancy house and car	Be real, be genuine, have friends, laugh
Happiness				
Good/Bad				
Love				
Marriage				
Parenthood				
Money				
Sex				
Beauty				

What do you notice as you fill in the chart? Do you see how much your own parents and culture have influenced you? Do you see how your beliefs impact your parenting? As you become aware of how such beliefs have been shaping you, you may be able to see how they have also created stress and anxiety. Healing occurs not only through gaining that awareness, but also through replacing those beliefs with new ones that are more empowering and conscious.

Step Five:
Dump the Savior Complex

I thought I could save you
From pain and strain,
From tears and fears,
From hurt and dirt,
Until I realized that this wasn't going to empower you.
It was going to cripple and enfeeble you
And destroy your ability to thrive,
For a life without these elements
Is death.

Here are some vital facts for you to remember: Our children did not make us parents. They had no choice in the matter. We made ourselves parents. It was our choice to become parents.

As you read this, you may wonder why I would think it imperative to state something so obvious. The reason is that on a subconscious level, we don't act as if this were an obvious fact. In fact, we act as if the opposite were true. We act as if we are doing our kids a favor by raising them and that they should be eternally grateful to us for having taken care of them—as if we were their saviors and creators. So filled are we with this air of largesse that we imagine we should win a prize for selflessness for having had our children.

We unconsciously embody a savior complex that says that because we bestowed on our kids the selfless favor of raising them, they should now treat us as if we were indeed their masters. As their creators, we think it is our job and right to dictate to them and influence their lives. Then, when they don't call us on our birthdays, don't return our texts on time, or make life choices contrary to our agendas, we lose our minds.

Here are two fundamental truths you need to absolutely accept right away to enter a greater state of clarity: (1) You didn't "create" your kids. They arrived here through biological cause and effect. (2) Having kids was *not* an act of selflessness. You had them to fulfill your own self-focused purposes. Your kids owe you nothing. Sure, they can give you respect and love, but they don't owe anything to you.

As you didn't create your children, you also are not their savior, nor the be-all and end-all of their lives. You might be thinking, "I *should* be treated like a savior. After all, I am expected to pay for everything when they f— it up. I'm the one who is supposed to clean up their mess and rescue them when they are stranded at a hospital or on a highway." I understand the feelings you likely have, but that is not how life works. While it sucks, this is the reality of parenting. No one said it was fair.

Understanding your role as a parent is a key to conscious parenting. When you believe your role is to play god, even though this sounds like amazing power, it is actually the cause of great suffering for both you and your child. Our savior complex is buried deep beneath our subconscious and isn't readily apparent. It resurfaces only when we observe our children behaving in a manner that's drastically opposed to our own ways. When we watch our children make life choices that feel horrific to us or are in dire polarity to what we think is best for them, we become highly triggered. The reason for this reaction? Our overidentification with the role of parent and savior makes us feel that our kids should succumb to our power and influence. When they don't, we are insulted and resentful. By taking things personally, we mess up our own equilibrium, and theirs. If our kids fail at life, we feel as if we have failed in some way, and we suffer tremendously. Or if they have social problems, we feel as if these are our problems to fix somehow. Without our conscious awareness, thinking we are our children's saviors places us under tremendous pressure to "fix" them. Moreover, we feel extremely resentful when we discover that they are *un*fixable. And do you know how your kids feel? They suffer huge amounts of shame for having messed things all up. That's right—this is yet another unliftable burden we unconsciously place on our kids.

The truth is that one of the goals of conscious parenting is to become irrelevant for our kids. You heard me right—irrelevant. This is an idea that our egos protest. We don't ever want to be deemed irrelevant. We want to be not just highly relevant, but supreme. The truth is that we need to raise our kids to not need us—and for this to happen, we need to allow them the space to fully step into their own lives. And to allow them that space, we need to back off and stop giving them our opinions at every turn. Do you see how this process works? We cannot desire independence for our kids and yet be sent into a tizzy each time they disregard our opinion or influence. The two simply do not go together.

The most effective way to release your savior complex is to ask yourself these questions:

How do *I* feel when someone thinks I need to be saved or tries to control *me*?

Do *I* like to be bossed around and lectured?

I don't think that you appreciate being dominated by another. No one does. Humans do not want to feel controlled. Like all animals—and we are animals—we don't like to feel cordoned off. While we may acquiesce to being controlled, like a caged bird or tiger, it isn't in our intrinsic nature to live according to the dictates of another. Living that way creates frustration and anger that one day will result in our lashing out and breaking free.

So accustomed are we to forcing our dominion over our kids that we don't even stop to think how it must feel for them to have to blindly follow us. So caught up are we in our delusions of power and grandeur that we just assume that our children need us and are happy to be our willing puppets.

No human likes to be a puppet—no one. Not you and not your children, no matter how small they are. With too much control, our kids will rebel, either against us or against themselves. When we understand this basic fact of human nature, we will be more attuned to the ways we try to manipulate our kids like puppets, and we will be mindful of creating space for natural rebellion.

Our children feel stifled by our domination of them. In fact, precisely because they are dependent on us in their early years and have no choice but to relinquish authority to us, they grow fatigued of this suppression. By their teen years, they crack. We call this adolescent rebellion and speak of it in negative terms, but what we don't realize is that this is a vital developmental process. When children are overly suppressed and not given space for this natural adolescent outcry, they will completely burst and snap in their early adulthood and go completely off track.

Why is teenage rebellion such a globally ubiquitous phenomenon? Can it just be a coincidence? Hardly. It manifests in such vociferous ways for one reason only: our kids are fatigued by their parents' god complexes and burned out from being compliant and obedient to our ways. When they were young, they had no choice. But the moment they turn into teenagers, they break away.

When we parents resist this rebellion, we do damage to our children's growth. It's only through rebellion against us that our children will be able to find their inner voice and sovereign authenticity. You see, this is where they kind of tell us to f— off with our god complex. While we feel they are rebelling *against* us, we need to realize that they are finally doing something for themselves. They are saying no to the god in us, sure. But they are doing something far more pivotal by saying yes to the god within themselves.

So how do we replace this god complex without losing all semblance of influence? There is a way—the *conscious parenting* way. We support our children from the side. Rather than leading them from the front, we move to their sides and walk with them, side by side. Instead of leading the way, we need to move into a new space of communion and kinship. Instead of seeing ourselves as the ones who are powerful and right, we need to enter a new way of interacting with our kids. Our rightful place is not in front of them or in their lane. It is by their side, in our own lane.

So many parents veer out of their own lanes and intrude on their kids' lanes. This intrusion is spiritually damaging for the kids. Being the "weaker" ones, our young kids are unable to shove us back into our own lanes, so they often acquiesce. This dampening of their inner will and autonomy is extremely threatening to their essence. Over time, this erosion creates great inner turmoil and self-loathing.

When we stay in our own lane, we won't walk in front of our children with domination and blind power. Instead, we will be careful to stay on our own path and walk by their side. If they take a step forward, we move with them. If they move to the right, we move after them. First we watch where they are going and attune ourselves to them, then we move along in the flow instead of resisting. Sometimes, of course, we guide them in different directions than their own steps might take them, but we do so gently, with respect and honor. We don't steer them our way through control, fearmongering, or manipulation. We steer them through conscious guidance and respect for where they are. A large element of becoming a conscious parent is to get off our pedestals of grandeur and stay in our own lane.

PUTTING IT INTO PRACTICE

Each day affords us an opportunity to walk in our own lane, alongside our children rather than before them. This is easier to do when we are grounded in our own lives and sense of worth. However, when we glean our sense of worth and identity from our children, it's harder to release the role of being their savior and leader.

Let's remember that our goal as a conscious parent isn't to give our children our opinions and sermons, nor is it to be their master or god. Our goal is to have them come up with their own opinions and leadership. All humans want to lead their own way and set their own path. Depending on their ages and developmental maturity, children want to feel autonomous, with the power to make their own choices in life. We as parents need to watch for opportunities to let them do this. We need to create such moments so that they can practice from a young age. When they are young, allow them to choose their own socks and shoes, or their own favorite cereal or glass to drink from. As they grow older, let them choose their dinner ingredients or the weekly family movie. Find ways to hand over power to them so they can learn to listen to their own inner voice.

Many parents protest by saying, "But my kid keeps asking me for my opinion!" My answer is this: They may ask, just as they ask to eat the tenth cookie. Just as you would not immediately give in to the cookie, resist giving your opinion, because doing so bypasses the crucial process children need to undergo to discover their own opinions about things. By looking to themselves for answers, they learn to practice inner knowing. If we parents keep robbing them of this process, we will engender great dependence on us and inner confusion within them. They simply won't know how to depend on their own inner GPS.

Children who are pleasers turn their power over to others readily. As parents, we need to be aware of this tendency and gently hand the power back. When they ask us what to do about something, instead of falling into the trap of giving our opinion, we can say, "Hmm, interesting question. I really have to think about it. I don't readily know. What do you think?" If your child doesn't come up with their own answer, it's far more powerful for them to sit with the unknown rather than depend on you for ready-made answers.

So, in order to put this into practice, parents can ask themselves these questions:

How can I give my child the power to exercise their own autonomy?
How can I show my child that they can trust their own voice?
How can I get out of my child's lane and allow them to walk their own way?

Here are some things you can say to your kid:

I don't know the answer. Let's find it together.
I need to sit with it for a while. Think about it yourself, too.
I know you want me to give you answers, but you need to find them for yourself.
You know what you need to do. You just need to listen to yourself more.

Helen's daughter, Tina, called her every day of her life. Sometimes it was several times a day. You would imagine Tina to be in her teen years. Nope. She was in her thirties, Helen in her late fifties. They spoke nonstop and knew everything about each other's lives. Now, on one level this could be thought of as a close and connected relationship. However, it wasn't a healthy relationship, because Tina depended on her mom for advice on every decision and choice the daughter faced. Tina relied more on her mother than on herself or any peer in her life. For this reason, this relationship was more enmeshed and codependent than it was healthy and empowering.

I began to see Helen because she was stressed out over Tina's divorce. It was almost as if Helen was going through it herself. She was involved in every decision Tina made and suffered the consequences along with her. They texted and spoke to each other at least a dozen times a day. Helen could barely work at her own job as a sales manager because she was constantly being distracted by her daughter's crisis. It was taking a huge toll on her.

I tried to help Helen deconstruct her codependency and enmeshment with her daughter, but she was extremely resistant. "Tina needs me. She always has, and I am never going to stop being there for her." Helen couldn't see the difference between being there for her daughter and micromanaging her entire life. I tried to explain that by trying to save her daughter at every turn of her life, Helen was actually robbing Tina of her resilience. Helen was resolute. She kept repeating, "I cannot let her down! I need to be there for her no matter what!" Even when I showed her that this level of fusion was causing her much stress, she refused to bend.

When we fuse with our children to a high degree, trying to save them from themselves, we don't empower them. On the contrary, we deflate their inner sense of worth and self-reliance—but we just don't realize this. We cripple our children by letting them depend too much on us at times when they are fully capable of relying on themselves. Helen protested, "But Tina is the one who keeps calling me to tell me her problems and ask me for help. I don't call her!" I tried to explain that it didn't matter who made the first call. What matters is whether and how the parent allows the dependency to continue. I explained, "You could easily just listen without offering any advice. When you give your kids, especially after their teen years, your advice—solicited or unsolicited—you cripple them. Instead of guiding them to their own knowing, you encourage them to bypass the struggle they need to go through to find their own answers. This struggle is pivotal for the development of resilience. You are robbing Tina of the ability to develop her own knowing. Don't you see that?"

Helen struggled with accepting her part in the dynamic. She kept displacing the blame onto her daughter, refusing to take ownership of her cocreation. To date, she remains one of my few clients who has simply refused to shift. I wish I could extol the wonders of my persuasive abilities and tell you that she disrupted her patterns, but

I would be lying. I would rather tell you the truth so you can be realistic about just how hard these patterns are to break. I finally told Helen, "Your need to be a savior is more important to you than allowing your child to grow in her resilience. Unless you are willing to see this part of you and heal the little girl within you who needs to be needed in such an extreme way, I will not be able to help you."

Helen was one of those parents whose identity was so wrapped up in her role of savior that she was unable to differentiate between her child and herself. She was so lost in playing god that she was fully self-absorbed in it. All that mattered to her was her embodiment of that role—not what her daughter needed from her mother in order to grow. The idea of being a savior fulfilled Helen so much that it was all she cared about—never mind that Tina was drowning in crippling overdependence.

When we identify with the role of parent as savior, we underestimate the power of our children to save themselves. When we overparent them, we actually dehumanize and limit them. We clip their wings. Instead of allowing them to trust in their own knowing, we steer them toward trusting in ours—and what a great disservice we do to our children.

As a conscious parent, it is up to each of us to find ways to express trust and to honor our children's ability to know who they are. This is a gift they desperately need from us. A failure to bequeath this gift to them incrementally as they grow, and increasingly as they mature, speaks to our own inner lack and fear, not theirs. Our children are ready to take their wings and fly—in an age-appropriate manner, of course. It's our inability to let go that causes them to doubt themselves and to flounder.

Entering our own lane and trusting our children to navigate their own destiny at the right age is a tremendous offering of trust and respect. Our children crave this from us. Open your palms and give this to them freely and abundantly. Once you do, you will shift from seeing your children as lesser than you to seeing them as your equal partners in this adventure we call life.

Step Six:
Discard Labels

My child is not a label,
Nor an adjective nor a title,
Nor an ornament nor a prize,
Nor an achievement nor a goal.
My child is a human,
Which means they are in constant formation,
In constant flux and process,
In rapid motion and commotion.
My desire to put them into a box
Comes not from them
But from my own resistance to their undefinable nature
And my fear of confronting my own.

At the cost of repetition, I need to remind you of a key fact: the dominant parenting narrative has really messed us up. Because it places us parents on top of the totem pole, it falsely bestows on us the power to judge our children ad nauseam. We don't think twice before we call them "good," "bad," "lazy," or "smart." We mete out labels without a second thought, as if they were pennies. These labels then influence our behavior toward our kids. We feel justified in treating them badly if we have just judged their behavior as bad. Then punishment feels rational. We don't stop to consider, "Am I right?" or "Is this true?" We think of the label in the moment and simply act as if this is who they are. What we fail to realize is that we are indelibly shaping our children's perceptions of themselves. These are powerful questions to consider: "What gives me the right to judge or label my child? Do I walk in their shoes or live in their circumstances?"

When we judge or label another, we presume several things. The first is that we are unquestionably right. This in itself may be one of the most dangerous things we can do in life—to presume the unchallenged superiority of our way of thinking over another's. It is the root cause of all the wars and conflicts in this world. When we judge our children, this is what we do, in essence. We assume we are superior, justified, and right. Ah, these are the very ingredients of relational disconnection and dysfunction.

The next thing we assume is an intimate knowledge of another human being—at a biological, emotional, and psychological level. Given that no human can know another human, not even our own child, at such a level, aren't the labels we assign to other humans completely delusional? Yet we keep assigning labels. Our judgments and labels of others are the basis of racism, sexism, and violence. Judgments and labels are the scourge of our existence and the root of our dysfunction in the world. By labeling our children consistently, we unconsciously train them to see the world from only one vantage point: black or white; good or bad. In this way, we unwittingly teach our children the fundamentals of prejudice. This primary social dynamic of disconnection and separation starts with the ways in which we parents judge and label our children and others. The good news is that the dynamic can end with us as well.

The two most common labels we place on our kids are "good" and "bad." These are overarching labels with plenty of derivatives: "clever," "lazy," "kind," "mean," and so on. We believe that if we constantly give our kids feedback about their behaviors, we can contour them to become the adults we want them to be. Now, some of this is true—but a whole lot of it is false. Let's talk about the truth part first. It is true that feedback helps shape behavior. Here is where things get false and tricky, though. If the feedback emerges from the ego of the one who's giving it, it is not designed merely to shape behavior, but to control it. You see, most of our labels about our kids emerge from our own egos—as in how those behaviors make us feel. For example, if you yelled at and judged your child for getting a B grade, this reaction would be coming from your ego and wouldn't really be about your child and their feelings. Do you see?

Here is the truth: most often we label our children as "good" because their behavior makes us feel like good parents, and "bad" when it doesn't. So the "good" kids are really the docile, achieving, servile, and compliant ones—those who hold our egos on a high pedestal. But if we probe more deeply into these labels and are willing to own our ego attachment to our identity as parents, we may be able to see that these "good" kids are actually not so "good" in terms of our own transformation, as they keep our egoic stronghold in place. And the kids we call "bad"? Now, while they may shatter the parental ego and cause much chaos in the home, these kids may actually be the "good" ones, as they hold the potential to awaken their parents. Do you see what I mean? Our labels of "good" and "bad" come more from how comfortable or uncomfortable our children make us feel and less from how wonderful they actually are. This is the reason I often say that in reality, "good" and "bad" are empty labels and can never be taken out of the context of our own ego attachments.

The truth is that our labels for our kids are heavily biased and tinged with our own past conditioning. If we are not willing to confront this fundamental truth, we will continue to label our kids and pretend that we are helping them to develop into more moral and ethical beings—when in reality we are just pushing them to develop into whoever it is that we want them to be.

When my daughter, Maia, was around fourteen years old, she decided to quit learning the piano after seven years of taking lessons. She literally went cold turkey. One week she was playing, and the next week she wasn't. I know that this sounds like a similar example to the one I shared earlier about her quitting horse riding. It is in some ways, but I am illustrating a subtly different point here, so keep on reading. The reason why many of my examples are about children quitting activities or going against their parents' wishes is because it is these decisions they make that feel like defiance to us when in fact they are acts of autonomy on their part. My ego wanted to rail against her and call this behavior "bad," "irresponsible," and "uncaring" toward her piano teacher. I wanted to yell, scream, cajole, and do everything in my power to convince her to continue. Why? I had loved playing the piano as a child and always wanted my kid to be good at it—better than I was. So when Maia chose to stop playing, it was heartbreaking—or rather, ego-breaking. I was taking her choice personally and literally was sad about it. My ego was trying to convince me that a "good" parent wouldn't allow their kid to call the shots on something so significant and just stop doing something whenever they desired. A "good" parent would be in control of the situation and demand that their child fulfill the responsibility of being a "good" piano student. I am so grateful that I had had enough practice in conscious parenting by then that I was able to ignore the manipulations by my ego.

The reason I was able to resist my ego's machinations was because I knew there was something else at play that was far more important than my ego. It was Maia's ability to listen to and embody her own truth about her relationship with the piano. While her clarity felt confrontational to my ego, I realized that it was far more important to her development that she honor her own truth in this matter.

If I had been parenting her from within the traditional paradigm, I would have unleashed my judgments, labeling her decision as "terrible" and "irresponsible." I would certainly have called her "bad" and tried to make her feel guilty. But I didn't. I knew that the only reason I wanted to judge this decision as "bad" was that she was making my egoic identity as a mom feel "bad."

I put the words "good" or "bad" in quotes to show you that these words are ultimately empty of intrinsic value and are mostly used to bestow on the "other" a standard or value that comes from the judger's own conditioning. These words are designed to give the judger credence and power. Yet on their own, these words are empty of power or meaning, since they exist in a context often embedded in the judger's perceptions.

The conscious parent within me knew otherwise. The fact that Maia was able to listen to her inner feelings about playing the piano and felt empowered to voice these feelings with clarity was beneficial to her development. To be able to listen to our own inner yearnings and manifest them in our lives is hands down the linchpin for living an authentic and empowered life.

Here is the deeper message I want to reach with you: We don't need to judge our children as anything—neither good nor bad. They are intrinsically just the same, all the time: they are human. Sure, sometimes their choices can be life-enhancing or life-destroying, but nothing more. As parents we need to ask, "Does this choice allow my child to feel liberated or encaged?" If the former, then the choice is life-enhancing; and if the latter, then perhaps it is life-destroying in some way.

In Maia's case, since she felt liberated after this decision, it was clearly life-enhancing for her, and for this reason it needed to be supported and celebrated. It all had to do with how she felt, not how I felt. She was the one who needed to deal with the consequences of her decision, not I. If she was okay with these consequences and was old enough and mature enough to understand what they could imply, who was I to stop her from making her own decision? Maia's decision to quit the piano was hard on my ego but good for her soul, because it allowed her to honor her own truth. At the end of the day that is what matters: What is good for our children's souls?

Now, what if Maia had been younger when she decided to quit? Would I feel the same way? Partly, yes. Do you know why? Even young children have the ability to listen to and embody their own truth. They are just more impulsive about it. Given that younger kids are often quick to make impetuous decisions, a good strategy is to say something like this: "I am aware that you want to stop playing the piano. I want you to do what you feel is best for you, but let's decide after another three months, because we have already committed to the teacher. If after three months you still feel the same way, we can talk about it." In this way we can honor their desires while at the same time assessing the situation more deeply over the passage of time. This is an example of coming alongside your child instead of leading the way with the ego.

Does this mean that we let four-year-olds run the house? Of course not. But it does mean that we consciously and actively participate in dialogue around their intrinsic desires and negotiate decisions with these in mind. We open the communication to let them hear their own knowing, and we negotiate choices with this in mind. This leads to our children feeling seen and honored for their own wills, voices, and leadership.

Most of our labels about the others in our lives, including our kids, come from our own conditioning and how their behaviors match this conditioning. The greater the discordance between their behaviors and our conditioning, the harsher our labels. Because we don't own that our own conditioning is at play, we put the pressure of the labels entirely on our kids. If labeled "good," they feel the responsibility to carry the torch for our happiness, and they are afraid that they will be labeled as "bad" if they don't continue to make us proud. We inadvertently make our children feel they are intrinsically "bad" if they behave outside the choices we have laid out for them. Such kids will base their life choices on how these choices make others in their lives feel rather than on their own inner barometer—and they will be left feeling shame and a dread of disappointing others. What a whole lot of pressure on our kids, indeed!

What we need to say to our kids, tailored to match their maturity level, is this: "Your decision is yours. If it makes you feel good and you are ready for the consequences, then I support you. If it is making you feel bad, then I can help you make another choice." If the child is younger, the parent might say, "I can see you don't like playing the piano right now. I will come with you to your next class, and we can see how you feel then. If you still don't like it, we can come up with a solution together. Let's try for a few times and see how you feel. I will listen to you and help you to decide the next step." In both scenarios, the children feel seen and honored for their feelings and trust that the parents will consider these with respect and gravity. Such children feel connected and empowered to listen to their own inner voices rather than being shamed for feeling a particular way. Do you see how we can entirely avoid putting our own judgment on them and let their choices be about their relationship to themselves? This is what conscious parenting teaches us to do.

Now you may ask, "What if our kid is doing drugs or engaging in criminal behavior? Isn't this bad?" The answer starts with a fundamental inquiry. Are you labeling the behavior out of an egoic reaction or because the behavior is truly detrimental to your child's soul? Without a conscious understanding of the fundamental difference, we can't answer this question with wisdom. If our kids do drugs or engage in criminal behavior, we can be pretty sure it will harm them. We can't be 100 percent certain, because in some cases, an individual becomes stronger and more resilient after such life choices. For example, I know of a teenage boy who got extremely drunk after a party, which led to an aversion to alcohol because he saw firsthand the ill effects of alcohol. He then became an amateur coach for friends who were struggling with their own substance addictions. This is an example of a "bad" choice turning out to be a "good" one in the end.

The fact is, we cannot simply label something or someone as "bad" without understanding the context and providing tools of change. These tools inevitably involve our understanding, empathy, and compassion, without which we create disconnection and fear. This topic will be discussed in more detail as this book progresses.

In conclusion, judgments and labels create separation between us and others, especially our children. For this reason, we must be extremely careful before we mete out these judgments. Our children deserve the space to grow and evolve without the burden of our labels and need to be given the freedom to make mistakes, with confidence that we see them as infinitely and immeasurably worthy at all times. Even if we may sometimes disagree with their life choices or behaviors, we need to communicate to our children that we are not judging who they fundamentally are. Our connection to their essence never falters, no matter what is happening on the surface.

When our children feel this level of assurance from us, they are able to remember their worth at all times. This holds true even when they go through phases of confusion or conflict. Seeing our children through the eyes of infinite worth is a game changer for them. It allows them to remember that their sense of worth stays constant, despite the vagaries of life on the surface. Isn't this a gift you want to bestow on your kids? Well, to give this gift you will need to practice discarding your judgment and labels for them. Do you think you are ready? Let's practice.

PUTTING IT INTO PRACTICE

Life is essentially neutral. It is neither "good" nor "bad." It just is—something that is brought about through infinite causes and effects. A tiger eating a deer is not seen by nature as "good" or "bad," but simply as natural. So it is with all of life; it is all the natural outcome of interminable causes and effects. To pick something out of this chain to label as "good" or "bad" is simply unwise.

We are going to practice neutrality. But the first place to begin is with an admission: we humans are inveterate judgers. We judge the weather, traffic jams, faces, bodies, clothes, shoes, homes—the list goes on and on. Little do we realize that our judgments are projections of our conditioning, period. They do not reflect reality in its purity. Judgments are always subjective.

One of the best practices for this step of our work is to go through a *label and judgment detox* for a week. What this means is that we become hyperalert and aware about the times we label things or use judgments when speaking and thinking. While both are hard to do, catching yourself when you have judgmental thoughts is obviously more challenging. Now, let me warn you that if you think you are not a judgmental person, this exercise will shock you. When I did my first judgment detox, I realized just how judgmental I truly was. I could barely go an hour without thinking or speaking through the lens of judgment. It seemed that my basic mental pattern was to constantly categorize things into "good" and "bad" boxes. It was fascinating and a bit discomforting to see how critical I was. Here is another fact I realized only after this exercise: how judgmental I was toward myself. I was even judgmental about being judgmental.

The point of this exercise is not to rail against ourselves and shame ourselves with judgment. The point is just to become aware. Awareness is always the first step in transformation. Without awareness of our own beliefs and thoughts, we will forever be in the dark. That's why we are focusing so much on our clarity in this section. Only once we are clear about our own inner thought patterns can we begin to make more conscious choices. Until then, we are robots shooting in the dark, hoping each arrow will land somewhere positive but never having a real sense of direction about our efforts.

So take out your journal and try to keep track of all the judgments you make in the next hour or day. At the end of the day, read through your notes with eyes of awareness and compassion. Try not to judge yourself or what you've written. Just read as an impassive observer. As you keep your inner eye on your judgments, you will begin to let go of them faster. You will become more and more aware when they show up in your mental patterns—and you will be able to drop them more and more quickly.

Here's an example of a list of judgments:

She is so rude and inconsiderate when she makes me wait for her at school pickup.
He is lazy and never helps me with the dishes.
He lies to me and doesn't really care about my feelings.

When we read our list at night, we have the opportunity to reflect and become aware of our own biases and conditioning. Are these people really the way I think they are? Are they truly as I judge them to be, or is there something going on within them or with myself that contributes to their behavior? This simple turning inward lets us connect to other people's experiences as human beings, as opposed to seeing them as simply players in our own movie.

The truth is that we will never reach a zero-judgment zone. The most we can ask ourselves is to be aware of our own conditioning so we don't project our judgments onto others—especially our kids. By owning our judgments, we begin to detach from our projections onto our children, letting them sort through their own mess-ups and mistakes without the added burden of trying to please us. Holding an attitude of neutrality around our children offers them a sense of space and freedom to experiment with different life choices without the fear of parental labels. We can hold this neutral approach only when we have cultivated compassion and patience toward ourselves. Our critical voice toward others is really a direct reflection of our critical voice toward ourselves. When we become aware of this relationship, everything changes.

So, fellow parent, I challenge you to see yourself through the eyes of neutrality. Instead of shaming and blaming yourself for this or that, try to lean into a new space where you soothe yourself with these words:

I am a human who is fallible and flawed. This is not a deficit but instead just a reality of being human. When I fall and fail I am not being "bad," I am just being a natural human. So it is with my kids. Instead of labeling them one way or another, I commit to simply observing them in their as-is reality, without casting judgment. When I give them the gift of my nonjudgmental observation, I show trust in their ability to self-correct and manifest their own knowing. This is a priceless gift to give to myself and to my children.

Hands down, the people you feel most comfortable around are those with whom you feel safest to be yourself—the ones who do not judge or label you. This is the same for our kids. So the question to ask yourself is this: Do I want to be a safe harbor for my children, where they can be who they are, or do I want to be someone they fear to be around? Your answer determines your willingness to shift from judgment to compassion. I am certain that you will steer yourself toward neutrality and consciousness.

You have made it through the first stage of the conscious parenting map. How are you feeling?

If you are feeling overwhelmed, then it is time to pause for a few days before moving on. During this time, you can wear the new glasses of awareness that you have been developing. Try to observe yourself with your children, and journal about whatever comes up. These reflections are vital for letting the concepts we've talked about seep into your being and become intuitive.

Conscious parenting proposes a way of being that is counterintuitive and certainly countercultural. It goes against what culture has ingrained in us for generations. For this reason, the process may feel lonely, strange, and alienating at first, and you may find yourself protesting or resisting. This is natural. Be gentle with yourself. Allow time and space for these new ways of being to percolate within you. If guilt is emerging, this is natural as well. Understand that guilt is a way for us to stay in self-loathing and pain. Notice it, write about it, and let it pass.

Perhaps you are not feeling overwhelmed and are ready to move on. In that case, I would suggest that you take a few moments now to write down your biggest takeaways and "aha" moments so far. Allow yourself to reflect and integrate. Once you have done so, we can move on.

We are about to go deeper into who you are and how you arrived at the place where you are. The next stage takes you into your own childhood and how it has deeply influenced your parenting. While this can be a challenging stage, it is also the heart of this book—because once you see how you came to be who you are, you will be liberated to make new choices and change your relationship with your children in a profoundly transformational way.

STAGE TWO

From Dysfunctional Patterns to Conscious Choice

I am tired of going around in circles with you, my child.
It pains me that I cannot reach your heart
And that I keep missing the mark.
I don't know what I am doing wrong.
All I know is that I want to do it right,
But something keeps getting in my way,
And it is creating an abyss between us so wide,
so painful and deep, that it hurts us both.
It is my greatest desire to meld our separation
And create a bond so deep
It will take our breath away.

DAVE, ONE of my clients, had a particularly difficult time seeing the dysfunctional pattern he was stuck in with his son, seventeen-year-old Scott, who was the star baseball player at his high school. As the forty-seven-year-old CEO of a tech company, Dave was extremely successful and competent. Playing baseball was one of his favorite things to do, and he had always volunteered at his son's games all through his childhood. When Scott's baseball coach fell ill and the team needed a temporary replacement, Dave was only too happy to step in. That's when things began to go south.

After Dave began filling in as coach, everything started blowing up between father and son. They were fighting and stonewalling each other on a daily basis. Things got so extreme that Scott threatened that he would stop playing baseball unless his dad quit as coach. Dave felt that Scott was behaving like a brat, since all the other players enjoyed learning from their new coach. Scott felt that Dave was bossing everyone around—especially his son—and he was embarrassed. He felt humiliated by his father.

When they were both in my office, I could have cut the tension with a knife. Father and son couldn't have been more emotionally distant. I encouraged Scott to share his feelings. This is what he said: "My father just doesn't understand how dominating he is. He thinks he is the best and knows it all. He barks orders at me and makes me feel really bad for all the mistakes I make. I used to love playing baseball, but now I absolutely dread it. He has turned it into a military camp where he is the dictator. He used to be like that when I was younger, too, and he used to tutor me. I just hate the way he is so condescending and rude!"

Scott had barely finished speaking when Dave interrupted, "I am not! I absolutely am not! Tell Dr. Shefali about your huge mess-up the other day. I am not your dad on the field—I am your coach. It is my job to point out your mistakes. I pay so much attention to you because I care. No one else would give a damn!" I was taken aback by Dave's emotional reactivity. I could see why Scott was having a hard time getting through to his dad. Dave continued his rant: "I am doing this because I love you. This is why I am taking the time to coach your team. If it wasn't for you, son, I wouldn't care!"

I could see that Dave was struggling with the situation. On one hand, he did love his son and was sacrificing his time out of this love. Yet, as many of us parents do, Dave was failing to see how his strategy was failing. His intentions were right, but his approach was all wrong. Instead of receiving his father's involvement as love and support, Scott was receiving it as abuse. The wires couldn't have been more crossed.

I am sure you have felt frustrated at times when, no matter how good your intentions, your child interprets your actions as coming from the devil itself. It's downright maddening, isn't it? The reason this disconnect happens is that without our conscious awareness, we are operating out of some sort of egoic control, and our children are resisting this. They feel manipulated and fight back in some form or another.

Parents often think to themselves, "But I'm doing X or Y in the best interests of my kids. My kids don't realize how their decisions in this moment are going to affect their lives later on, but I do. I need to let them know." Or, as Dave was thinking, "I need to help my son become a better player, and I will do whatever it takes to get him there." When as parents we harbor an intention to "train" our kids to become "better" than who they are in the present moment, we don't realize how degrading and disempowering this can feel to them. We fail to see that our desire to make them "better" for the future often comes from our own fears and sense of lack in the present moment. In our desire to make things better in a future that may never come, we end up making things worse—way worse—in the present moment.

I called Dave for an individual session the following week. I tried to explain Scott's point of view, but Dave wasn't having it: "Scott is a complainer and a whiner. He always finds something to be negative about. I am sick and tired of pandering to his protests. He'd better buck up or he will be thrown off the team for a bad attitude. All I am trying to do is help this kid, and he is behaving like a damn brat!" Dave was furious and couldn't begin to see how he was even slightly in the wrong, let alone how he was severely damaging his son's sense of self-worth.

Dave was in a complete parenting fog. He had lost track of his mission as a parent. Instead of being there for his son as a benevolent guide, Dave had made it all about himself. It is not uncommon for us as parents to have something completely eclipse our compassion and heart. It's as if we have been overtaken by some alien force so powerful and seductive that we have no control over it. Do you know what this thing is? It is all our own childhood crap. I will explain more as we proceed.

I said to Dave, "Your son is feeling displaced and controlled by you. Didn't you join his team to offer support? Do you realize that your approach is doing the opposite and creating a huge disconnection between you and your son?"

I couldn't even continue before Dave jumped in. "How can you say that! I am being so supportive. Scott is just ungrateful and thinks he's entitled. I would have given my left arm if my father had shown me even a tenth of the support I give him. I would have died to have a father who cared the way I do! I do so much for Scott!"

There it was! The childhood wound.

Dave believed that he was being a loving father by giving his son the things he himself had never received from his dad. Dave was projecting his own past wounds onto Scott and filling his own image of what he thought a father should be. Dave's behavior was rooted in his own past pain and had nothing to do with what Scott wanted or needed. Dave was filling his own bucket and neglecting his son in the process.

I had to find a way to gently show Dave the mirror. "You are try-ing to fix your own past, Dave. This is what you yearned for from your dad. Because you never received it, you are now trying to make sure Scott doesn't feel the way you did. But this is not how your son feels. You are projecting your needs onto him. You are driven by your own agenda to right the wrongs of your past. By doing so, you are messing up your relationship with your kid."

Dave struggled with this insight for weeks. He just couldn't see how he was trying to control his kid. All Dave saw was his "good" intention. It was only after many explorations of his past that Dave began to touch on his own childhood pain. He revealed that he had grown up with a neglectful father who never paid attention to his son. As a result, Dave grew up thirsty for his dad's validation. He worked hard at school and on the field, becoming a star student and athlete. Even these achievements couldn't bring his father to attend any of Dave's games. He then kept being more and more successful, hoping that his dad would finally see his worth.

It never happened. To this day, they have a strained relationship. "I didn't even realize that I was holding so much pain around my dad and my childhood," Dave finally admitted. "I thought I was just fine. It is only after you brought all this up that I could see how crazy I have been acting. I cannot believe how I have treated my son. This was exactly what I was trying to avoid."

Dave began to see how his own lack of self-worth was driving his desire to coach his son. He wanted to give his son what he'd never had and to be the "good" dad he'd wished he had. When he wasn't receiving validation from his son, he began touching upon his inner pain. The moment he felt "lesser-than," his ego roared like a tiger and acted out. As he had done in his childhood, Dave tried to become the best. In this case, he tried to become the best coach, at all costs—even at the cost of his own son's well-being. Dave soon began acting like an out-of-control child. It was only when he explored his old patterns that he began to have insight into his childhood pain. Only then did he finally begin to see his own projections onto his son and how they were creating a serious dysfunction in their relationship.

Once I showed Dave his patterns, he was able to observe when they came up in his relationship with his son. As he did so, he was able to disrupt these patterns, and his relationship with his son improved immediately. After a year, he had truly changed his patterns for good and had reached another level of awareness as a parent. As Dave began to take each small step, Scott responded as willingly as a flower to the sun. This is the beauty of our children. They don't want to remain walled off, yet they will only reveal themselves when they feel it is safe to do so.

Dave's initial resistance was not uncommon. Most of us live on autopilot, moving through life robotically, emotionally reactive and impulsive. We think we are reacting consciously to the present moment when we are actually reacting to moments from our own childhoods. But we can move away from unconscious parenting and connect with our kids in a more attuned way when we're able to stop in the middle of a reaction and ask ourselves, "Where is this feeling coming from? Is it from my past or the present?"

Just as Dave was unaware of the impact his wild emotionality had on his son, most of us parents fail to realize how our past impacts our children in the ways that it does. Until we become aware of our own childhood patterns, we will not be able to parent our children consciously. We won't be making our choices; our past pain will. At this stage of the parenting map, you are going to become aware of how many of your present-day behaviors and reactions come from the past instead of the present. As this awareness grows within you, you will be better able to make new, clear, and conscious choices grounded in the present moment rather than the past.

There are lots of opportunities for revelations during this stage. You will figure out your patterns and diagnose your style of parenting when you are triggered. Are you a yeller? A negotiator? A pleaser? Wouldn't you like to know? It is only when you become aware of your typical patterns that you can begin to break out of them. In a concrete and simple way, you will learn to break out of dysfunctional cycles, just as Dave did. Go through the following steps with curiosity and playfulness. These are not intended to blame or shame you, but rather to spark your interest and to inspire you to recognize your patterns and begin to change them.

Step Seven:
Discover Your Two *I*'s

How can I ever hope to connect to you, my child,
When I am so disconnected within myself?
I barely know who I am.
I barely understand my own essence.
It is only when I can reclaim my own authenticity
That I can hope to honor yours.
It is only when my inner holes heal
That I can connect to you in wholeness
And you can soar as you are meant to.
It all begins with my own soul's redemption.

Whether or not we like to see ourselves as psychological beings, the fact remains that our psychology profoundly shapes us. And the one fundamental stage of life that shapes our psychology more than anything else is childhood. Although I find psychology fascinating, I am aware that many may not. For this reason, I am going to keep this section, which is heavily rooted in psychology, as engaging and accessible as possible. Remember, everything in this book is about understanding yourself better so that you can make more conscious choices in your relationship with your kids. To achieve this, some awareness of your own psychology is key. Let's start at the beginning.

Childhood is the ultimate game changer. Not only is it the blueprint for all our later relationships, but it is the time when we learn everything about ourselves and how we are to be in the world. Quite simply, it's the most profound phase of our lives. Something very significant begins to happen in childhood that many of us do not fully understand. We begin to be *conditioned*. We begin to be brainwashed by our parents and our culture—without our own conscious realization or consent. Let me explain further.

When we are born, we are psychologically "unconditioned": we are "empty" of parental and cultural rules, values, beliefs, and traditions. We are the purest manifestation of our psychological essence. We are simply present to this moment, then the next, and then the next. We just show up as we are, the most beautiful expression of the human soul. This is the reason children are often called "pure."

Of course, we aren't completely blank slates. We each come with a unique flavor. We have a genetic blueprint and an emotional temperament that is undeniable. Some of us are born calm and serene, others hotheaded and loud. Parents often like to say things such as "Oh, you have been like this since day one!" What they mean is that our own unique temperament shows up early, and this tends to imprint itself on our daily existence.

While we are unique in genetics and temperament, as human children we all have the same intrinsic emotional desire. Do you know what this is? It's the desire to be seen and validated for who we are. To be honored for "ourselves" is our greatest desire as humans.

Yet this was not to be our fate. Once we encountered the adults in our life, we were jolted into *their* ways of being. We were forced to think, feel, and act in ways that matched *their* realities. We couldn't just unfold in our own ways.

For each of us to be celebrated for our authentic self, our parents needed to attune themselves to us. Sadly, most parents were not conscious enough to do this consistently. Instead of allowing us to blossom as our true selves, they raised us to be *other* selves—conditioned by our parents' own fantasies and expectations. This is the current status quo. Parents project their wishes, expectations, and fantasies onto their children from the very beginning. We do so unconsciously, and it has become a fundamental aspect of the parenting role. Think about the conversations we have about our children and how we dream up this and that about their futures. We think we are meant to shape our children's futures, and the first step is to determine who they will be in the world. The problem, of course, is that who we want them to be and who they are likely differ. In this way, the conditions for disconnection with our children begin to be established at an extremely early age. These conditions often have nothing to do with our children's intrinsic natures and everything to do with our own desires, hopes, and projections.

Before you've even emerged from the womb, most everything is predetermined for you: your family traditions, your religion, your values, and how to be your gender! Now, you may say, "Of course my parents did that—they had no choice! That's what every parent does." My rebuttal is this: we always have a choice as to how we raise our kids. We can either choose to follow the ways we were raised, or we can choose a new way that breaks free from the past and dares to contour itself to the present moment. A parent who chooses the latter path might say, "I choose to raise my child without cultural impositions and blind beliefs. I choose to consciously connect with my child first, to understand their temperament, before I plan out nearly every aspect of their life." Barring a few basic practicalities—such as giving their children names—conscious parents are mindful of the subconscious prescriptions they subscribe to and use to control their children.

Not only did our own parents indoctrinate us with entire prescription lists for how to live our lives, including whom to worship and eventually whom to marry, but they also laid out the consequences of noncompliance. To defy parental dogma was unthinkable, even blasphemous. With their love came clear conditions: *follow my will or deal with my rejection.* Our parents didn't need to explicitly state these conditions. We just felt them. We learned to do everything in our power to avoid the painful consequence of losing our parents' love.

There is no one to blame for this process. Our parents, too, were victims of a similar fate. They also went through an abduction of their true selves in childhood. This is just the way the wheel of unconsciousness turns as generational patterns are set in place. Each prior generation seals the fate of the next one. Over and over, the pain of unhealed emotional patterns and wounds moves like waves through the ocean of humanity, taking many down in its lethal riptides and undercurrents. Rest assured that you are now well on your way to ending this cycle.

Children intuitively know that they'd better follow their parents' program, or else. Children know that it is far more important to be who their parents want them to be than to venture off trying to be themselves. If they want their parents' approval, children had better be "good." And they know that being "good" means suppressing their authentic selves. Children implicitly know that they are involved in a *barter-and-exchange* program, in which getting love equals giving up one's true self. Over the years, these expectations build. What was once the light of our children's authentic selves grows dimmer and dimmer.

This process happened to all of us to some degree. Instead of being given the freedom to blossom into our authentic selves, we were—mostly through implicit programming—coerced to abandon our authentic manifestations of ourselves. As this inner self muted itself, we slowly became a carbon copy of our parents' ways. We masked our true selves and eventually buried them, hoping that our new personas would provide a sense of worth and significance.

Think about this grave reality: instead of feeling as worthy and empowered as we truly are, we were made to feel like aliens in our own lives. We were granted citizenship only if we embodied the customs and traditions of the dominant culture—in this case, our parents'. If we refused, we faced deportation. So instead of experiencing this, we buried our own souls far away from plain sight.

Instead of being celebrated for who we truly are, each of us soon came to be left with an insecure and needy replacement—a pseudo-self hungry for worth, approval, and validation from our parents. This hungry part of us is often referred to as the inner child. This is the first *I* that I reference in this chapter.

Now here is a profound fact to contemplate:

We aren't supposed to have an inner child filled with fears and inner "holes," so to speak. We are supposed to feel full, complete, and worthy. We would feel that way if we had been celebrated for our authentic selves and raised by parents who celebrated their own authentic selves. We developed this fearful inner child because we were raised by unconscious parents in an unconscious culture.

Imagine that! All our current insecurities and unworthiness don't have to exist. Tragically, instead of being celebrated for our whole selves and accepted for exactly who we are, we have been invalidated and slivered into pieces, with many holes. Our holes grew larger and larger, depending on how unmet our inner needs were. These holes created our *inner child,* plagued with unworthiness and fear—our first *I.*

Monica, during a therapy session with me, remembered how her own inner child must have developed way back in childhood. "I used to be such a gregarious and outgoing child. I remember wanting to play with my siblings and the neighborhood children all the time. I was filled with a joie de vivre. I was a bit chubby as a young kid. I only knew that because my mom was always telling me to exercise and eat less cake. I hated exercise, and I loved cake! I must have been around six years old when I think everything began to change in my life. I had just started kindergarten. Mom began to treat me differently. She began to restrict my calories and put me into sessions with a nutritionist. She didn't do this subtly or in a disguised way. No! On the contrary, she blasted it to everyone, repeating all day, 'Monica has a weight problem!' She even told me that if I wasn't careful, I wouldn't be invited to any birthday parties at school. It felt as if my change happened overnight. I stopped eating and became overly conscious of how I looked. I wasn't even seven years old. I also changed from an outgoing, fun girl to a shy, insecure kid. I became withdrawn and quiet, as if this would protect me from being rejected. Truth be told, I hated myself!"

Monica is not unlike the rest of us. The severity of the disconnection may differ, but the result plays out psychologically the same way. Like most of us, she began her life with a bright inner light that began to dim in its wattage in her early years due to an onslaught of insecurity and doubt. Instead of celebrating her essence, her mother forced Monica to obsessively focus on her external appearance, so much so that she forgot she even had an essence. Her external form became her entire focus.

You see, when we lose touch with our true selves in childhood, everything gets messed up. Now, instead of operating out of intrinsic worth, we operate out of intrinsic loathing. So what do we do now? We create a false self to cope with this inner lack of worth. We employ this false self to purchase love, validation, and approval. This is our second I—our *impostor ego*, which is in essence a collection of all the masks we wear to fulfill our innate desires to be seen as whole, complete, and worthy.

In Monica's case, she employed the mask of a withdrawn recluse. This allowed her to feel safe in a shell, so that she didn't have to face her fears of being rejected. What masks we employ depends on our temperament and unique childhood circumstances. Some of us become comedians, some withdrawn depressives, and yet others divas. Then there are some of us who create an *I don't give a f—* persona because we feel it's futile to chase after our parents' validation.

These masks all represent our desperate attempts to do two things: (1) protect our inner child from further parental invalidation and, (2) if possible, create ways to artificially "buy" love, validation, and worth. These ways are often inauthentic to our true essence and involve some sort of manipulation of either ourselves or others. Before long, our entire existence is predicated on these masks, and soon our original true self fades to become a distant memory.

Let's look at an example of how the dynamic of the two *I*'s—the inner child and the impostor ego—begins to take root in childhood:

1. A parent wants their child to take violin lessons. The parent is a musician and dreams of their child becoming one. The child has no wish to learn the violin or any instrument at this time. The child is more athletic than musical, but because the parent always dreamed of the child being a musician, the parent overrides the child's will and pushes the violin onto the child.

2. The child wants to express their authentic feelings of not wanting to play a musical instrument. Each time they state their feelings, the parent gets upset with them. The child feels afraid of their parent's disapproval.

3. The child faces a difficult choice—to fight for their will or to suppress their true feelings. Although they want to express their authentic truth, they know that the price will be high. They begin to push their true self from view.

4. The impostor ego kicks in to protect the child from the pain of parental rejection. The child wears the mask of a compliant, pleasing, "good" child and tells the parent, "I love playing the violin." This gets the child the praise and validation they so desperately seek from their parent.

5. Over time, the child begins to wear more and more masks in order to gain the parent's approval, adding on the titles of

superachiever and pleaser. The more the parent applauds the child, the stronger their false self grows. It's only after many years that this self will crack under the pressure of pretense, and the person will be given an opportunity to heal.

This example of the violin lessons may seem trivial, even inconsequential—and if it were a one-off event, it might have been. However, such abductions of the true self show up again and again in our lives, until we manage to shrink this part of ourselves from our own awareness.

Becoming aware of these internal hijacks of our authenticity is vital if we are to ever grow into a new and empowered self—not just for ourselves, but also for our children. As we claim our authentic freedom, we liberate our children to do so as well.

PUTTING IT INTO PRACTICE

Your authentic self is waiting for you to reclaim it. In order to begin the process of discovery and reclamation, we need to activate old memories from childhood. Let's do this exercise. Close your eyes and let your mind wander to some painful memory of your younger self, between the ages of two and ten. Once you have a memory, write it down.

Make sure to note not only the event, but also the feelings you had.

How did the event make you feel?
How did your parents react to you?
Did it feel safe to express yourself?
Were you nurtured and validated, or were you made to feel ashamed and dishonored?

If you were not validated or nurtured, you probably suppressed or denied your feelings. Those feelings then began to block your authentic self.

Getting to know your inner child is an important step on your path to empowerment. Let's get to know your inner child intimately through this exercise. Maybe you want to give your inner child a name or a color. Maybe you want to draw how your inner child felt. Find some way to memorialize this being as an image or entity. Doing so is important, so that you can observe your inner child, own it, and call it out in a way that lets you reference it in real time.

An additional practice that I have cultivated over the decades to attune to my own inner child is to close my eyes and ask myself:

What is my inner feeling right now? Am I feeling fear or calm?
Is my response coming from a state of lack or one of abundance?

I once did an experiment in which I challenged myself to respond to situations only when my answer was a yes to calm and abundance. If the answer was no, I chose not to take action until my inner state changed. I literally didn't speak much for the first seven to ten days of this experiment, because I discovered that most of my responses were habitually conditioned from fear and lack. Asking ourselves these questions allows us to recognize just how much we have been living in our inner child of fear, doubt, and lack. Remember: each time you are in your inner child, it's likely that you will activate your impostor ego in order to compensate for that inner child's fears and insecurities.

Can you commit to turning inward and asking yourself the previous two questions over the next twenty-four hours? Here are some additional questions that could help in this discovery process:

Am I needing validation and approval right now?
Am I afraid of rejection and abandonment?
Am I afraid of conflict and being seen as bad?
What are my exact fears right now?

It is imperative to be in touch with our inner fears, because it is through our fears that the inner child speaks to us. The inner child's language is fear-based: "Don't say this or else!" or "They will think you are a bad person, so don't speak up!" and so on. While some caution is natural, the fears of the inner child are crippling. They displace us from a position of authentic empowerment and take us to an inauthentic place of tremendous inner impoverishment: the stomping grounds of ego.

I encourage you to write these six questions on cards and place them where you can see them throughout the day. As you attune to your inner voice, you may be surprised by what you discover. You may find yourself awestruck by the way lack and fear permeate your beliefs and responses, as happened in my case. If you become aware of this condition within you, don't panic; you are simply getting in touch with the voice and needs of your inner child.

I will be honest with you. It's very hard to pay attention to the buried whispers of the inner child. So buried is this part of us that we can barely hear the inner child's voice. Given this difficulty, what is another way to start the healing journey? An easier place to start is at a more obvious level—the level of our reactions. This is the level of the impostor ego. Why is this an easier place to begin? The reason is that the ego is easy to observe. It typically causes havoc, conflict, separation, and dysfunction. It acts out and implodes. As a result, the reactions of our ego are easier to spot than the subtle and deeply buried feelings of the inner child.

The next step on your parenting map will help you identify your impostor ego and discover the ways it has been creating conflict with your kids. Once you become aware of your impostor ego, you can begin to break the dysfunctional patterns it creates and change your entire relationship with your children.

Step Eight:
Catch Your Ego

Who am I beneath my hundred masks?
Am I this or that, or all or none?
I have abandoned all of who I really am.
In all my desperate searching, I lost my way.
In my need to be right, I ended up so very wrong.
In all my bravado, I was actually crouching in fear
And dumping this all on you, my child.
It is now time for me to go beneath my masks
To find who I truly am
So I can allow you to revel in who you are.

We wear our ego masks whenever we feel afraid or insecure. Because
we are not in touch with the fears of our inner child, we can only observe our outward reactions—those of the ego. Did you know that

you are wearing your ego mask each time you engage in the following behaviors?

Yelling, screaming, or cursing at your child
Self-blaming or self-criticizing
Withdrawing in rejection or fear
Isolating yourself or shutting down

Through our dysfunctional behaviors, we can identify our ego and begin to understand what it is trying to protect. Starting with the outer reactivity is always an easier place to start. This is why I always tell my clients, "Let's start with your ego reactions, as they are easy to spot!"

Before we move forward, let me check in with you. Do you believe that the ego is the bad guy here? You probably do. While it is easy to get mad at the ego for creating so much havoc in our lives, we need to understand that it is not to blame. Again, the point is not about blaming yourself or another, but about understanding *why* your ego has been in place and why it acts the way it does.

I need to reiterate that there is a reason for the ego, and that reason is protection. What is it here to protect? Our scared inner child. No one took care of our inner child in our childhood. Because the ego was created during our childhood as a means of survival, it employs mechanisms that are primitive, immature, and childish— including yelling, screaming, addiction, self-harm, and sabotage. We didn't learn adult ways of coping, only childish techniques. Sadly, these techniques never work. Each time we deploy them, we make our situation worse. The fears of the inner child grow greater and greater. The only way *out* of this quagmire is by going *in*—by doing the inner work, which is what I'm teaching you. As you do this work, you will learn to tend to your inner child in empowered and transformative ways.

Have you heard of your body's "three *F*'s" response during stress—*fight, flight, or freeze*? Based on these, I have constructed five parental ego categories to help identify your impostor ego. These "five *F*'s" are the Fighters, the Fixers, the Feigners, the Freezers, and the Fleers. Of course, I have created these with full awareness that our psyches are infinitely complex and that no one wears just one egoic mask throughout life. These are categories I have gleaned from anecdotal experiences with clients over time, and they are intended to further your awareness about yourself; they are not empirically verified or scientifically proven. They are meant to provide you with snapshots of common reactions so that you can easily identify those that match your unique style of reactivity. Be aware, though, that how we show up in one relationship may be drastically different from how we show up in another. And we can be a bit of all categories at the same time, or we can be one category for part of our life and then switch to another. Understanding our egoic categories is just for the purpose of understanding, not to blame or shame—just to create an awareness within ourselves of how we react when we are triggered.

As you read through these categories, have a curious and adventurous spirit. You are about to discover new parts of yourself and others who are in your life. Approach this journey with an open and playful mind, as if you are diagnosing yourself: "Ah, I am a Fighter!" or "Yes, I am a Fleer!" If you start reading up on a category and find that it doesn't resonate with you, I encourage you to keep reading anyway, as you never know how it may spark an understanding of someone close to you or a past relationship. Remember, every single one of us wears an ego mask—or many. There is nothing to be ashamed or afraid of. Discovering and identifying your unique ego masks is a huge step in breaking out of your cycles of reactivity to reach empowerment and connection with your children.

If any of the following masks sound familiar, these may be masks that you wear or that you have observed others wearing while you were growing up. I encourage you to get in touch with the feelings beneath these masks and find a way to explore them through any process or creative expression that feels right to you, such as journaling, meditation, or drawing.

THE FIGHTERS

When triggered by your child, do you find yourself raising your voice and shouting commands? Do you threaten, punish, scream, or curse? Well, if you do, you may be a Fighter. Let's see whether this is true for you.

Who are the Fighters? In a nutshell, they are the angry and controlling ones. The main emotional arsenal for Fighters to manage their fears is *anger*. When their inner child feels fear, the ego mask of anger is put on. Fighters use their anger to control others. They yell, scream, punish, and degrade. All of this behavior makes them feel powerful. They have learned from childhood that to be heard and validated, they need to wear this mask of an angry controller. Those with more masculine and dominating temperaments take on these masks the most easily.

Fighters hold these beliefs:

I feel worthy when I am in control of everyone.
Anger is how I gain power and dominance over others.

Do you think you react this way in moments of stress? Do you find yourself raising your voice, stomping your feet, and exerting force or control over others so you can feel significant? If so, you are probably a Fighter.

Many Fighters grew up around other Fighters in childhood. Perhaps you observed one or both of your parents using Fighter strategies with you or your siblings, and you learned through osmosis that these techniques lend power and significance. If this behavior is what you saw around you, it's quite natural that you equate domination over others with worth and power.

Does this sound familiar? The Fighter has different subtypes. As you read through, you can reflect on whether you utilize any of these strategies. Again, these are just guidelines and not definitive categories. As I said, most of us are a bit of each.

The Enforcer

When triggered by your child, do you sometimes find yourself saying or thinking things such as "Because I said so!" or "'It's my way in this house, and if you don't like it, there's the door!'"? If so, you may be wearing the mask of an Enforcer.

This mask is worn by the parent who thrives on having carte blanche power in the home—as a mini-tyrant, if you will. While mostly emotionally and physically absent, this parent is called to the scene to enforce law and order, making sure rules are followed and laws are adhered to. Enforcers are often emotionally disconnected from the needs of others, busy in their own lives and achievements. They are black-and-white thinkers, preferring to be right more than to be connected.

This is what they believe:

Rules matter more than feelings.
Kids should obey parents at all costs.
Kids should be punished for disobedience.
It's the parent's way or the highway.

Children who grow up with an Enforcer learn to shut down around that parent and pretend to be angelic. They are terrified to be their true selves because all this parent's ego cares about is "my way or the highway." This parental mask is extremely controlling and dominating. To survive, children of such a parent typically withdraw and fly the coop at an early age, often to their own harm and detriment. This is how an Enforcer might sound: "This is the last time you break my rules. You are a disgraceful human being. You are grounded for two weeks. You need to learn a lesson so you'll never think about disobeying me again!"

If you deploy this mask or know someone who might, it is worthwhile to go beneath this mask to the feelings it hides and find a way to explore these deeply.

The Exploder

When triggered by your child, do you find yourself losing your mind and screaming at the top of your lungs? Do you feel okay one moment and then lose all semblance of control the next, maybe breaking things or throwing them against the wall? If so, you may be wearing the mask of an Exploder.

This mask uses extreme fits of rage to get its way. While the rages may be few and far between, they are sufficient to make the entire household tremble. These are the parents who go from zero to one hundred in a few seconds. They don't express their emotions but explode into them. Boy, are these parents terrifying! Unregulated and unpredictable, they are unable to verbally process their emotions in a mature manner. It's almost as if they don't think anyone will listen to them unless they explode. By inflicting extreme fear on others, this person feels empowered and worthy.

This is what these parents believe:

Parents need to show dominance and supreme control.
Children learn through fear.
Creating fear through punishment and anger brings results.
Children need to be submissive to parents.
Parents should never be friendly with their children.

Children who grow up around such a person live in the shadow of turbulence and mortification. They feel trapped to either comply and be servile or to pay a high emotional cost. They become accustomed to walking on eggshells, since they don't know when that mask will be set off next. They live in constant anxiety about when the other shoe will drop, catching them unaware. This is not a comfortable feeling for children. They spend a lot of energy trying to overplease so this parent won't blow up.

This is how an Exploder might sound: "I am done with all of you! I am done, done, done! I don't want to hear another word. I am going to hit the wall if you say one more thing. All of you are insane! I am sick of you all!"

If you deploy this mask or know someone who might, it is worthwhile to go beneath this mask to the feelings it hides and find a way to explore these deeply.

The Litigator

When triggered by your children, do you find yourself getting into arguments with them on a constant basis? Do you try to get in the last word in conversations with them? Is it important for you to win the debate and get your point of view across? If so, perhaps you wear the mask of a Litigator.

This mask is that of an extremely relentless and cerebral lawyer who thinks life is a constant court battle. This is a parent who loves to intellectually debate and argue in order to cut an opponent to shreds. The Litigator incessantly asks tons of questions, like a detective, controlling the conversation and forcing the opponent to answer. Winning the debate is of extreme importance to the Litigator, who cannot lose gracefully. To dominate the other, the Litigator may use underhanded techniques and lie, cheat, and slander. There are no limits to what such people will do to win a battle. They just don't realize that they are constantly losing the war.

This is what they believe:

Life is a game of winners and losers, and I need to be a winner.
I cannot be wrong, and I will prove that I am not.

It is more important to be right than to be connected.

People are objects within this game. Children are pawns to be used to win.

The way to get worth is to manipulate others on a mental level.

Arguments and debates are more effective than dialogue.

Children who grow up around this mask are made to feel like sinners and criminals at the mercy of a judge and jury. Being around this kind of parent makes them feel worthless. They feel as if they are guilty until proven innocent, rather than the other way around. It is really hard to feel significant and powerful around a Litigator, and one way to cope is to shut down and withdraw.

This is how a Litigator might sound: "It is a yes or no question. Don't give me a reason, just give me the answer—yes or no. You said X, but now you are saying Y. You are inconsistent and irrational. Your answers are all over the place. Did you or did you not lie when you said X? You obviously are not telling the truth."

If you deploy this mask or know someone who might, it is worthwhile to go beneath this mask to the feelings it hides and find a way to explore these deeply.

The Critic

When triggered by your child, do you find things to criticize them for? Do you analyze every microelement of their actions? Do you tend to focus on what's wrong and the negative? If you do, then the mask of Critic may be yours.

Ever been around someone whose favorite hobby is to criticize everything from the paint on the wall to the lighting in a room? Well, such people wear the mask of the Critic. So uncomfortable are they with just going along with a situation that they need to create adversity and discord wherever they go. They gain significance and power by introducing negativity into situations and disrupting how things are flowing on their own. Those who wear this mask feel that giving their feedback makes them important.

This is what they believe:

My opinion matters a lot, and others should hear it.
Nothing is good enough as it is; it can all be improved.
Accepting reality or others as they are is simply too soft and
passive.
Criticizing others makes me feel better about myself.

Children growing up with critical parents develop an abysmally low sense of worth. As they are constantly being told that they are not yet good enough, they are filled with a sense of hopelessness and worthlessness. They feel as if life is a constant uphill battle in which they simply cannot achieve worth or completion. There is always something more to do or to become. They feel frustrated and helpless.

This is how a Critic might sound: "Why do you never do things correctly? What you have done is absolutely a disaster! This is terrible. Have you made a plan for how you are going to fix things? Are you sure it's a good plan? I don't know if that is the best plan. I would do it another way."

If you deploy this mask or know someone who might, it is worthwhile to go beneath this mask to the feelings it hides and find a way to explore these deeply.

The Passive-Aggressive

When triggered by your child, do you find yourself using sneaky or indirect ways to communicate your displeasure? Do you have a hard time expressing yourself clearly in a straightforward way? If so, you may be wearing the mask of a Passive-Aggressive.

This mask is a more sinister one, because it doesn't present as the other masks do. It's more subtle. Its emotional missile isn't an explosive outburst, as it is for other Fighter masks. Instead, this mask relies on passive-aggressive withdrawal. But the outcome is the same: mass control and manipulation. Those who wear the Passive-Aggressive mask use attention, or the lack thereof, to control those closest to them. If these parents feel that their children are not following their way, the parents withdraw their attention from the children and set them up to fail.

This is what Passive-Aggressive parents believe:

I am in control, and I will use that control to teach others a lesson.

I will withdraw my love and affection to teach them to obey me.

I want to "show" the other who is right. They will learn through my absence.

I will win at the end of the game.

Children growing up with a parent who wears this mask feel betrayed and abandoned during their times of need, especially if their need is something this parent doesn't agree with or believe in. They pay a price for going astray from the parental plan and daring to experiment with their own authenticity. The price is parental withdrawal and neglect. As a result, these children are wary of going against the stream and their parents' ways. They know that the penalty will be excruciatingly painful. They are faced with only two choices: follow their inner voices or follow their parents. These children often succumb to the latter choice, much to the chagrin of their true selves.

This is how the Passive-Aggressive might sound: "I don't care anymore what you do. Don't involve me. Don't call me when you crash and burn. Deal with things on your own. I am not going to concern myself with this nonsense anymore."

If you deploy this mask or know someone who might, it is worthwhile to go beneath this mask to the feelings it hides and find a way to explore these deeply.

THE FIXERS

When triggered by your child, do you find yourself in a huge inner panic and tizzy? Do you feel as though you need to save everyone

from a sinking ship? Are you always in search of things to fix so that you can feel in control? If so, you may be a Fixer.

Who are the Fixers? They are the overdoers. The main emotional response that Fixers employ for managing their fears is to rescue everyone and solve everything. Fixers are panicky, insecure worry-warts whose main goal is to be viewed as the "good" one. Unlike the Fighters, the Fixers are terrified of conflict. They use the techniques of pleasing, indulging, pampering, solving, and saving to assuage their inner tempests and to buy love and worth. They have learned from childhood that to be heard and validated, they need to wear this mask of overdoer and pleaser. Those with a softer and more feminine temperament wear these masks most easily.

Fixers hold these beliefs:

I feel worthy when others see me as the good one.
Pleasing and rescuing others is my vehicle for gaining power.
I am loved most when I am fixing other people's problems.
I need to be needed, because that helps me feel significant.

Many Fixers, like Fighters, grew up observing this model in their own home or perhaps learned to follow this path because they had no choice. While the Fighter wants to control the actions of others to feel good about themselves, the Fixer wants to control others' perceptions of them so they are viewed as good. So fearful are they of being rejected or deemed "bad" that they bend over backward in order to control others' perception of them.

Does this model sound familiar? As you read about the following Fixer subtypes, reflect on whether you utilize any of these strategies.

The Enabler

When triggered by your kids, do you rush in to take over their lives and do things for them, even though your children are fully capable of doing these things on their own? Do you see your kids as needing you and unable to manage their own business? If so, you may be wearing the mask of an Enabler.

In psychological parlance, the term "*en*able" doesn't have a positive connotation. It really means to "*dis*able." These parents weaken their children's *ability* to do things for themselves. The Enablers are the classic rescuers and overdoers. They do so much for others that they literally suck the willpower out of the people they enable. While these parents may appear lovely on the surface, their subconscious agenda is lethal and crippling, especially for their children. They manipulate others to become needy and dependent, so the Enabler can feel like the "good" one coming to the rescue. Enablers need others to ask for their opinion or help in order to feel competent and worthy.

Enablers gain significance through others fusing with them and needing them. Enablers insert themselves into another's life even when there's no real need or real request to do so. In this way, they slowly but surely get the other to be superdependent on their presence and influence.

Enablers have these beliefs:

My worth is defined by how much others need me.
When others depend on me for every decision, I feel in control.
It's easier to jump in and fix situations than to watch others
     struggle or fail.
Controlling other people's lives gives me a sense of control over
     my own life.

Children growing up with this kind of parent can feel all sorts of ways, from feeling entitled to receive all kinds of rescuing to experiencing apathy and helplessness in their own decision-making. They often become accustomed to being passive and letting the Enabler do the hard work for them. Because these children don't know what it means to take risks and suffer the consequences, they often develop a sense of inadequacy and insecurity.

These children may also feel resentful toward their Enabler parent on some level. They intuitively know that help comes with jagged edges of control and manipulation. This causes them to be angry and frustrated, but they don't know how to express that. Deep down they feel helpless and anxious, because they've rarely been given the chance to practice tolerating frustration and building resilience. Having a parent swoop in at a moment's notice sounds luxurious, but it has long-lasting hidden consequences that are ultimately detrimental to the child's sense of autonomy and empowerment.

This is how an Enabler might sound: "Let me do that for you. I am free right now, and I would be happy to take it off your back. Just leave it to me, and it will all be handled. You can just rest while I do it."

The tricky part of this mask is that Enablers sound really nice. But here is how you can spot this sneaky impostor:

They give help without being asked.
They interfere in people's lives without being invited in.
They don't give the other the right to refuse.
**They presume that they know what's best and that their help is
    the answer.**
They don't collaborate; they take the situation hostage.
They sulk and withdraw attention when refused.

Does this pattern sound familiar? Maybe it's a mask you wear or one you observed while growing up. Get in touch with the feelings beneath this mask and find a way to explore them through any process or creative expression that feels right to you, such as journaling, meditation, or drawing.

The Superhero

When your child triggers you, is it your instinct to take control of everything? Do you like feeling that you have the ultimate word and are the boss? If this description sounds like you, maybe you are wearing the mask of a Superhero.

The Superhero is the one who knows it all, does it all, and puts out all the fires. Unlike the Enabler, who's like a worker bee, the Superhero is the queen bee, with the demeanor and air of someone who needs to always have the last word. Unlike the Enabler, who is involved in the nitty-gritty details of another's life, the Superhero doesn't bother until there is a huge decision to be made, a calamity, or a crisis. That's when Superheroes swoop in and take over the entire shebang. They are ruthless, relentless, and righteous. They ignore all the efforts made by anyone else up until that moment and hold others hostage to their power, influence, and competence. Superheroes are the ones who will undo all the preparations for a party at the last moment and call in an entire new team to make it their way. People in the Superhero's family often don't finalize any plans until the Superhero agrees, because everyone knows that this parent's consent must be obtained before any final decisions are made or any plans are set in stone.

Superheroes are usually people with status, influence, and power. While others may engage in the daily grind of life, the Superhero has the real power to make a difference. For example, if one parent is helping their kid study for final exams, doing the daily grind with them, it's the Superhero who swoops in at the very end and hires the tutor who actually makes a difference. Superheroes create dependency in a way that's slightly different from Enablers. While Enablers may have the illusion of control over daily minutiae, in the final analysis they dare not do anything without the permission, consent, and approval of the Superhero.

Superheroes have the following beliefs:

I am the ultimate authority in this household, and without me nothing can function.

My decision has the most votes, and others need to follow
   my way.

I know how to do it best, and others should bow before my
   competence.

I am a genius and need others to acknowledge this.

Children who grow up with this kind of parental ego are often
thwarted from having ownership over their lives, even as adults.
They have a nagging sense that they need to seek approval and permission from the almighty power in their life, their Superhero parent. They are also aware that this parent is highly competent, so it's
a double-edged sword for these kids. On the one hand, they have
respect for the competent authority of this parent, but on the other
hand, they feel crippled, undermined, and even resentful of the
Superhero's presence and power. Children of such parents often feel
inadequate and insecure, unable to fully depend on their own inner
authority and leadership. They feel overshadowed by the ominous,
gigantic presence of this Superhero parent.

This is how the Superhero might sound: "You know I never make
mistakes, and I know exactly what to do here. I told you this would
be a mistake, but you didn't listen. I don't know when you will learn
that you don't know it all and start listening to me. I know what I am
talking about. I am much smarter and more successful than you. Let
me clean up this mess you have created!"

If you deploy this mask or know someone who might, it is worthwhile to go beneath this mask to the feelings it hides and find a way
to explore these deeply.

The Nervous Nelly

When you are triggered by your child, does your mind go straight
to imagining the worst possible catastrophes? Are you typically a
worst-case-scenario kind of person? If so, you may be wearing the
mask of a Nervous Nelly.

This is a parent who wears the mask of an overly obsessive prophet of doom and gloom—a worrywart. A Nervous Nelly controls the environment by micromanaging the minutiae. If a child has the sniffles, this parent imagines bronchitis or pneumonia. If the child gets an A-minus, it's the end of the world. This is the parent who has the umbrella ready, the lunchbox in place, and the fridge stocked. Sadly, such parents don't operate out of an inner mindset of abundance but rather from a sense of great inner lack and scarcity. They try to foresee, preempt, and prepare for every potential calamity. They are the ones who buy ten backups for everything so they'll never run out. They are those we often refer to as "helicopter parents," who hover and buzz around their children constantly, worrying about everything. They are forever tidying up, making lists, and planning things six months in advance.

They have the following beliefs:

I am the only one who can prepare for calamities.
If I am not extra cautious, things will fall through the cracks.
Life needs constant micromanagement.
I need to be hypervigilant at all times to keep things under control.

Children who grow up around this kind of energy may not only absorb the massive anxiety it represents, but also become extremely apathetic. Since there's not enough room for two hyperanxious people, children often relinquish their own self-governance. They come to expect that the parent will be hovering around them to manage everything, so they disconnect from their own autonomy and power.

While this mask seems eerily similar to that of the Enabler, it's different in its manifestation. An Enabler gains a sense of significance by becoming enmeshed in the life of the other. The Nervous Nelly has more anxious thinking and an obsessive energy that spirals into labyrinthine thought patterns. Being around the overpowering energy of the Nervous Nelly mask is both exhausting and daunting. It's just easier to shut down and wither away in the shadows. Children of such parents often absorb their nervous energy and become anxious themselves.

This is how the Nervous Nelly might sound: "This is terrible! I can't believe this has happened to us! How will we ever recover? Everything is falling apart, and nothing is working well. If I don't make big changes, nothing is going to work out."

If you deploy this mask or know someone who might, it is worthwhile to go beneath this mask to the feelings it hides and find a way to explore these deeply.

The Fixer-Upper

Do you get particularly triggered by your children's tears or anger? Do you find yourself wanting to erase their negative feelings so they can return to being happy? If so, you may be wearing the mask of the Fixer-Upper.

This mask is worn by those who just can't tolerate "sad" or "bad" emotions. Unhappiness in others makes them unhappy and anxious. Fixer-Uppers seem cheerful at first, but after you live around them for a while, you quickly realize that they are avoidant and highly controlling. They are so fixated on making everyone else happy and presenting a happy face to the world that they dismiss, invalidate, and bypass any emotion that suggests sadness or anything they consider negative. They are constantly cheerleading and rallying others to feel the way the Fixer-Uppers think that others should feel.

Fixer-Uppers believe the following:

Unhappiness is bad.
I am responsible for making people happy.
When I make others happy, I feel happy.
I don't like to feel sad emotions, so I ignore them.
Big feelings are scary and bad.
No one will love me unless I am happy.

Children raised by Fixer-Upper parents intuitively realize that they need to suppress their more negative feelings around them. They grow to be averse to such emotions themselves and see them, not as normal, but as signs of badness or weakness. These children resist being unhappy to such a degree that being unhappy makes them even more unhappy. So obsessed are they with happy feelings that they contaminate their experiences in the present moment with this obsession and miss the actual lived experience of whatever they are feeling right now.

The Fixer-Upper might sound like this: "Why are you sad? Don't feel sad! What will people say? There's nothing to feel sad about! You need to be happy about your life. Don't be ungrateful and waste your life in sadness. It isn't fair to me if you're sad, when we do so much for you and give you so much."

If you deploy this mask or know someone who might, it is worthwhile to go beneath this mask to the feelings it hides and find a way to explore these deeply.

The ATM

When triggered by your child, do you look for ways to buy yourself out of the situation? Do you distract yourself and your kids with purchases when you're going through a rough time, or show your love with gifts? If so, you may be wearing the mask of the ATM.

This mask is typically worn by successful parents who identify their worth with their wealth. As a result, they are accustomed to "buying" the love and allegiance of the significant others in their lives. ATM parents are typically not very present or attuned to their children and bypass real connection through purchases and acquisitions. Their love has strings attached—strings of money and power. This mask helps parents feel significant and worthy, because they know they hold the money strings and therefore have ultimate power over others. Their love is often conditional, replete with the "if-then" sentiment: "If you comply, then I will give you money. But if you don't, I won't."

ATM parents have these beliefs:

Money makes the world go round.
Money and success are the source of my identity and worth.

People will love me if I give them money.
I will never be hurt if I have the power of money over people.

Children who grow up with such parents learn to play the game of conditional love. They realize that their parent is invested in and draws their sense of identity from being the ATM. The children "use" these parents to purchase what they need. As the children realize that the parental relationship is superficial and transactional, they learn to behave the same way in return. On a deeper level, they feel resentment for having to depend on these parents in such a perfunctory way, though the children realize they have no other choice. They also feel pain about being objectified and about the fact that their parents glean a sense of worth from the control of money rather than a deep connection with their children.

This is how an ATM parent might sound: "I am always bailing you out and giving you so much financial support. You need to be grateful. Do you realize how much you get from me? Other children are not as lucky as you are! I never got anything from my parents. You need to work hard and make me proud."

If you deploy this mask or know someone who might, it is worthwhile to go beneath this mask to the feelings it hides and find a way to explore these deeply.

THE FEIGNERS

When triggered by your child, is your first thought "What will people think?" or maybe "How does this look in public?" Are you constantly aware of people's perceptions of you? If so, you may be wearing the mask of the Feigner.

The main emotional strategy used by Feigners to manage their fears is attention-seeking. Feigners are publicity hounds and attention desperados. They are desperately insecure within, parasitically thriving on the attention and praise of others. Everything is basi-

cally all about them. They try to create the perfect outer appearance
by "curating" the perfect life—dressing themselves and their kids in
the trendiest clothes and living in the fanciest neighborhoods.

Feigners are the quintessential boastful braggarts, seeking constant adulation and validation. They manipulate situations—and
their children—to place themselves front and center in order to receive the maximum spotlight. Their homes, their belongings, and (of
course) their children (whom they see as possessions) are all fodder
for the insatiable desire to be seen as special.

Feigners hold these beliefs:

How another sees me is how I see myself.
Public perception is of supreme importance.
My worth comes from how I fit within social circles.

Do you think this could be you some of the time? Are you fixated
on what others think of you? Do you base your sense of self on the approval of others? Do you spend hours obsessed with what people are
saying or thinking about you? If so, you may be wearing this ego mask.

Many Feigners have grown up observing this way of being in
their homes; others may have learned to adopt this mask through
their life traumas and situations. Feigners, like Fixers, want to control the perceptions of others. But even more, they are desperate for
the attention and accolades of others. Unlike the Fixers, the Feigners don't try to help others in any way; they are too self-absorbed.

They simply want to passively receive all the validation they can get. It's a one-way street. It's all about just one person—the Feigner.

The Feigner, too, has subtypes. As you read through, consider whether you utilize any of the strategies that are described here.

The Stager

Do you set your life up to look perfect to the public, taking pictures and posting on social media? Do you find yourself searching for validation and feedback from others? Do you need praise and attention constantly? If you do, you may be wearing the mask of a Stager.

Stagers set up their lives based on how things look to the external world; everything about them—especially their children—is constantly on display. This display is how Stagers accumulate a sense of significance. Grossly disconnected from their inner voices and worth, Stagers live in heightened drama, careening from one talent show or popularity contest to another.

They have these beliefs:

How other people perceive me is of great significance to me.
I am only as worthy as others deem me to be.
Outdoing myself in comparison to others is important to me.
All of life is a show, and I want to be the star.

Children of such parents are frequently put on display and used as pawns to attract the attention their parents so desperately crave. Often, these children are objectified at an early age and made to perform in the parent's *show and tell*. These children's lives are led for documentation and memorialization, for others to fawn over. To help keep up with the Joneses, the children are taken all across town as part of their parents' entourage. They feel the pressure to be "star children" and typically do one of two things: balk under the acuity of the stress or succumb before eventually bolting and rebelling.

Such children intuitively understand that they aren't being seen for who they are, but instead exist to perform a vital function for a parent's sense of self. These children are raised by narcissistic parents who use them as part of an award show. The children's true feelings and experiences aren't important; only the awards are. Such children know they serve as functions rather than human beings in their own right, and they feel trapped in this awareness.

This is how a Stager parent might sound: "Appearances matter! You need to impress everyone by how you look and act. Don't let yourself be average or ordinary. Always maintain the perfect image, because people are going to judge you. How people perceive you is how you will perceive yourself."

If you deploy this mask or know someone who might, it is worthwhile to go beneath this mask to the feelings it hides and find a way to explore these deeply.

The Transactor

Do you find yourself engaging with your kids through "*if-then*" arrangements, always looking for the best "deal" or outcome for yourself? Do you view relationships as you would a business arrangement, trying to come out on top? If so, you may be wearing the mask of a Transactor.

Transactor parents set up relationships based on what they get in return. Everything is about the return, as in "What's in it for me?" Their giving always has the secret agenda of getting something back for themselves in return. They are highly conditional, binding others to themselves through obligation and guilt. Transactors are so afraid of being connected from a heartfelt place, lest they be hurt, that they make sure they're receiving something from the outset and never have to experience the vulnerability of sacrificing for another. They have the following beliefs:

If I don't get something from this relationship, I won't give anything.
Relationships are painful, so I will engage only if I get significant value back.
I feel safe only when I'm in a transaction.

Children of such parents are often fearful of breaking what they perceive as a contract between themselves and their parents. It's as if these children implicitly understand that they are under an obligation to fulfill their part of the agreement. Failure to do so will result in disapproval, invalidation, or complete ostracism. These children feel as if they owe their parents more than just loyalty and love— they owe them their lifestyle and life choices. Such children feel controlled and micromanaged. Their ability to roam through life with freedom and joy is stifled.

This is how a Transactor parent might sound: "I have taken care of you and sacrificed for you my entire life. I bear the heavy weight of your decisions and pay for it all. You need to do your part to give me what I need in return. You owe me so much. I want to be considered in all your life decisions. This is the least you can do for me in return."

If you deploy this mask or know someone who might, it is worthwhile to go beneath this mask to the feelings it hides and find a way to explore these deeply.

The Star

When triggered by your child, do you focus on yourself and what's going on for you instead of what's going on for your child? Do you tend to bring attention to your own life and issues rather than to those of your child? If you do, you are probably wearing the mask of the Star.

The Star is the diva of the family, and everyone knows it. Stars have a natural flair for drama and histrionics that automatically draws the attention of others. They are the ones with larger-than-life personalities, who are accustomed to the adoration of others. When they don't get the attention they're used to, they rev up their emotions to draw others back into the drama. They often do so by creating upheaval and chaos in everyday situations, making much ado about nothing. They will do anything to get the attention they crave: exaggerate, confabulate, and catastrophize situations to the extreme. If they need to act like victims, they will. Attention is so important that they often work themselves into a tizzy to pull others in. Naturally fragile and sensitive, these parents create drama by unconsciously becoming the prey of others. Attention makes them feel important.

The Star parent has these beliefs:

I gain my worth from the amount of attention I get from others.

My feelings are so important that everyone needs to pay attention to them.

Rejection, real or perceived, will make me fall apart.

I feel insecure and unworthy unless I am getting attention from others.

Children are trained early to be attuned to the needs of such a parent, their radar directed toward the parent instead of themselves. The parent's needs are more important than their own. They have bought into the script that their parent's emotions need to be managed more than their own do. Such children typically suppress their own inner life to be present for the parent, which ensures that the children don't place too heavy a burden on their parents. These children become reclusive, obedient, and "good," sacrificing their own internal worlds for their parents.

This is how a Star parent might sound: "I have many needs that require tending. Do you see all that I have to deal with in one day? I am handling so much! My life is so difficult, and I am going through so much. You can never understand what it feels like to be me. I have a million responsibilities, and I need support. I cannot believe you are not there for me when I need you. You need to be there 24-7 and help manage my life, because I have way too much on my plate."

If you deploy this mask or know someone who might, it is worthwhile to go beneath this mask to the feelings it hides and find a way to explore these deeply.

The Child

When triggered by your child, do you feel overwhelmed by the responsibilities of showing up as a parent? Do you feel it is just too much for you to handle? Do you feel burdened by all the things you have going on in your own life? If you do, you are probably wearing the mask of the Child.

The Child mask is worn by parents who abandon their responsibilities and expect to be parented and raised by their own children. Such parents have a consistent air of helplessness and fragility, forcing their children to step in as leaders and parents. They stay in bed too long, are disorganized and sloppy, forget to pay their bills on time, miss appointments, and shy away from taking charge of situations. Simply put, they are a bloody mess! Their general demeanor of incompetence and ineptness creates a void around them that someone else has to jump in and fill to save everyone from catastrophe. These parents have literally never grown up and display immature decision-making skills. They often engage in promiscuity and substance abuse, as reckless teenagers might. Watching these parents is kind of like watching a seven-year-old driving a car: it's a wreck about to happen.

These are the Child parent's beliefs:

I am entitled to be taken care of.

I shouldn't have to be responsible; others can take control.

I prefer to have fun and enjoy life rather than be bogged down with boring stuff.

I don't need to grow up.

I want others to manage my life for me.

Children of such parents grow up old beyond their years. These children are thrust into the roles of caretaker and parent before they are emotionally ready to embrace such burdens. They forsake their own childhoods to manage the irresponsibility of their parent's decisions. They feel the pressures of this enormous struggle and buckle under its weight. They often become depressed or suicidal as they burn out from all the caregiving. They don't feel nurtured or tended to in their own lives but instead are swept away by their parent's emotional needs, to the neglect and detriment of their own. These children are not allowed to be children and suffer the consequences throughout their adulthood.

This is how a Child parent might sound: "Life is so difficult. I can't cope. I can't handle my bills. I don't want to work in a boring job. I hate having all these responsibilities. Why can't you grow up so you can take care of your own life? Why do I have to do everything for you? You need to help in the house. I can't manage it all."

If you deploy this mask or know someone who might, it is worthwhile to go beneath this mask to the feelings it hides and find a way to explore these deeply.

THE FREEZERS

When triggered by your child, do you wish you could run away and escape it all? Does the stress and conflict in your relationship with your child make you wish you could just disappear? If you feel this way, you are probably wearing the mask of the Freezer.

Who are the Freezers? They are "*nonparent* parents." They are there, but not really there. The main emotional strategy used by Freezers to manage their anxieties is to avoid intimate relationships altogether. They avoid confrontation and real connection like the plague. The *idea* of being a parent and having children appeals to them, but not the real work of being emotionally present for their kids.

Human emotions are scary for Freezers. They seek safety and refuge by erecting walls around their hearts. They want connection but are terrified of being traumatized, so they have learned to *zone out*. They are the classic couch parents who don't want to be bothered by the day-to-day of their children's lives. Freezers' reluctance to be involved or to participate is apparent. They give those around them, especially their children, the impression of being uncaring and unloving.

Freezers hold these beliefs:

If I get emotionally involved with others, I will experience pain. Conflict is painful and could lead to abandonment.

Do you think this could be you sometimes? Do you withdraw your emotional investment from others because you're afraid of rejection and betrayal? Do you find emotions messy and bothersome? Were you so rejected as a child that you now wall yourself off from others to avoid feeling that pain again?

Many Freezers experienced trauma in childhood, which taught them that it's safer to stay away from the muck of relationships. They were probably so hurt and betrayed that they found it is easier to build walls than connections. They yearn for connection but are too wounded to drop their Freezer masks, which would enable them to nurture deep emotional bonds in their life.

As you read through the Freezer subtypes described here, think about whether you utilize any of these ego masks to help you cope with your parenting and life struggles.

The Half-Assed

When triggered by your children, are you filled with a sense of dread about dealing with their feelings? Are you taken over by a need to just be left alone, as if there's too much stress for you to handle? You may be wearing the mask of the Half-Assed parent.

This mask is worn by parents who are around but not invested in any of the nitty-gritty of life. They participate, albeit reluctantly, but don't care to add value. They need to be dragged into things and persuaded to be part of the mix. It's as if they are doing everyone a favor by bestowing their presence. They don't get into the dirt of things to avoid getting messy. They push their kids onto nannies and other caregivers. They stay at a long emotional distance from others and watch the action from afar. When they do engage, it's half-assed, almost to the point that others wish these parents weren't there at all. They may offer assistance, but then do the job so incompetently or with such indifference that they're almost assured of not being asked again.

Half-Assed parents have the following beliefs:

Relationships involve vulnerability, and I don't want to be vulnerable.
I am afraid of being connected to others.
I reject and eject myself before others can do it to me.
It is safer to watch from the sidelines than to jump in.

Children of such parents feel as if they are a burden on their parent. These children are confused and wonder why they aren't important enough to get the attention and care they so desire. They feel rejected and neglected by their parent to the point that they might turn themselves into star achievers and perfect children in order to be seen and validated.

This is how a Half-Assed parent might sound: "Why do I need to stay for the whole performance? Why don't I just come for the last part? It's so long and boring to sit through. There's no parking, anyway, and I'll have to walk at least a mile. I really don't like watching shows. I'd rather see you after. I don't know why I even bother."

If you deploy this mask or know someone who might, it is worthwhile to go beneath this mask to the feelings it hides and find a way to explore these deeply.

The Deadbeat

Do you find that the mere presence or idea of your children triggers you? Do you find that you're not interested in being involved in their lives? If so, you may be wearing the mask of the Deadbeat.

This kind of parent is just dead weight around the family, stoic and emotionally absent. In simple terms, these parents are checked out. They show no real emotional interest in the family or its care. While they take up physical space, they don't extend themselves emotionally. They are there, but only one step away from not being there at all. But because they are physically in the home, they suck up resources and affect the energy of those around them. Deadbeats typically put pressure on the other spouse or the older children to compensate for their refusal to play any role themselves. Deadbeats want to be a member of the household without contributing to it.

Deadbeats have the following beliefs:

I don't need to give to others, just take from them.
I am incapable of contributing to others, and unwilling to try.
I am scared to fail and show my vulnerability.
No one cares about me, so why should I care about them?
I am unworthy of participating in relationships in any
meaningful way.

Children of Deadbeats may take this parent's lack of care personally and wonder why their parent isn't more engaged. These children may create the narrative that the reason is that they aren't good enough. Depending on their own temperaments, they may feel a pervasive sense of an inner lack and learn to emotionally disconnect themselves. Or they may try extra hard to get the parent's attention by being the extra-good one or the extra-bad one. Either way, a valuable opportunity to feel connected is lost when there's no response from the parent.

A Deadbeat parent doesn't say or do much, so it's hard to imagine what they would sound like. This is the energy Deadbeat parents emit: "Nothing around here is worthy of my interest, resources, or time. Everything here is a waste of energy. I don't belong with these people. I wish I wasn't here. I am an outsider."

If you deploy this mask or know someone who might, it is worthwhile to go beneath this mask to the feelings it hides and find a way to explore these deeply.

THE FLEERS

The Fleers aren't even present enough to be triggered by their children. They disappear altogether. The main emotional strategy used by Fleers to manage their fears is to abandon ship altogether. They discard, bail, bolt, and run. Their modus operandi is to escape pressure and responsibility. It's easy to disparage such parents for their lack of investment, but we need to understand that they are trauma victims themselves. Their inability to bond and connect comes from past childhood wounds, not from evil intentions. I am not condoning their behavior, but understand that this *bail and run* mentality comes from deeply ingrained conditioning that they are so lacking within that no one needs them around.

Fleers hold these beliefs:

**I have nothing to contribute or give to anyone. I don't
    exist.**
**Nothing means anything to me, and I don't mean anything
    to anyone.**

Could this be you sometimes? Do you feel so unworthy that you run away from relationships or situations because you genuinely believe you have nothing to contribute? Do you stay away from intimate commitments because you fear being rejected and traumatized the way you were as a child?

Fleers have learned through experience that committing to others could bring about trauma and abandonment. It's therefore safer to stay away from any emotional entanglements. You can reflect on whether you ever utilize this ego mask yourself.

The Yo-Yo

Yo-Yos are constantly on the move. Commitment of any kind terrifies them. These parents come and go whenever they feel like doing so; there's no rhyme or reason to their presence or absence. They refuse to stick to plans, and if they do make plans, they are likely to be late or not show at all. You never know whether they will make an appearance. When they do show up, they often act as if nothing is wrong, then disappear into the ether again for months or even years. Yo-Yos are often grossly commitment-phobic and dependency-averse. They cannot bear to have people expect anything from them, so they cut all consistent ties.

This fear of dependency appears highly selfish, and on one level it is. However, it's bred from a fear of being a disappointment to others and being abandoned themselves.

Yo-Yo parents have the following beliefs:

Don't invest in others or you will be hurt.
Do the abandoning before the other does.
I have nothing to give to anyone.

No one wants me in their life.
People are unreliable and will abandon you.
It is too risky to depend on others.
If others depend on me, they will be disappointed.
I am unworthy of giving or receiving love.

Children of such parents feel neglected and betrayed, and often confused by the unpredictable nature of the relationship. They may spend a lot of their energy and resources waiting and hoping for these parents to appear in their lives and taking their parents' absence personally. These children may wonder why they aren't good enough for their parents to spend time with, making them feel dreadfully insecure.

Yo-Yo parents are rarely around, but when they are, they emit this energy: "I don't have time to stick around. I have a whole life somewhere else that needs my attention. I can't get bogged down in your troubles. I am a traveler through life who needs to be free to come and go as I please."

If you deploy this mask or know someone who might, it is worthwhile to go beneath this mask to the feelings it hides and find a way to explore these deeply.

The Abandoner

Abandoners are just as the name suggests—not there. Period. These are traumatized individuals who outright abandon all parental responsibilities and may simply disappear for years on end. It is almost better for their children to think of Abandoners as dead, because then being abandoned wouldn't feel so personal.

These parents often suffer from a combination of some sort of clinical psychological disorder and a substance addiction. This condition typically results in their being completely ill-prepared to manage the responsibilities and pressures of parenthood. These parents simply cannot cope. Moreover, they don't believe their abandonment is causing anyone pain. They feel so unworthy within that they aren't able to fathom the possibility that anyone is affected by their absence.

Abandoner parents have these beliefs:

Connecting with others is traumatic.
I have no significance or worth.
I have nothing to contribute.
I don't enhance anyone's life by my presence.
Others are better off without me.

Children of these parents often feel ruthlessly abandoned, discarded, and neglected. Unless some compelling narrative gives these children a meaning to attach to their abandonment, they are likely to take it personally and believe that it's because they aren't good enough. The abandonment and "not good enough" narrative will run through the course of their lives. They will need to work hard to heal so they don't pass this narrative on to their own children.

Although Abandoners aren't around to say much, their absence speaks volumes. This is what their lack of presence says to their children: "You are not important enough for me to heal my wounds. You are not important enough for me to change my ways. I am too messed up to care about your messes and struggles. I am in deep struggles and pain over my own life and can barely stay afloat. I need to take care of myself. I cannot take care of you."

If you deploy this mask or know someone who might, it is worthwhile to go beneath this mask to the feelings it hides and find a way to explore these deeply.

We have now covered what I believe are our major ego masks. Several of the characteristics of these different masks probably resonated with you, and perhaps you were able to "diagnose" yourself or your loved ones. It's important to note that we can wear many different masks, depending on the situation we are faced with. At times, we might wear the Fleer mask; at others, the Fixer. Or sometimes, we may wear several masks in sequence—for example, starting with the Fixer mask, and then donning the Fighter mask, and ending up wearing the Freezer mask.

As Trisha, a client, recently said to me, "I first start off in a panic. I rush to the rescue. I overplease. I overcompensate. I do everything for my kid. I put on her shoes, fix her bed, comb her hair. I do everything just so she doesn't throw a fit. But when she keeps on fighting me and resisting, my anger begins to boil. I feel helpless and frustrated. Before you know it, I am screaming at the top of my lungs. Then I am so mortified at what I just did, I withdraw and clam up. It's a crazy cycle, and I don't know how to break it."

Trisha is not alone in her sense of inner chaos. Most of us wear many different masks in different situations with different people. Becoming aware of this tendency is a powerful tool in the awakening process. Remember, we are fluid beings who cannot be typecast. The categories I've described provide a helpful frame of reference, but are not meant to bind us or box us in. They are here to provide insight and guidance.

Each of these impostor ego masks creates predictable communication loops with our children that can cause pain, stress, and conflict. It's only once we can spot our own unique impostor egos that we can uncover the habitual patterns we create with our kids. I call these negative patterns our "dysfunctional loops." We keep going round and round within them and don't even realize we are caught up in a cycle. Are you ready to go deeper to uncover your own typical patterns and loops?

Before we move to the next phase, take a moment to check in with yourself. How are you feeling about all this information? Perhaps you are noticing the ego within yourself and others for the first time. This awareness may feel overwhelming, even intimidating. Becoming aware of our inner dynamics is never an easy process, but it is a vital one if we are to break our dysfunctional loops and create greater connection in our lives.

PUTTING IT INTO PRACTICE

The reason I have described our ego masks in such clear and simple categories is to help you spot them in your own life, either in yourself or in others. If you find yourself stuck in negative feelings about this part of yourself, remember these extremely important points:

Your impostor masks are not bad.

Your masks have saved and protected you from pain.

Spotting your ego doesn't make you a bad person; it makes you human.

Becoming aware of your masks is a key step in breaking old patterns.

What is your most predominant style of mask? What is your secondary style? Perhaps you recognized the styles of the masks worn by your parents or your loved ones. The chart on the next page may help you organize your thoughts.

This is a time for you to be aware of your feelings. What is coming up for you? Maybe you have shame or guilt about your past, or perhaps you have anger toward others. This could set off another cycle of ego reactions. If you can remember that the ego rises to the fore as a means of survival, maybe you can show compassion and empathy—for yourself and others.

To put these new awarenesses into practice, it is important to begin spotting these masks as they arise in the moment. Awareness of when you are in mask mode is essential to begin breaking cycles. Let me warn you that something else could occur at this stage of the process—an ego regression. Let me explain:

When our ego senses that we are about to dismantle its stronghold, it kicks in even more powerfully in the form of self-sabotage and sends us back into old, dysfunctional states of being. I cannot even begin to describe how many times this regression has happened with clients.

When my client Brandon was about to make serious headway

Relationship	Primary Mask	Secondary Mask	Memories	Feelings
Mom	Fighter	Fleer	I was around 8 years old and my mom yelled at me for breaking her beautiful China dish. She thought I was being purposely careless. She called me a no-good loser. After that she literally didn't speak to me for days.	I felt like disappearing. I hated those long periods of silence. I was terrified of them.
Dad				
Siblings				
Self				

with his gambling addiction and had truly begun healing childhood wounds during therapy, bam!—one day he just stopped coming. No matter how many times I tried, he didn't answer my calls or texts. I immediately knew what had happened. He had regressed. His ego had panicked and dug its heels into his psyche, sweeping him back into old patterns so it could stay in place. He was so close to breaking free, but he was terrified of being healthy. Our psyches are complex, aren't they?

Brandon finally emerged more than a year and a half later. Crestfallen, he apologized for his absence. I told him there was nothing to be sorry for. He reported that during this time away, his addiction had kicked back in big-time, and he'd had the worst plunge into addiction ever. It was only when his wife discovered that he was hundreds of thousands of dollars in debt and threatened to divorce him that he chose to call me. I felt compassion for Brandon. Given his past trauma, I understood that choosing health over destruction was unfamiliar to him. So habituated do we become in our patterns that no matter how unhealthy they are, they feel more familiar than new ones. It feels more comforting to stay stuck and dysfunctional than to move into the new terrain of consciousness and wisdom.

It took Brandon another year of therapy to uncover how he had created a pattern of scarcity and lack in his life from childhood. During his time with me, he uncovered innumerable instances of never having money and, when he did, being so uncomfortable with it that he would spend it all at once. This pattern of acute scarcity had created a complicated relationship with money throughout his life. This pattern laid the foundation of his gambling habits, as these allowed him to stay in eternal uncertainty and lack around money. It was only when Brandon began to connect the dots and see how his past was contributing to his present that he slowly began to undo these narratives and replace them with healthier ones. His story is not so unlike the story of any one of us; we are all mired in our past patterns without even realizing it.

You may be experiencing some fear by this stage. If so, be gentle with yourself. Your ego will be whispering all sorts of things in your ear: "This is all nonsense." "You have been fine all this time and you can just continue the old ways." "Your friends and family will be mad at you for changing so much." I want you to know that these kinds of statements are your ego's ways of staying in place. Just by being aware, you are helping to release its control in your life. The ego is not something you need to kill in a brutal way. Instead, as you become grounded in yourself, you can release it layer by layer, step-by-step.

Step Nine:
Face Your Triggers

My ego masks blind me
And keep me stuck in chaos
And disconnect me from my children
And make me forget how much I love being a parent.
It is only when I begin to see them in the mirror
And break the chains they imprison me with
That I will finally be free
And finally see the beauty that lies within my children.

Once you have identified your ego masks, you will be able to see exactly how they have set up dysfunctional communication loops that have kept you stuck in chaos with your children. This is an exciting step on your growth journey as a parent, because you are about to see your patterns up close and personal. What's more, you are going to start using tools to help you break your dysfunctional cycles with your children. Isn't this a hopeful prospect?

When we are triggered by our kids, we act out in habitual ways. These loops are so predictable that they can be charted on a graph. Your kid does A, you say B, your kid says C, and you say D. Before you know it, you are in an argument. It's as though you and your child have memorized the movements of a dance and keep repeating them over and over. Here is the good news: You can absolutely break out of these loops. You just need to know how. This step will teach you. Only when you break the pattern can new dynamics be created and new connections made.

If you are a parent who finds yourself getting stuck in one dysfunctional loop after another with your kids, it's time to take a pause and start disrupting your own patterns. Believe it or not, you have the power to do so for yourself. Breaking old patterns is what this step is all about. Disrupting your patterns will help you attune to your children and connect with them in a brand-new way. Isn't this connection what we all yearn for with our kids?

To start, we need to ask ourselves: What is the flame that lights the entire cycle? Every dysfunctional pattern you have with others starts with a common element. Do you know what that is? It's a trigger. We traditionally define a trigger as something on the outside that sets us off. While this definition is accurate, it isn't the whole picture. Let's break down what triggers are and how they operate.

A trigger doesn't start off as a trigger. It starts off as an event, a situation, or a statement. Maybe it is a birthday party, a plane delay, or someone's comment at the store. Simplistically stated, the trigger starts as a "thing," and it could be any "thing": a dish served wrong at a restaurant, a traffic jam, your mother's judgment about your hairstyle. If you documented a hundred people's reactions to such things, each person would respond differently; some would not respond at all. If these were truly triggers, they would trigger everyone in roughly the same way.

So a trigger starts off as a "thing." What turns it into a trigger isn't the thing itself, but *how it* is interpreted and metabolized internally. This—internal interpretation and metabolism—is the key, the lynchpin, to determining whether a thing stays a thing or turns into a trigger. This is probably one of the most important data points along your growth journey, so vital that we need to pause here so I can reiterate: what makes something a trigger is not the thing itself, but how you emotionally metabolize it. If you can understand this truth on a deep level, you will be well on your way to breaking your negative patterns with your children.

Let's take a simple example: being caught in a traffic jam. If it is a beautiful day and you are not in a hurry to get somewhere, you likely experience a traffic jam as a neutral event. You might even be able to turn it into something positive by listening to a favorite podcast or catching up on calls. But what if you had a crummy day and are late for an evening obligation? Suddenly this traffic jam could cause an explosion. Do you see what I mean? The effect of this event all depends on what is going on for you internally. If you are filled with calm water, you react differently than if you are filled with gasoline, say, or an even more combustible explosive.

The "thing" is just a flame that could either grow or die out. But whether or not it sets fire to our inner dynamite depends on something inside us. What is this something? Ah, it is what we have been talking about all along—the ego masks we have been wearing. Are our masks made of water, something volatile that causes an eruption, or something even more destructive that results in a huge explosion?

Here is the truth about our triggers. They are just flames. What transforms these flames into something destructive is one thing only: our ego. The bigger our ego, the greater our inner emotional explosion.

Take the event of your child not listening to you. At the basic level, this is just a situation called "child doesn't listen to parent." That's all. Now, what makes this situation turn into a trigger? The parent's reaction based on their ego. Do you see? Do they just lovingly care for the child, or do they blow up? It all depends on the

#1

parent's inner ego, doesn't it? The more the parent feels invalidated or insecure, the greater the force and velocity of the ego that shows up. And the greater the ego, the more combustive and explosive the parent's reaction will be.

A simple way to represent this idea visually is to imagine the parent's inner world. Is the parent filled with many holes or a few holes? Is the parent filled with calm water or with dangerous explosives? Of course, the fewer the holes and the calmer the parent

#2

is within, the smaller the combustion will be when the parent reacts; the more holes and inner explosives, the greater that combustion will be.

In this illustration, those with fewer inner wounds, or "holes," as symbolized by the first heart, have a less egoic reaction than those with more holes. In each case, the trigger, or "flame," is the same. But the way it sets off each person's "inner bomb" is different: the more flammable we are, the greater the size of our inner bomb

#3

and the more severe the destruction it can cause.

Which one of these hearts do you most identify with? Perhaps you notice that in some situations you have the energy of water, but in others, you have the capacity to explode. It's useful to understand yourself in terms of your inner chemistry so you can take conscious steps to protect yourself and others from your own combustion. In general, the more our inner holes are healed, the less reactive we will be. Take a moment to reflect on the last time you felt triggered.

What was the flame or triggering event?
What were your inner holes? Were you filled with water,
  gasoline, or explosives?
How did you react?

One of the most touching examples of how our internal world dictates the way we perceive our external reality comes from Jake, who attended one of my seminars. He came up to me after the event and broke down in tears. "I finally see how I have been creating my own nightmare," he said. "I have been fighting with my eight-year-old son almost every day for years because of my own crap. I finally see it! All this time, I thought there was something wrong with him, but today you have shown me that it was me. I was my own trigger. He wasn't the trigger. It was me, all me." Jake explained how he had been highly triggered by his son for years because Max wasn't as masculine and athletic as he'd imagined a son would be. Max also suffered from speech and learning delays. All of these qualities in his son were very difficult for Jake.

Jake, even though he loved his son, was getting into daily battles with him. The final straw was when he threw a glass of water on his son and dragged him by his jacket, slamming him into a wall. It was then that Jake realized things were beyond his control and he needed drastic help. This is when he signed up for one of my workshops. After doing work with me on his childhood triggers, Jake uncovered a key memory from childhood that helped him understand a lot of his issues around his son. He remembered being cornered in a school bathroom at around age ten and being violently bullied by several older boys. They called him a "sissy" and laughed at him when he cried. Jake had buried that memory but still carried the shame about his fear that day and how he had been too terrified to fight back. He had blamed himself for a lack of masculinity. In fact, when he returned home, his father derided Jake for not standing up for himself and made him feel ashamed for lacking courage.

Since that day, Jake had grown an ego mask of hypermasculinity. He forced himself to be more athletic and buffed himself up as he grew older, and he started spending a lot of time at the gym. If you saw him today, you would never imagine that he had any issues around masculinity. Fast-forward to his male child, Max, who was not the prototypical "boy's boy." On the contrary, Max was more effeminate, sensitive, and "soft." The divide between who Max was and what his father expected set the two of them on a collision course of tragic conflict.

What Jake was completely unaware of was his own inner trauma and how it had been bubbling like hot lava below the surface. Jake had buried his inner pain so deep that he thought he didn't have any. Disconnected from his own inner trauma, he projected this pain onto his son. He thought Max was at fault and needed to be fixed. Jake's old childhood trauma lay buried deep in his unconscious, driving his current behavior toward his son. He tried to fix his son so that Max would not go through the pain that had brutalized Jake. It was only that day, after years of berating and shaming his son, that Jake looked deep enough to discover his own unresolved wounds. The watershed of insight was forceful. Jake's inner child was finally seen in its pain. It had been screaming under Jake's "Fighter" ego, but no one had paid attention. The ego had always won—until that day, when the ego finally shattered and the pain of the wounded inner child gushed out.

I could see the raw pain in Jake's eyes as he realized how he had been transferring all his past pain onto his child. I embraced Jake and his inner little boy. They both needed so much attention and tenderness. I asked him to promise that he would return to his inner child and allow that child to cry out all the pain Jake had suppressed for all these years. The more he healed his own inner boy, the more he would accept his son and allow him to be who he truly was. Jake had been projecting onto Max the hurt that he himself had experienced in his own past. This is how "hurt people hurt people." Do you see how, if we are not aware, we can pass our unresolved childhood pain on to our kids? That's why the growth you are about to experience is so important—for you and for your kids.

When you understand that a "thing" outside only triggers you because of your internal emotional explosives, that is a turning point. This can change every dynamic with your children. The more you become aware of your inner pain and fears, the closer you will be to understanding yourself more deeply and being more connected with your children. The more inner explosives or holes you have, the more you will project them onto your kids. Your projections in turn will create holes in your kids that they will use as explosives in their own adult relationships. This is the cycle that we are ending by doing this work.

PUTTING IT INTO PRACTICE

One of the most effective ways to recognize the triggers in our lives is to do an exercise called "Flip It Around." In essence, we take something that is a trigger for us when we see it in someone else and flip it around to ourselves by asking, "Have I ever been triggered by this part in myself?" If the answer is yes, then we have carved out the first step toward understanding a deeper wound within us.

This is exactly what happened with Jake in the example that we just discussed. Once he flipped the trigger back to himself and asked, "Have I ever been triggered by my own feminine side or my own lack of masculinity, as I am being triggered by Max?" the answer was clear.

Another recent case echoes this process. Victoria came into a session with me one day clearly triggered. Her thirty-year-old daughter had filed for divorce a few months before and had only recently revealed to her mother that she had suffered physical and emotional

abuse from her husband. Victoria was livid. She wanted to file a police report against her son-in-law. She was also frustrated with her
daughter for what she perceived as passive behavior: "She is so weak
and immature. I didn't raise her to be this way. I want her to fight
back and stand up for herself. I can't believe how she allowed her
husband to get away with this abuse."

I could see that Victoria's ego was highly activated. "It is not your
job to take action against your son-in-law. It is your daughter's,
isn't it?"

Victoria continued to rant. "I am furious about this. I worked so
hard to raise a strong female child that I cannot believe, after all my
efforts, that she turned out like this." Victoria reported getting into
a serious argument with her daughter and banging the phone down
in frustration.

I knew there was something about Victoria's past that was being
reactivated, so I did the "Flip It Around" exercise with her. I asked
her, "What about your daughter's behavior do you not like in yourself? You feel she is being passive and weak. Was there a time in your
life when you were passive and weak?"

Victoria answered in a heartbeat. "Yes! I was exactly like this
with my own first husband, in my marriage before the one with my
daughter's father! He used to physically and verbally assault me. I
had to file many reports against him. Each time he said he was sorry,
I would believe him, until the next beating. After four years of hell,
I finally had the courage to leave him. I worked so hard on myself to
never allow this to happen to me again. When I married for the second time, I made sure to choose a docile and quiet man who adored
me." And there it was. Do you see how predictably our old wounds
surface?

Victoria's intense reaction toward her daughter was evoked by
her own painful past. She had worked so hard to rid herself of any
passivity and weakness toward men that when she saw this passivity
emerge in her daughter, Victoria couldn't bear to look in the mirror.
I gently encouraged her. "You may have grown strong, but you still

have not healed. To heal, you need to forgive that old part of yourself and treat it with compassion. You have just killed it, buried it, and moved on. This is not healing. We know this because you want to do the same thing to your daughter's 'weak' parts as you did to your own: kill them, bury them, and move on. You have to let your daughter take control of this situation. But it is only when you own those parts in yourself and see them through the eyes of compassion and understanding that you will accept yourself for your past. Once you accept yourself for all your 'weak' parts, you will accept your daughter. You will have compassion for her pain and struggle. This will bring you both closer."

The parts within us that we have rejected, disavowed, and abandoned don't just disappear. They are simply buried deep inside us. When we see them rise up in our children or others we love, we become extremely triggered and try to do to those parts what we have done to our own. Our own past wounds wash over us with such pain that we enlist our ego with a furor. Our ego roars to the scene with great velocity and attempts to drown out our inner pain by lashing out against our children's pain. Instead of connecting to their pain and seeing it for what it is—separate from us—we thrash against our children with control and degradation, and they end up feeling unseen and invalidated. The tragedy is that we don't even realize what we are doing; this all happens unconsciously. Such is the power of unresolved inner pain.

Step Ten:
Break Your Dysfunctional Loops

Round and round we go,
Missing all the exit signs.
Instead of breaking the chains free,
The chain knots us further into our cage.

Most of us parents have gotten stuck in negative communication loops with our children at some point or another. And boy, are these loops painful to be in. They cause stress, tension, and conflict. They feel yucky. The reason we get into them is that we are not aware of our own egos and how they mess up our relationships with our kids. Unless and until we are able to see our patterns clearly—our egos in action—we won't take responsibility for our part in the dynamic and will try to blame our kids. That blame sets them off even more, and the pattern continues.

The key question is this: Who will break the loop? Who will disrupt the pattern? Will it be you? Do you dare to be the pattern disrupter in the family? The beautiful reassurance is that you have the full power to be the one to make the changes. Our children are not going to be able to be the changemakers, because they are molded by our egos. They cannot help but be in reaction mode. Therefore, the onus is on us. As daunting as it may feel, I encourage you to embrace this challenge with courage, because doing so will free not just your children but yourself as well.

Zina had been coming to me for coaching for more than six months when she finally experienced a breakthrough. She had been stuck, cycling again and again through the same dysfunctional loop with her seven-year-old daughter, Angela. What was their cycle? Zina was a Freezer. She hated conflict and always tried to shut it down. She simply couldn't cope with her daughter's issues because of her own PTSD—a condition she wasn't even aware of. Angela, on the other hand, was a Fixer. She desperately wanted her mother to like her and would try anything to please Zina. When Angela felt that she was failing to please her mother, she would cry uncontrollably and even self-harm. The more volatile her daughter's emotions, the more Zina shut down. And the more she did, the more Angela perceived herself as "bad" and "shameful." The cycle wouldn't stop.

When I probed into Zina's life, she was able to explore her dynamic with her own mother, in which she had felt terrified by her mother's alcoholic rages. To cope, Zina had learned to numb herself by dissociating from the trauma. Zina had continued this pattern into her own dynamic with her daughter. When Angela was needy and clingy, Zina felt intimidated and afraid. She was unable to touch her maternal, giving heart. She didn't believe her daughter could truly need her, since she felt so unworthy of being a mother. When Angela became more and more vociferous, Zina took it personally—as if Angela were going to attack and harm her. Zina basically went into PTSD mode.

It took six months of intensive work for Zina to crack her Freezer mask so she could touch the pain within. Once she did, the dam burst. She collapsed into a frightened little girl desperately seeking her mother's love. She sobbed, saying, "My mom never loved me.

She loved the alcohol more than me. She never truly wanted me around. I felt worthless all my life. I couldn't compete with alcohol." Zina was shaking and trembling. After many moments of crying, she began to rock herself into a calm state. I gently asked, "Do you think Angela feels the same way you did, and this is why she is crying for your attention?" Zina got it! Seeing her own inner wounds in action permitted her to get in touch with how her daughter might feel. She realized that Angela just needed a mother, much as Zina had when she was a little girl. Their pain and craving were the same. Slowly but surely, Zina began to melt toward Angela. As Zina thawed out her Freezer mask, she began to be more compassionately attuned to Angela's needs. As Angela felt her mother's presence more and more, she became less needy. Soon, they began to bond at a deeper level.

It doesn't matter what mask we wear. Since all these masks come from our egos, all of them are bound to create dysfunctional patterns with our children. Each ego mask sets up unique communication loops with our kids. Let's take a look at these loops to see whether any of them resonate with you. I will be examining these on a generic level, but make sure that you use these examples to pry into your own patterns and see whether the lessons apply to you.

We will use the same event for each scenario and observe how each mask shows up. Let's take the event of a child being "rude" and saying "I hate you!" to their parents. I use this example because almost every parent is bound to be somewhat reactive to these words. Most parents interpret them as a sign of not only disrespect, but also ingratitude. For traditional parents, these are huge triggers that inflame the inner wounds of insignificance. Let's examine how each impostor mask might react in this situation.

THE FIGHTER LOOP

When Fighter parents hear "I hate you" from their children, they first interpret the words as a personal attack. They immediately

want to respond with something like "What did you say? How dare you talk to me this way!" Their anger and indignation begin a dysfunctional loop.

If Fighters perceive their children's reaction as an attack, they use anger to regain a sense of power. Fighters interpret such events as something that they need to stop right away. Their modus operandi is to stop this behavior by using shame, degradation, or punishment. They scream at their children and scare them into compliance. Before such a parent, a child feels invalidated and unheard. The child feels shut down and shut out.

In this loop, a parent's reaction creates negative feelings within the child. These don't disappear, but instead set off a cascade of new negative patterns—and the cycle continues.

THE FIXER LOOP

Fixer parents, too, take it personally when their child says "I hate you." But instead of trying to control the child's behavior, Fixers try to control the child's perception of them as parents. They are scared to lose the child's love, so they will do their best to retrieve it at all costs. They use techniques such as enabling and rescuing to ensure that their children don't abandon them. Their MO is to stop the bad

behavior through acquiescence and pleasing. Let's see how this loop might look.

The child before the Fixer parent feels neglected, the child's true feelings ignored, as the parent seems concerned only with converting the child's feelings from hatred back to love for the parent. Fixer parents don't seem concerned about why the child is feeling that way or about doing any deep repair. In this loop, too, the parent's reaction creates negative feelings in the child. These don't disappear, but set off a cascade of new negative patterns—and the cycle continues.

THE FEIGNER LOOP

When they hear "I hate you" from their children, all Feigner parents can think about is how the situation will look to the outside world. Feigners' image and public persona are more important than anything else. They will do anything to avoid negative attention being placed on them. Their MO is to gloss over the problem in any way, shape, or form in order to appear a certain way to the rest of the world. The children's feelings are completely disregarded, as Feigner parents' focus is only on how others perceive them. These

children realize that their feelings are being disavowed and may feel shunned.

Once again, in this loop the parent's reaction creates negative feelings in the child. These don't disappear, but set off a cascade of new negative patterns—and the cycle continues.

THE FREEZER LOOP

When they hear their children say "I hate you," Freezer parents also interpret the situation as being personal. They put up frozen walls to

hide behind. Conflict is a huge trigger that causes them to shut down. Freezers become paralyzed and reject any pleas from their children. Their MO is to hide. Instead of reaching toward the child and showing concern for the child's emotions, such parents prefer to tend to their own comfort and retreat behind an emotionless, cold wall. Their children receive the message that their emotions are falling onto icy hearts. This leads to a feeling of isolation and unworthiness in the child.

In this loop, the parent's reaction creates negative feelings in the child that don't just go away, but instead set off a cascade of new negative patterns—and the cycle continues.

THE FLEER LOOP

Fleer parents interpret "I hate you" as something to run away from. They don't take it personally, since they are completely disconnected from any personal responsibility due to their own traumas. They simply don't see the child's problem as their problem. Fleers run from responsibilities and struggles. Their children feel invisible and realize that they are insignificant to their Fleer parents. These feelings create a general distrust of others, coupled with a piercing sense of betrayal and abandonment.

Do you notice something alarming in these loops? Do you notice how the child is being ignored in all of them? These loops are toxic for our kids, because when we are caught up in them, we end up completely disregarding our children's feelings and worldview. We focus only on how *we* feel and how *we* can protect ourselves.

The degree to which we display our ego masks to the outside world is directly commensurate with how deeply we are wounded within. The more our inner pain, the greater our outer outburst. And to a large degree, our children are helpless, hostage to our moods and fancies. They cannot just run away and live in another city. They are dependent on us and prey to our egoic inner monsters; they are innocent prisoners with no recourse or escape route. This is one of the greatest reasons for us to do our own inner work to heal, so that we don't unleash our pain on them.

It's hard as parents to own that we can operate so unconsciously. However, this is the brutal reality. We were raised unconsciously, so it is no surprise that we pass our wounds on to our children. But when we can clearly see our patterns in action, we can begin to break them down. Only then can we start being attuned to our children for who *they* are and what *they* feel.

Once we heal from within, we can finally stop reacting from our inner holes and instead respond from a place of inner wholeness. This inner wholeness will allow us to raise the child *before* us rather than the child *within* us.

PUTTING IT INTO PRACTICE

It's hard to break our patterns when we are in the middle of them, isn't it? It's hard to spot our ego while we are in it. It is hard to break out of a loop once it is underway. Our only hope is to stop the loop before it starts. For this to happen, it is important to recognize how our body reacts when it is being triggered.

You see, our body tries to signal us when it enters a state of alarm.

There are definite signs and symptoms—we just need to be aware of them. They show up in our bodies. So how do we start paying attention? We tune in. Tune in to what? Our bodies' alarm system. Is my heart racing? Do I have palpitations or sweaty palms, a heaving chest, trembling lips, teary eyes? What is my body trying to tell me? Tuning in to such signals can help us identify when we are about to have an explosion. In this way, our emotions act as signals that something is awry. Recognizing our patterns at the emotional level is a huge step toward breaking free from our patterns.

To make it simple, I have categorized our typical emotional signatures as the "five A's." Understanding yourself via these five A's can ground you in your body and help you keep your ego from reacting. Let's reflect on these emotions now:

The **Fighter's** emotional style is *anger.*
The **Fixer's** emotional style is *anxiety*.
The **Feigner's** emotional style is *attention-seeking*.
The **Freezer's** emotional style is *avoidance*.
The **Fleer's** emotional style is *abandonment*.

Can you identify your own predominant emotional style? How does your body express that style? Since I am a Fixer by nature, my emotional signature is anxiety. Recognizing the signs of anxiety in my body before I go into a tailspin has been useful for me. When I feel anxiety and stress, my body immediately speaks to me. I feel my chest begin to heave and my eyes tear up. Nervous energy then wells up inside me. My stomach feels queasy, and my mind races with thought after thought. It's obvious that I'm about to have a meltdown.

When I pay attention to these warning signs and pause, I can engage in self-care practices such as meditation and journaling. Sometimes when I'm in an emotional storm, I call a friend or take a few hours off work to exercise in nature. These things help me center and ground myself. However, there are many times when I miss the signs—or rather, I observe them but pretend they aren't signaling me. Then I shoot straight into reactive mode and explode into my Fixer mask. Once the explosion begins, it's hard to rein it back in. That's why I want to help you learn how to change your own patterns, before an explosion.

Let's take a look at what this cycle looks like and where you can begin to break it.

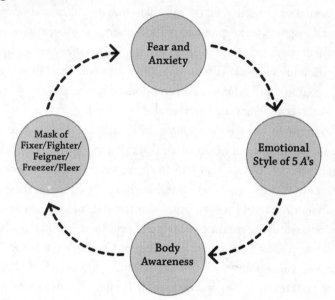

My client Becky, as an example, uses attention-seeking when she's feeling an inner lack. As an overachiever, she's used to receiving external validation and goes into attention-seeking mode in overdrive. Stuart, another client, is the eternal avoider. Conflict and any emotional drama terrify him, so he shuts down and freezes. This response causes tremendous emotional tension in his family. My friend Jonathan uses anger to feel significant and powerful. He typically explodes and then withdraws. (I find anger a common default for many males conditioned to use control and domination to show their worth.) Debbie's ex-husband is a classic abandoner, who was so traumatized by their divorce that he completely cut off all contact with her and fled the country.

I needed to show each of my clients how to recognize their own and their loved ones' ego patterns and discover their underlying emotional styles. Once they became aware of their emotional patterns, I helped them to notice these patterns in their bodies. As they became better at body awareness, I could help them pause and change the patterns. Fighters, for example, may notice their teeth grinding or their jaws clamping. Fixers may have sweaty palms and heaving chests. Feigners may experience panicky shortness of breath because they feel they are being caught by others. Freezers may notice heart palpitations, since any emotional conflict terrifies them. Fleers may have cold feet and experience an emotional desire to run away.

I call these "emotional" styles and not "feeling" styles, because I differentiate between emotions and feelings. Emotions are the outward embodiment of our inner feelings and are often ego-based and protective. We use emotions to express that something is amiss within us. It's our signal that something has gone awry. But these are nowhere close to our true feelings. Our true feelings are just that—feelings, which are meant to be felt and processed within ourselves. For example, helplessness is a feeling, but blame is an emotional reaction; vulnerability is a feeling, but anger toward another is an emotional reaction. The feeling is something we feel deep within us that can be experienced silently and privately. The emotional reaction is what we deploy to run away from the feeling or to express the feeling. Expressing the feeling is not the same as feeling the feeling. Do you see the difference?

It is only when we notice our emotional reactions that we can begin to address them with a calming presence. Perhaps we can soothe ourselves by saying something such as this: "I am in an emotional tsunami. I am about to react in destructive and toxic ways. I need to stop the pattern here. I *need to* understand what I am really feeling within."

Just this pause has the potential to stop our egoic patterns from acting out, allowing us to go deeper to do some inner-child work. The two keys to healing are to notice your emotional reactions before they become masks, then to go beneath those reactions to the actual feelings they mask. The following exercise can help you do this work.

On the left side of a blank page, write down your ego-based emotional reactions to your triggers, as in the examples that follow. On the right side of the page, try to uncover your inner child's true feelings about those happenings, as also shown in the examples. Unless we go to the feelings beneath a reaction, we run the risk of having our emotions run amok. Reactions that are left unchecked lead to our impostor ego masks becoming solidified. Once these masks come into play, it's hard to shed them, because they set other dynamics in motion.

For example, the five *A*'s might be unearthed in the following manner:

Emotional Reaction Style	True Feelings
Anger: "I hate you. I don't want to be near you"	"You are hurting my feelings"
Anxiety: "I will fix it. I am good. I need you"	"I am scared you won't love me"
Attention-seeking: "Do you see me? Do you care?"	"I feel empty without your praise"
Avoidance: "I don't want to be near you!"	"I am scared you will reject me"
Abandonment: "I don't care about you!"	"I fear being abandoned again"

To recap, these are the steps to follow to change destructive emotional patterns and break your loops of dysfunction:

1. When you feel strong emotions in your body, pause.
2. Notice the physical signals.
3. Be forewarned that unless you take care of yourself, these emotions are going to burst forth in some kind of explosion.
4. Say to yourself, "What am I truly feeling right now? What's going on inside me? Before I jump into action, let me spend some time with myself to uncover my true fears."

Emotions are messengers telling us that an internal tsunami is forming. They speak through our bodies. If we don't pay attention to the emotional manifestations of anger, anxiety, attention-seeking, avoidance, or abandonment in our bodies, we will react all over the place without knowing why. Soon we will be embedded in a harsh dynamic of dysfunction and dis-ease with our kids, wondering how we got here. The truth is that there were plenty of clues along the way; we just didn't know how to pay attention to them. This map is laying out the steps to help you do just that.

Step Eleven:
Activate Your Third *I*

Caught in the tsunami of my ego
I have wrecked and destroyed my love
And in turn made you, my child, feel shame.
Yet if you only knew that it has nothing to do with you,
You would realize that it is I who am wounded within
And it is I who needs to heal myself
Before I can learn to parent you.

The reason your fearful inner child exists is that your parents struggled to honor you for who you were in childhood. When you tried to be your authentic self, you received pushback and rejection. You lived in fear and avoidance of this rejection. You craved validation.

Suzie spent her whole session with me sobbing. "My mother said that she wished she had never had me. She said that I was an embarrassment to her because I was fat and not smart at school. Every day I tried to starve myself and study hard, but it was never good enough for her. Even though I am thirty years old now, I am still filled with self-hatred for all the ways I could never measure up to my mom's wishes for me."

Suzie's inner child was desperate for validation. She blamed herself for all the ways her mother projected her own lack onto her. She couldn't see that it was her mother who was lacking, not her. Suzie was an obedient little girl who believed her mother when she was told it was her fault that her mother was upset with her. Children do this, you see: they believe their parents. If their parents are angry with them or disappointed in them, children automatically believe it is their fault. They don't have the maturity to realize, "Oh, my mother is projecting her own pain onto me!" They simply believe in their parents, trusting that their feedback is true.

To protect us against this parental rejection and get the desired validation, we create the masks of our impostor egos. Suzie, for one, created the mask of the superachiever. She worked hard all her life to receive the validation she so desperately desired from her mom. However, she didn't become thin. In fact she went in the opposite direction and ate in an obsessive way, even binge-eating at times. She said to me, "This is my way of staying in control, you know. If I gave her my body, too, then I would have nothing for myself." I worked for many months with Suzie to help her learn to accept and validate herself. She had to carve out an entire new sense of self and release the one that was desperately searching for her mother's approval.

Now, imagine this: you had a parent who accepted you just as you were. You would never have needed to create all those false selves to gain validation, would you? Our children suffer greatly when we parents are in our egos. When we as parents are not in touch with our own true feelings, we inevitably ignore our children's true emotional needs and invalidate their authentic experiences. As you have seen in the prior steps, we make it all about us.

The ego's mission is just this: to protect the self at all costs. It doesn't care that it hurts our innocent children. Can you imagine how we would treat them if we weren't wearing our masks? Can you imagine how we would be as parents without our egoic reactions? Well, this is what your healing is going to lead you toward and what you are learning to do. But here is the catch: our ego is recruited by a silent and hidden boss. It doesn't function on its own. Who is its boss? As I have mentioned before, it is our inner child. As long as our inner child lies buried and wounded, our ego will be on call to protect its feelings. So in order to truly heal, we need to go to the core of our issues—the pain and fears of our inner child. When we take care of the inner child, we will automatically take care of our ego. The more our inner child feels nurtured and cared for, the more our ego will calm down and retreat. That's what this step on the parenting map is all about: the healing of the inner child.

To heal the inner child, it is key to understand why it exists in the first place. It exists because a conscious parent was not present to nurture and accept it for who it truly was. So to heal the inner child, this is what we need to activate within us: an all-nurturing inner parent. Do you think you are up for this? I will show you how you can re-parent yourself and help yourself to heal in the most trans-formational and powerful ways. That's what this step is all about: cultivating an internal loving parent, one that I call your Third I, or your *insightful* self.

When your inner child begins to feel the internal loving energy of your insightful self, it will start to transform in a profound way. Your inner child will begin to feel nurtured and validated. It will begin to heal. And as your inner child heals, the ego will no longer need to be called on to protect the inner self—because the inner self will no longer feel rejected or invalidated. It will feel seen and validated—by you, yourself. How powerful this process is!

The ego will slowly fade into retirement. Of course, it won't disappear overnight. First, it tests us to make sure we are truly on our way to healing. The ego is a tough cookie. It has been protecting us for decades, after all, so it isn't going to fade away without testing the power of the Third *I*, even trying to sabotage it. The ego needs to know that we are in good hands. Once it sees the power of this nurturing Third *I*, it will quietly recede into the background and let the Third *I* calm the inner child.

Our insightful Third *I* is the self that you should have internalized from your parents in childhood. It's a self that is soothing and nurturing, a self mirrored by an unconditionally loving parent who sees you for who you are. Most of us were raised by unconscious parents who had their own rage and anxiety issues to deal with; these parents couldn't be present for us in a loving way. In fact, for the most part they projected their angst and inadequacies onto us—just as we do with our own kids, as we now see.

I am going to show you how you can birth and cultivate this new part of you. You *can* re-parent yourself—it just takes time and a renewed consciousness. It takes practice to consolidate this part within us. Your children need you to develop this part of you so that you can manage the dynamic between your inner child and your impostor ego. When your inner child is managed, your ego calms down.

The steps we need to take to calm the ego are the same for each impostor ego mask. Let's outline them:

1. *Become aware of the dynamic between your two I's*—between your inner child and your impostor ego. Understanding that your ego responds to the fears of the inner child is key. Until now, you have just been in ego mode. Now you are beginning to understand that the ego is only reacting to the scared inner child inside you. This awareness needs to be embedded in your consciousness in order for healing to begin. It looks different for each of the ego masks: the Fighter, Fixer, Feigner, Freezer, and Fleer.

THE FIGHTER

THE FIXER

The Feigner

The Freezer

The Fleer

Being aware that your ego is always reacting to a fearful inner child is a powerful step on your healing journey. It lets you see that the real threat is something felt within you, not on the outside. The next step is to catch that fear while it's coursing through your body. Body awareness is key. Remember the five *A*'s? Catching how these emotions show up in your body will allow you to pause.

2. *Create a pause through body awareness of the five* A's. Checking in and attuning to your body throughout the day is key. Emotions will show up in your body. Your body pays attention to your subconscious faster than your own conscious mind does. Asking yourself these questions throughout the day is a powerful way to stay attuned:

> **Is my body feeling the emotions of anger or anxiety?**
> **Or is my body needy for attention, or wanting to avoid the present moment? If so, can I pause and check in at a deeper level?**

How can I honor what I am feeling and take care of these feelings without activating my impostor ego?

This pause is vital to our growth. Taking a pause allows us to center ourselves in our bodies and choose different plans of action. Before, our egos would kick in with knee-jerk reactivity, but now, we are able to pause and discern what is really going on inside us.

Once we viscerally get in touch with the needs and fears of our inner child, we are ready to activate a new way of being and develop a new consciousness. We are ready to birth our Third *I*.

3. *Activate your insightful self.* The voice of the insightful self is a calm, soothing, and loving one. It listens to the fears of the inner child and soothes it. Let me give you an example of how this works through the story of one of my clients, Linda.

Linda was having chronic relational difficulties with her seventeen-year-old daughter, Tracy, who wanted to take a gap year before college to work and live on her own. This idea freaked Linda out. She was afraid that once Tracy got off the academic train, she would never get back on. Linda herself had never gone to college, because her parents couldn't afford to send her and she didn't qualify for student loans. The prospect of her daughter following in her footsteps terrified Linda. She had experienced firsthand the perils of not having a college degree and didn't want her daughter to be in this same situation. Linda's inner child—the one that so badly wanted the validation of a college degree and felt insecure without it—was having a panic attack. She was spinning out of control with insecurity, doubt, and fear. The more her inner child cried out, the more her Fixer ego came into play. She begged, cajoled, and pleaded with Tracy. She offered to get tutors, fill out applications, and pay for any college of Tracy's choice. But no matter how hard she tried, Tracy refused her mother's help. In fact, Tracy dug her heels in even further. After a few weeks of trying to salvage the situation, Linda activated her Fighter mask. She began to have tantrums all over the place. She fought with Tracy at every chance she got, spewing all her anxieties onto her child. Tracy fought back. There were nonstop battles. Both of them were exhausted and frustrated.

When I showed Linda that she was not actually reacting to Tracy, her "real" child, but to her own inner child, she was shocked. I explained, "You are terrified because of what happened to you. You never felt good enough because of your own lack of a college degree. You felt ashamed and insecure. These feelings still live in you. Your ego has masked all of this for years. Now that your daughter is choosing to give up something you desperately wanted for yourself, your inner child is out of control with fear and projecting these fears onto her."

Linda was aghast: "You are right. I am panicked because this is how I felt. It may not be what she feels. She is not me. We are different."

I then helped Linda to cultivate her Third I. I encouraged Linda to go through the steps we have been talking about. "Each time you feel anxious in your body, pay attention. This means your ego is about to get activated. I want you to tune in and listen to what your body is trying to tell you. Get in touch with the scared little girl within. Begin soothing her. Tell her that she is okay and safe. She doesn't need a college degree to feel worthy. Tell her that Tracy will be okay, too."

I gave Linda a bunch of sentences to say to herself in moments of panic, including the following:

I am going to be okay, no matter what decisions my child makes.

I don't need my child to make me feel good enough.

> **I am a good enough parent, no matter what my child chooses to do with her life.**
> **I am a worthy person even if my child makes unconventional choices.**

Linda began to do this inner work of re-parenting herself on a daily basis. She began to self-soothe in moments of panic. Tracy felt the shift immediately. The fights stopped, calmness ensued, and connection flourished. Linda began to see Tracy as her own being. Instead of fighting her daughter, Linda now supported her. Tracy was grateful for that support and began to respond in a positive manner.

Once we soothe our inner child, we not only attune to our "real" children, but also free them to live their lives with autonomy and freedom. That's the power of this inner work. The Third *I* will look different for each of the ego types as you can see in the illustrations for the Fighter, Fixer, Feigner, Freezer, and Fleer on the following pages.

Do you see how reassuring and validating the voice of the insightful self is? It soothes our fears and assuages our insecurities. It lets us accept our inner fears as they are, without judgment or shame. It's the voice we never internalized as children and have been missing all this time.

Talking to ourselves in the voice of the Third *I* is key for our healing. If we are constantly ping-ponging between our inner child and our ego, how can we ever hope to be a voice of calm and reason for our children? Only when we re-parent ourselves can we hope to parent our children in the way they deserve. This is the crux of conscious parenting.

We can now begin to attune to our own feelings in a conscious manner. We can live with a calm and centered inner world. This gives us the emotional bandwidth to take care of our children in the manner they require. No longer blinded by our own fears, we can provide them the comfort they need. It's no longer about how they make *us* feel, but about how we make *them* feel.

THE FIGHTER

THE FIXER

THE FEIGNER

THE FREEZER

THE FLEER

We understand that our children—like us—also have an inner child and an ego at play. We can now get in touch with the inner dynamics and lives of our children to help them deal with their own inner struggles. Now, because we have raised ourselves to a state of calm and equanimity, we can show up for our kids the way they need us to be. This is the foundation of conscious parenting.

PUTTING IT INTO PRACTICE

Activating your Third *I* is going to take a lot of observation and practice. I have filled out the first of the following two charts to provide examples for these three parts of yourself: the inner child, the impostor ego, and the Third *I*—your insightful self. You can fill out the blank chart yourself.

There are no fixed rules as to what your insightful self can say to you. You can be creative and flexible in your approach. You could give affirmations, such as "You are loved and worthy!" You could gently cajole your inner child into a place of self-acceptance by saying, "Remember that your worth comes from within you and not from your achievements." Or you could write a song or a poem to remind your inner child that it is seen and validated. Compassion, empathy, and nonjudgment are the hallmarks of the insightful self's voice.

When you are not reactive, you are calm and in a state of equanimity. This is the nature of your insightful self. Try to observe yourself throughout the day as you move between these parts of yourself. Tune in to your body and pay attention to the emotional messages it gives you. This will allow you to pause and choose new directions. As you do, you will calm down from within and feel an inner expansion. From this sense of internal spaciousness, you will feel empowered to put aside your egoic reactions and attune to your "real" child.

Let's take a look at what these inner voices might say. I have filled out a sample (see the chart below), and you can fill out your own chart to practice.

Once we understand that we need to look within ourselves, we are able to create a ripple effect of positive changes that allow us to break our dysfunctional loops. Here is a summary of the steps we need to take to break our patterns.

	Inner Child	Impostor Ego	Insightful Self
Fighter	I'm a failure.	I will fix you.	You are scared. You feel out of control. There is nothing to control.
Fixer	I'm not loved.	I will please you.	You are scared. You want to fix it all. There is nothing to fix.
Feigner	I don't belong.	I will make you like me.	You are scared. You want them to like you. You are liked as you are.
Freezer	I'm not good enough.	I will ignore you.	You are scared. You want to ignore it all. There is no need to ignore it.
Fleer	I'm not worthy.	I will leave you.	You are scared. You want to leave it all. You can try to stay.

	Inner Child	Impostor Ego	Insightful Self
Fighter			
Fixer			
Feigner			
Freezer			
Fleer			

Step One: Let's Break This Loop

In the illustration, we see a typical scenario between parent and child. The child says something that the parent feels is disrespectful, and the parent reacts in the usual egoic way—by employing one of the five *F*'s. In this case, it is the Fighter parent. If the parent keeps reacting in this way instead of breaking the loop, the dynamic between parent and child will remain toxic and dysfunctional.

Step Two: The Parent Looks Within

To break our toxic patterns as parents, it is essential that we connect to the inner child in each of us that activates our egos. In the illustration, you see the parent pausing and listening to her inner child.

Step Three: The Parent Soothes Within

Here, the parent is aware enough to give her inner child what it needs and to soothe herself. When the inner child feels taken care of, it doesn't employ the ego as protection.

Step Four: The Parent Attunes to the "Real" Child

Once the parent has calmed her inner child down, she is ready to turn to help her "real" child soothe herself. The "real" child feels connected and attended to. This is the ultimate pathway to the connection both the parent and the child yearn for.

Step Five: The Ultimate Parent-Child Connection

When you look at the illustration, what feelings come up for you? Do you know that this could be your reality? Absorb this image, and allow yourself to envision this relationship for yourself and your children.

Re-parenting ourselves is not an easy job. Not only do we need to get rid of all the old voices within us, but we need to implant new ones. We literally need to learn a whole new language. This can be a discombobulating process. You may feel as though you are traveling in a foreign country with no map. If you're experiencing this sort of discomfort right now, be patient with yourself. Allow yourself these uncomfortable feelings, and try to hold them in a loving embrace. Understand that you're having these feelings because all of this is new for you. Applaud yourself for getting to this stage of the journey.

This inner work is going to continue for a lifetime. There is no end to it. Our goal isn't to arrive at any particular destination but simply to keep shining the light within so that we can become more and more whole. The journey toward wholeness never ends. However, we can keep moving closer. Getting just this far will make a huge difference in your relationship with your kids. By becoming aware of your inner dynamics and calming your inner fears, you are profoundly transforming your ability to connect with your children.

The next section is all about concrete ways in which this connection can become more viable and lasting in our everyday lives. Are you ready to learn new tools so that you can create a deeper and richer relationship with your children? I know that they will be eternally grateful for this massive effort you are undertaking. I celebrate you on this path. Let's take a deep breath and continue.

STAGE THREE

From Conflict
to Connection

When I am present with my kids
And accept them for their unique essence,
They begin to blossom under my gaze.
Their chests swell with worth,
Their feet root with resilience,
They feel extraordinary in their ordinariness.
They have nothing to do, nowhere to go.
They are at home right where they are.
They are at home within themselves.
This gift of my presence reaches deep
and allows their wings to spread wide.
My unconditional celebration is worth gold.
It begins with how I celebrate my own inner treasures.

THINK ABOUT the people in your life you feel the most connected to. I can bet that the list is short. It will encompass those you have felt you could be *yourself* with.

What does "be yourself with" really mean? In my opinion, it means that you feel honored and celebrated for being your true self, your essence. You feel safe to be *you,* whatever shape or form that takes. When we are around people who make us feel this way, we feel both worthy and empowered. We feel emboldened and invigorated. We feel as if we are golden. This is a wonderful feeling, isn't it?

Guess what? This is what our children desire from us more than anything else. They, too, want to feel safe and golden in our presence. They want to feel accepted for who they are. This is the entire goal of conscious parenting: accept your kids for who they are, period. Parenting isn't about their grades, talents, or trophies. It is about unconditionally honoring them for who they are.

Just accept your kids! It sounds so easy, right? How hard could it be? Well, if you are very honest, it's extremely difficult to unconditionally accept anyone. Do you know why? We don't accept ourselves. We didn't get this acceptance from our parents, and we don't give it to ourselves. Acceptance of self and others is probably one of the hardest spiritual tasks. It takes a whole lot of consciousness. Why is it so hard? It's because of all our cultural conditioning about how things "should" be. It's because of our preloaded mental ideations about things and people that we cannot simply be present with them.

If we see a rose, we want to pluck it. If we witness a stunning sunset, we want to take a photo of it. We cannot simply *be* with things. We feel the need to *do* something with them. Being present to the essence of things—whether these are our own feelings and inner conflicts or those of another—is something we are not conditioned to do. Instead, we are conditioned to *react* to things. Hence the state of affairs in our world today. Whatever we don't accept within ourselves, we project onto others through an egoic reaction.

Of course, all of this reactivity comes from the lack we feel within our own inner child. It is because of our own inner lack that we see lack in the outer world, our kids, or our life situations. That's why completing Stage Two is so important before we go on to Stage Three. We simply cannot consciously connect with anyone else until we have first connected with ourselves.

Children who receive unconditional acceptance from their parents experience an indelible worthiness. They feel accepted for their true selves, you see. And because each of these true selves is intrinsically whole, such children grow up feeling complete just as they are. These children don't need to earn their parents' trust or approval; it's theirs already, as natural and obvious as their own breath. These children feel accomplished just as they are, without needing to win a single medal or race. They feel seen, heard, and validated. The core desire to be fully honored and celebrated for their authentic selves is satisfied. Such children are self-directed, self-initiated, and self-governed; they are entire universes unto themselves.

Children with self-worth can still make mistakes, lose jobs, earn C grades, and get divorced. They can still get frustrated or cry themselves to sleep. They are not exempt from life or emotions. The difference is not that life throws them no curveballs. The difference is that they are able to draw on their own inner resources to handle hardships without sinking into shame and self-loathing.

Wouldn't you like your children to be able to feel this way? The good news is that you can give this to your kids right from this moment. You just need to know how. That's what this stage of the process will illuminate for you: how to connect to your children's essence and let them feel seen for who they are versus who you might wish them to be.

Consciously connecting with your children's essence is the linchpin of conscious parenting. It is the ultimate game-changing strategy of this work. And while this strategy may seem passive or simple, it is far from that. It is active and complex. It takes work—your inner work. It takes moment-by-moment awareness and consciousness. It takes a parent with a healed inner child. It takes *your* growth.

Step Twelve: Learn KidPsych

Although I want to mold and shape you like clay
And re-create you into a version of myself
And thrust you into a rendition of my fantasies,
I realize that the anguish of your self-abandonment
May be too painful for my heart to endure.
So my only choice is to change myself
And release my blind fears and expectations,
And finally connect to who you truly are
And through this finally learn true love.

Do you know who your kids are? I mean really *know*—at the level of their essence, their true selves? We get so caught up in the *doing* of raising our kids that we miss the *being* of them. This is the vital ingredient missing from our own childhoods: the *being* of it all. It is really the missing ingredient of life, period.

We are all so busy doing, doing, doing that we miss the real point of it all, which is to connect to our children and our own beings. Instead of molding our approach to our children, we expect them to mold their natures to us. When we engage in these psychological gymnastics with them, our kids lose out and are forced to create their own false impostor masks. In order to minimize the degree to which our kids create inauthentic versions of themselves, we need to create space for them to be themselves. The onus is on us.

Our own parents likely missed truly celebrating our essence. They may have celebrated us for our grades or accomplishments, but may not have allowed us to feel just as worthy in our ordinariness. As a result, we went on a quest for significance and worth by foraging in all the wrong places. For this reason, our own impostor egos may loom large and threatening. Perhaps the inner work you just did in Stage Two will now help you tame your ego so that you can begin to enter a new realm of understanding your child's true self better. This is what this stage is all about: connecting to your child's true nature.

Just as we ourselves once did, our kids arrive with their own unique essences. When we don't honor them for these essences, they are likely to create their own kiddie versions of our impostor egos: their own mini-versions of the five F's, the Fighter, Fixer, Feigner, Freezer, and Fleer. When either parent or child gets triggered and enters ego, the battles for power and significance can be quite dramatic. Each of them, parent and child, has the potential to set off the other's ego more and more. Who do you think may suffer more? Obviously, the child—right? They are younger and more innocent, more trusting and dependent. The effects on their psyches are far greater because of their young ages. So the onus is on us parents to try our best to tame our egos as much as possible. As we release our own egos, we can enter our heart space and connect to ourselves more deeply. And as we do so, it is natural for us to connect to our children more deeply.

Remember: the more ego we parents have, the more ego our

children will have. They have to have ego around our egos, you see? There is no other choice. Their egos are formed in reaction to ours—almost as a coping strategy. If we tell them to do something and they yell at us or are insolent, we may see their behavior as rude and disrespectful. But in truth, it's likely a result of how they feel about something we said. Sure, it's rudimentary and unpleasant, but it's a coping strategy for them. So it is when our children withdraw from us or shut us out. Are they being rude, or are they trying to cope with our egos? I'm not saying that we are the only cause of our children's egos. Of course not. After all, they have hundreds of other encounters that can cause their egos to rise. What I am saying is that when parents are stuck in their own egos, their children may have no choice but to be activated in their own egos as well.

When Angie came to see me, she was in her late thirties. She was frail, with a body covered with tattoos. She had extremely thin hair with bald patches all over her scalp. Her nails were bitten to the quick. She said that she had been suffering from hairpulling, nailbiting, and repetitive behaviors since she was seven years old. She was clearly suffering. When we worked through her history of traumas, it was clear that Angie had inherited a deeply ingrained belief that she was unworthy at her core. Her father was a rageaholic and frequently used corporal punishment on her. Her mother was often depressed, withdrawing from life for weeks at a time. Angie had no one to help her with her feelings and struggles. She remembered first pulling her hair out at around the age of seven: "It hurt, but that pain felt good. It was like all the pain I felt in my heart was finally given an expression."

Angie's hairpulling became so bad that she had to wear a hat to school. The more she pulled, the more upset her father was with her. She then began to pick at her skin and bite her nails. She was ostracized at school and shunned by her peers. She had no one to turn to. She looked at herself as the greatest failure possible. When I began to coach her, I reframed her behaviors—all of them, from the tattoos and piercings to the hairpulling and nail-biting—as coping strategies in the face of the inordinate pressures of her childhood. I told her, in the most loving voice I could muster, "You were a little girl who was neglected and abused. You had no one to help you. Your parents dumped all their crap on you. You couldn't share your voice with anyone, so you found the only way you could to express your inner pain—through your body. This was 100 percent your absolute coping strategy. It was your way of saying 'Help!'"

Angie looked at me in shock. It was as if no one had ever soothed her in this way before or shown her any grace. She had been so used to excoriating herself that to receive this kind of tenderness felt alien. Slowly, over months, I was able to help Angie see that she had been the victim of a traumatic childhood that had resulted in her having no recourse but to harm herself. Her entire body became a display screen for her pain. She was shouting from every pore, "I am in pain! Can someone help me, please?" No one had heard her until now. In fact, the more she had expressed her pain, the more she was slammed with one diagnosis after another. Her psychiatrists kept giving her labels and medications as if she were crazy. Angie said to me, "I felt like I was defective my whole life, like I should be locked up in an institution."

Do you see how Angie was taking on all the mental illness of the others in her family? Because they had not done their inner work, they were dumping all their crap on her. And she was actually sane enough to say, "Hey, this is driving me nuts, help me, I am only a kid!" But because her parents were so caught up in their own pain, no one heard her. It was only through our connection that she was able to slowly reframe her beliefs about herself and create a new foundation of worth and empowerment.

So many of us have just been in survival mode, creating defense patterns to cope with traumas from our childhood. Our parents' egos were so entrenched that they overwhelmed our true selves and devoured them. All that was left was unadulterated, piercing pain. Understanding ourselves through a lens of compassion is key for healing ourselves. Reframing our behaviors, from "crazy" to "coping," is pivotal if we are to change the narrative.

What if our parents had healed their own pain and hadn't had gargantuan egos that massacred our true selves? Can you even imagine what being raised by such parents would have felt like? Imagine feeling complete within yourself just as you are. In this state of inner completeness, our true home would not be a mansion or an island with lapping ocean waters, but the abode we carry within ourselves. In this state, we would be our own best friends, leaders, and partners. We would carry the sense of being at home wherever we are—because we would have ourselves wherever we went. If we all lived with this inner wholeness, there would be a vast difference in how we lived in the world. No wars, no violence—only a deepened interdependence and greater conscious connection.

I am going to be brutally honest with you. During my own child's early years, I was wrapped up in my own egoic agendas about who she should be, and I wasn't even aware that I was. When I began to observe my daughter's true essence, when she was around the age of two or three, I was shocked. She was so unlike who I had been as a child. I thought she would be my mini-me—or, better still, a mini-Buddha. She was anything but! Who was this creature?

I couldn't wrap my mind around who she was in her authentic self. Whereas I had been a shy kid and a compliant people pleaser, she was the opposite. She was bold, even confrontational with other kids, and absolutely uninterested in pleasing anyone, least of all me. Where I was soft and pliable, she was stubborn and defiant. Where I was hesitant and passive, she was bold and aggressive. I wanted her to be different, darn it—like me! Easy to raise, moldable, and submissive. She was anything but that. She was a little spitfire—energetic, feisty, and confrontational. It was because she was so much the opposite of my fantasy kid—or rather, because she was not a mirror version of myself—that I struggled to accept her for who she was. You see, I had not done enough inner work on myself.

I tried my best to squeeze her into my "Shefali movie" so I could script her moods to my fancy. I wanted to create a new shape for her. I wanted a carbon copy of myself. Inevitably, we clashed and disconnected quite a bit. I was trying to shove my agenda down her throat, and she wouldn't have any of it. The more she fought back, the more my ego rose, and the vicious cycle continued. It wasn't until I began the conscious parenting way that things began to move in a positive and healthy direction.

As I write these words, I am aware that you might judge me. I am consciously exposing myself in this transparent way on these pages because I want you to see how none of us, including myself, is beyond the devouring seduction of our egos, and that every one of us has to do the inner work required for healing. Projecting an image of perfection would be untrue and full of inauthenticity. I have no interest in such a projection. Only through the baring of our wounds can we heal. I want you to witness my honest sharing of my ego so that you feel safe to encounter your own. This transparent disclosure is the only way we can heal ourselves—and until this deep healing occurs, we will project our inner pain and our lack onto our kids.

I can still remember the moment I witnessed my daughter abandoning her true self when she was a feisty and adventurous three-year-old. I was extremely upset and reprimanding her for not listening to me. My voice was raised and my attitude was self-righteous. I kept going on and on and then, in one split second, I saw something heartbreaking take place. I saw her bend her head down in shame and slump her shoulders. Her entire body went limp like a deflated balloon and the flicker of fire in her eyes died out. My ego immediately stopped in its tracks. I knew right then that I was way off course and if I didn't get my ego under control, I would destroy my daughter's essence.

My ego was hitting rock bottom again and again. That was yet another turning point in my life when I began to heal my own inner wounds and started practicing conscious parenting. My daughter's strong personality spurred an entirely new way of being in me. I had to ask myself the tough question "Why aren't you accepting your child for who she is?"—and I realized it was because I wasn't accepting myself for who I was.

I repeatedly tell Maia, who is now twenty years old, "You are the reason I teach conscious parenting. You dared to be you despite my ego's attempts to squash you. You stayed true to your essence so that I was forced to shed my ego." I am forever grateful to have birthed such a courageous and indomitable spirit. If she had been any different, I might never have understood the power of my unconsciousness, and I might never have dared to transform myself.

When we don't recognize our children for their authentic essences, we drive a wedge in our connection with them. You see, we cannot help but do so when we see them through the eyes of our egos. Entering our heart space and connecting with who they are simply cannot happen without all the work outlined in Stage Two. No one tells us when we have children that a huge element of parenting is raising ourselves, right? We enter the journey completely clueless, and before we know it we've dumped all our past traumas onto our kids and think *they* are the ones who are messed up. Ah, the irony of it all. That's why this parenting map is so vital—to teach us *how* to heal so that the cycle of pain doesn't go on and on.

Using Maia's example again, had I remained a supercontrolling and domineering parent, I would certainly have destroyed her sense of self. Had I continued to perceive her as "bad," I would have shamed her for her natural temperament. It wasn't her fault that she was the way she was. She was just being herself. It was my inadequacy and insecurity that were creating the problem. It had nothing to do with her.

Aneika was the opposite of Maia. She was the daughter of a client who came to me looking for help. Aneika was the same age as Maia, but they couldn't have been more different. Aneika was soft-spoken and docile—a follower, not a leader. Afraid of her own shadow, Aneika allowed her parents and friends to boss her around and lead the way. Her parents were thrilled with how "good" she was. You see, Aneika was the "dream child." She obeyed without delay and listened to her parents' every word. They praised her as consistently "perfect," and the more they praised her, the more she tried to be flawless. Aneika didn't just try to be perfect; she tried to become superhuman.

Everything seemed fine until Aneika entered high school. Then the s— hit the fan. She turned into a "bad" girl overnight. She threw perfection out the window and began to cut classes, take drugs, and rebel in all sorts of ways. Her parents were flummoxed. What had happened to their angel daughter?

I explained to my client, "This happens with 'good' children— girls, especially. What happens is that because their natural way is to be compliant, a parent who's not attuned to this can domineer over these children. 'Good' children make it easy for their parents' egos to take over. And this is what you did. You thought you could just boss her around, which you did until she couldn't take it anymore. One day, Aneika snapped. She couldn't be your ideal, perfect girl anymore. And everything fell apart. But this is a good thing, actually. What was falling apart was her mask of superperfectionism."

Without conscious intention, Aneika's parents had devoured her natural goodness until their own egos had consumed her completely. Her naturally pleasing nature ratcheted up one gear and then another, until one day it went into overdrive and she completely lost herself in pleasing them. She sought an unblemished immaculateness that no human can achieve. This burden led her ego mask of perfectionism to eventually crack. Although the change in Aneika hurt her parents, they needed to understand that Aneika had to do this for her own essence to survive. While the relationship between Aneika and her parents had looked perfect on the surface, it was actually perfect only for her parents' egos. For Aneika's essence, the relationship was oppressive and toxic. The real truth was that she was a match for her *parents' ego*, instead of them being a match for *her essence*.

Aneika's mother had a hard time adjusting to these new ideas. She had been so used to having the perfect child that she couldn't relate to this new Aneika. It took the mother a long time to accept her part in the dynamic and own up to the ways she had projected such unrealistic expectations onto her child. Parents of "good" children have a hard time accepting the changed situation when their children stop being so good. The egos of these parents have been so used to getting their way that they simply cannot change course midway. In my case, Maia's strong essence didn't allow my ego to get its way right from the start. So (thankfully) my ego was checked very early on. Regardless of whether our egos are kept in check early on or the child's ego reveals itself more slowly, as in Aneika's case, the fact remains that we parents have to confront our own egos. The earlier in our child's life that we do so, of course, the better.

Just as we used categories to understand our egos in Stage Two, I'm going to introduce ways to help you understand your child's essence. Clearly, on some level, your child's essence can never be boxed into a category; I would never suggest such a thing. Kids cannot be categorized. However, they do fall along a continuum, and this is what I have loosely outlined in this section to get you thinking about who your child is in their essence. The more we tune in to their true natures, the more we can create stronger connections with them.

The categories that follow are not based on a *good-to-bad* spectrum but instead on a *high-to-low-anxiety* spectrum. They indicate how intrinsically anxious our kids are at the basic level of their wiring. Some come high-strung, others more chill and easygoing. Take a look at these categories and try to identify where along this spectrum your kid falls. Then ask yourself:

Am I attuned to their temperament and authentic essence?

Can I give them space to be without controlling or dominating them?

Can I honor and celebrate their authentic self without judgment or shame?

These same categories can be applied to you, too, and to anyone else you know. They speak to the inherent, basic nature of each of us.

Every nature is a superpower when alchemized in a conscious way. We have to remember that each one of us has something to contribute and just needs the right conditions to highlight those strengths.

When I finally began to accept my own daughter's essence, everything changed. I began to match myself to her temperament instead of the other way around. Instead of resisting her natural power and leadership, I began to flow with it. I saw her defiance as confidence, her stubbornness as self-governance. I began to admire her and learn from her. I began to enjoy her! Today, as a twenty-year-old, Maia is still hotheaded and supremely independent. She doesn't take much advice or direction from me. Even now, I watch my ego rise in protest—"Why can't she just be obedient and dependent on me?"—and realize that this is my Fixer parent self, the one who needs her to be needy, and not my authentic self. For example, I now know to reframe her hotheadedness as self-empowerment and her independence as a positive trait. When I do, I lean into her with respect and honor instead of criticism and judgment, which directly improves our relationship. In my Fixer mask, I need her to be broken and dependent on my direction. Only when I am in my whole self can I let her be who she is and see this as worthy of celebration. Only when I am in my own true self-celebration can I see her as the light she truly is instead of seeing her from the shadows of my unworthiness. It all depends on my internal state and whether or not I project my own lack onto her.

Do you see how we create a dysfunctional dynamic when we fail to attune to our kids and instead project our own internal lack onto them? Tuning in to our children's essence doesn't just help us become more conscious and facilitate a more conscious relationship with them; it also helps our kids understand themselves better. When we're able to help them understand their authentic selves, they can better own who they are. In this way, we can teach them to celebrate themselves and hold on to their own truths as they journey through life.

As you read the categories that follow, enter a heart space instead of a head space. These categories are intended for you to use, not to judge yourself or your children, but to help you understand them better and grow into greater acceptance. Conscious parenting is all about seeing ourselves and our children as whole, complete, and worthy. When we are in self-acceptance and self-celebration mode, we are able to honor and revere our children for who they naturally are, without adornments or accolades attached.

Remember to enjoy this process without being too rigid about any category, because, after all, human nature is neither rigid, absolute, nor categorical. Remember, I am moving along the spectrum in these descriptions, from high anxiety to low anxiety. All of us are fluid beings who move along this continuum at different points in our journey. So keep this in mind as you try to identify your child's essence.

THE ANXIOUS EXPLODER

Do you think of your kid as a hot wire ready to snap, or a bomb about to explode? Are they highly fussy, irritable, and edgy? Do they complain and whine? Do they get triggered by the slightest thing? Well, if this is your kid, you may have a highly sensitive child.

Highly sensitive kids are porous. This is their beauty—they can feel everything. But as a result, they react to a lot of things. This reactivity can make it difficult for parents to cope. Because this kind of sensitive child has so many feelings much of the time, they absorb the anxiety around them. What do they do with all this anxiety? They explode. It's too much for them!

These kids are challenging for parents to be around, as they are incessantly being triggered. Clothes, smells, and words can set them off, causing them to need a high degree of attention and patience from their parents. Their acute sensitivity makes them pick up on other people's energy constantly, which leads to their forming strong opinions of others—both likes and dislikes. That can make it challenging for a parent to help these children negotiate their way through life.

Crying and panicking are common for these kids. They also have wild imaginations, which conjure all sorts of ominous futures that create irrational anxieties. They are the kids who ask "What if *this* happens?" or "What if *that* happens?"—with no answer ever really satisfying them. These kids are sponges, picking up on every cue from their external environment and reacting to it.

Do you feel as if your kids are often this way? Being around them can feel exhausting, right? It's understandable that you feel burned out at times. These kids need a lot from their parents. Depending on their own temperaments, parents may react in one of two unconscious ways: overcontrolling or overindulging. Overcontrolling parents try to thwart their kids through anger and control, making them feel bad and lesser than who they really are. Typically, a Fighter, Freezer, or Fleer parent reacts this way. Or parents might overindulge their children and create a high degree of enmeshment, as a Fixer parent might do. Fixer parents—being highly anxious themselves—seek to micromanage their children's anxieties by trying to solve their problems. They overfix their kids' environments so they don't feel their feelings as much. As a result of this overdoing, the parent is often depleted, and what's more, the kids become even needier and more dependent. These are the kids who incessantly call their parents for advice and help—even as teenagers and adults. This may appear to be a close relationship, but it's actually a highly fused one.

So what do these kids really need? They need a parent who is grounded, firm, and calm—neither a Fighter nor a Fixer. They need a parent who can alchemize their anxieties into intuition and power. They need conscious parents who can help them reframe their anxieties and discover their own self-direction. For their part, parents need to maintain a steady, calm state in the presence of these kids. If a parent becomes reactive, either in anger or anxiety, that can set off a tsunami of emotions. The only path forward with these kids is for the parents to use the antidotal energy of supreme calm and centeredness. This is not easy, but it's what these kids desperately need.

If you have this kind of a child, you may be at your wits' end, ready to throw in the towel at times. You may be exhausted from all their high anxiety and may feel utterly scorched and burned, as if nothing you do really makes a difference. So how can we as parents celebrate these kids? The way to make a true difference is to alchemize their sensitivities into power. Praise them for their abilities to feel and process their environment, but also teach them to go within themselves to create the answers and solace they need. For example, you might tell them:

> You are like a dry sponge soaking up everything around you. You are sensitive and soft, absorbing everything around you. It is hard for you to separate your moods from other people's moods and because of this you often explode. When you feel nervous, close your eyes and repeat to yourself, "I am safe right now, I am home right now, I am going to be okay." You are not a bad person for losing your calm. This is what happens to extra-sensitive people. As you learn to feel safer in this world, you will become calmer. When I see you explode, I know it is because you feel anxious and unsafe. I will do my best to remind you that you are safe in this moment. Your sensitivity is a superpower if you learn to use it in this way. It is a radar and a GPS that helps you know another person's moods. You will soon learn to use it without letting the information overpower you. When you do, you will be able to use this sensitivity to your own benefit.

Do you see how such an explanation can help these children feel understood and accepted? You are communicating that you see their essence as something pure and invaluable, not inconvenient or bad. By addressing their anxiety, you are teaching them something valuable about their inner worlds and how their ego shows up. You are helping them create a narrative of worth and self-respect. This will be hugely healing for them as they move on their life journey.

By using this gentle approach, you can honor where they are without feeling that you need to control, fix, or shame them. You can show them that they are fully capable of finding their own solutions and strengths.

THE HYPERACTIVE EXPLORER

Do you have a kid who just cannot sit still, who is constantly on the go and never where you last left them? This is a child who constantly has scrapes, bruises, and cuts; who is always in trouble; and who always has that glint in their eye that you know means mischief. If so, you may have an Explorer on your hands. If you do, attempting to control or constrain your kid is going to cause nightmares. The more you box these kids in, the more agitated and uncontrollable they become.

These are children who need to be on the move constantly, creatively exploring their worlds. These kids are often labeled "bad" by their parents, teachers, and society at large for no reason except that they are more active in their body and mind. They are likely to be diagnosed with an attention deficit disorder or an oppositional-defiant disorder and made to feel lesser-than. The truth is, these kids are just different. They don't thrive within the conventional standards of society. These are the *wild ones* and need to be honored for their passionate spirit instead of being degraded and shamed.

I bet many of you are reading this right now and nodding, "Yup, that was me as a kid! I was the wild one. They tried to tame me!" If we are honest with ourselves, most of us have some of this wild energy within us. However, we learned to bury it, because we saw what happened to other wild kids. We learned from the treatment they received that to be wild means to be in trouble.

These kids need parents who "get" them and honor them for their unconventional and wild ways. They need parents who admire them for their adventurous spirits, not parents who shame them for it. Parents who are too conventional might feel threatened by kids who are like this and try to control them. Or parents might be afraid of their child's "big" energy and withdraw altogether. It all depends on how parents view such kids. Parents can see these children in admiring ways or in degrading ways, depending on how the parents were conditioned in their own childhoods.

These children desperately need their parents to take their side and not cage them in conformity and traditional structures. Such children thrive in wide open spaces of freedom and experimentation. They feel stifled in conventional habitats. If freedom is not willingly given to them, they will fight for it, biting and kicking. This need for freedom could get them in trouble at school and with the law. The solution for these kids is to have parents who appreciate and understand them deeply but also help them manage their wild energies in constructive ways. These children thrive best in spaces of autonomy and self-direction. Their parents need to bestow a tremendous amount of trust in them to let them flourish on their own terms. If these kids feel overmanaged or overcontrolled, they will either wither away or rebelliously protest.

If you have this kind of a child, you may fear that they will be outcast from society and never find their way in "normal" life. Out of fear, you may label them as "bad" or a "derelict." The truth is that they are neither. They are just very different from the average, conventional kid. These kids think and behave differently. They need an entirely different approach from the standard parental protocol. Accepting that your kid is not within the standard bell curve may feel like a disappointment and a letdown. Here is the truth that may relieve you: your child is absolutely okay as they are. It's just that society is too narrow for them. If society were more fluid and expansive, it would be able to accept your child without making them feel ostracized or "weird."

The best approach is to remember that your child is not abnormal; they are just larger than life. They need to receive your unconditional acceptance so that they can accept themselves in a world that may repeatedly shun them. You might say something like this to your child:

> *You are like the sun, exploding with power and energy. You are filled with creativity and adventure. You are an explorer by nature! You are different from most kids. This is what makes you unique. There is nothing to be ashamed of or sad about. Being different is cool. The world is going to make you feel bad about yourself, but we cannot let them. The world is afraid of humans like you who think outside the box, and people will keep trying to squash you into the box. You need to trust in who you are. I see you and admire you for your creativity and imagination. Your different ways of thinking and being are your superpower and can help you do amazing things in your life. Let's find a way for you to feel honored and safe to be yourself.*

By taking this soothing approach toward your child, you can help them honor their difference, while at the same time helping frame this difference as a superpower.

THE OVERDOER, OVERGIVER, OVERPLEASER

Do you have a child who is like butter—soft and pliable, easy to mold and shape? Ah, your ego is in luck! You have the empathic, overpleasing kid of the parental ego's dreams. Such kids are the perfect prey for our parental need for control and domination. With no pushback or resistance, they easily knuckle under. They make themselves into any shape you desire without putting up a battle. Shy and docile, these kids are soft at heart and always willing to comply.

Overly feeling and empathic, these kids don't have the internal bandwidth to tolerate the pain or wrath of others. Rejection or anger from another crushes their internal worlds. They can't handle any "big" emotions and fall apart. As long as they don't have to take risks or be blamed, they are happiest as followers. This proclivity to say yes makes them naive, gullible, and easy prey for predators. However—like Aneika, the girl I talked about earlier who fell apart in high school—these kids eventually crack under the pressure of following everyone else's wishes. It is a struggle for them to learn how to follow their own inner voice and heart. Eventually this separation from their true self catches up to them and breaks them apart.

These children need their parents to understand just how soft and pleasing their kids are. It is incumbent on parents to watch their own egos and not hijack these kids' inherent docility for the parents' own comfort. If parents are not extra careful, these kids can go from docile to servile, from loving to sacrificing, from giving to self-annihilating, from performing to overachieving. These kids possess the prototypical emotional ingredients to convert them into adult codependents, so we need to be extremely mindful to nurture their goodness without exploiting, overriding, or dominating them with our own egos.

These kids will do anything to make parents happy. These children are often superachievers and overdoers. They fill in gaps, take over chores, and get gold stars for achievement. They are inherently primed to give of themselves. Once they feel rewarded for this giving, they often go to extreme lengths and cross over into self-sacrifice and self-abnegation. Because they are so eager to help others, they often overstep their lane and take over parental tasks and responsibilities, becoming the "parentified" adult in the home and carrying the burdens of the parent. Doing so robs them of their own childhood joy and innocence. These naturally empathic kids may become their parents' therapists by helping them manage their feelings. In such ways, these children can be used by their parents' egos and lose their own sense of direction and leadership.

There are many ways we can and should help these children maintain their essence without falling prey to our own egos or the egos of others. For example, when these kids ask us for our opinions—and they do, a lot—instead of rushing to offer answers, we can allow them to arrive at their own conclusions. We need to give them space to struggle and fumble so that they can discover their own truth. Even when these kids push parents to take control over their lives and hand over the keys to let them do so, parents need to resist the temptation. We need to rein in the urge to dominate our kids and work on appeasing our own desire for control. If we don't, these kids will become accustomed to being subservient and therefore will be easy prey for the domination of others.

Overpleaser children need to understand how their naturally giving hearts make them vulnerable in today's world. Parents can teach these kids how to protect themselves from predators and honor their internal and external boundaries by attuning to their own needs and fulfilling themselves from within. Without alarming them too much, we can say to them:

> You are an extremely giving being who wants nothing more than to make others happy. This is your nature. This can be taken advantage of by others if you aren't extra protective of your heart. You need to realize that unless you please and love yourself first, you will neglect yourself. You don't have to be perfect for others to love you. You are allowed to be ordinary, and even to fail. You don't have to please others all the time. You will meet many who are not as caring as you. You are a giver, and you will encounter many who will keep on taking from you. You need to discern between who is worthy and who isn't. If you learn to open your giving heart to the right people, it will be your superpower. The most important person in your life is you; always remember that. You come first. Listening to yourself and honoring your own truth is paramount.

Maybe these words will be soothing for you as a parent, especially if you are a pleaser type, too. Remember, these are just ideas for what conscious parents might say as they seek to create a better relationship with their children. Adapt these ideas to the situation and needs at hand. At their core, these words demonstrate a parent's capacity and willingness to see the child's essence through the eyes of honor and celebration. When parents are able to stand up against culture's narrow norms and advocate for their children, helping them to better understand and accept themselves, these kids can see their differences as superpowers instead of as limitations.

THE DREAMER-RECLUSE

Do you constantly catch your kid staring into space, doodling in their notebook, playing for hours with their imaginary toys, or sitting in a corner journaling day after day? Do you have a kid who spends hours on their own so much that you wonder if they are even in the house, or a kid who cannot be around friends for too long before they grow tired of the company and want to come back home? Does your kid shy away from rough play or aggressive competitive sports, preferring to be out of the spotlight? If so, you may have a kid whose inherent nature is that of a dreamer and an introvert.

Such kids are quieter and shyer than most. They can be forgetful: so lost are they in their imaginations and overdreaming minds that they often even forget to brush their teeth or tie their shoes. They are the proverbial absent-minded professors and may grow into artists or computer programmers.

These kids often get into trouble with teachers and parents for forgetting their keys, homework, or backpacks. They lack organizational and time-management skills. Their external worlds are of less interest to them than their internal worlds. They also may lack social and conversational skills. Awkward and gawky around company, they may tend to be loners and hermits. Shy and sweet in temperament, such kids are prone to being bullied and picked on at school by rowdier, more aggressive classmates. This treatment results in further withdrawal. These kids are sometimes the more studious or "geeky" kids who like to do things that most kids their age don't. They may not like rough-and-tumble sports, drinking when they are in high school, or engaging in highly sexualized behaviors. As a result, they can feel outcast and ostracized—causing them to withdraw from the social scene around them even more.

Parents of such kids could become extremely triggered if they are more conventional. I have observed dads, in particular, becoming upset if their children, especially their sons, are of this nature. It's as if we are particularly conditioned to believe that boys are not supposed to be introverts or dreamers. The conventional conditioning is that boys are supposed to be extroverts—boisterous, athletic, and competitive. Having a son of this nature is therefore extremely challenging for this kind of father.

These kids need help and encouragement to feel secure in who they are, since the world gives them the message that they should be the opposite. To be quiet and shy is not considered a positive trait, and kids are often forced to be more social than they authentically feel. After all, culture favors the more extroverted, outgoing, and friendly kids rather than the more reclusive ones. Because of familial and societal pressure to be assertive and bold, these kids often end up feeling ashamed of who they are, and thus they grow up with a pervasive sense of unworthiness. They compare themselves to others their age and realize that they are not like them. This realization brings them insecurity and disempowerment.

Parents of such children need to intuitively understand how hard it must be for these kids to be themselves in mainstream culture. These parents need to work extra hard to be mindful of not pushing their kids to join the mainstream crowd, instead seeing in their children the strengths they uniquely possess. Parents need to work on their own expectations and realize that there are many positives to be found in a kid who is "off-center" and perhaps even "off the grid." The million-dollar question is whether the parents of these kids appreciate their difference and find the positive in this rather than viewing their kids as lesser-than.

Precisely because these kids tend to be more unusual and different, parents need to work even harder to honor them for what they bring to the table. Criticizing and comparing them to other kids is just going to make these kids feel even more ashamed and withdrawn. To help them amplify their self-worth, parents need to encourage these kids to feel positive about who they are and to feel valued for themselves.

Highlighting their strengths is extremely important for these kids, because they don't get much external validation from society—especially when they are young. Parents could do so by saying:

You are a unique soul. You have a rich imagination and inner world. You are filled with ideas and dreams. These are beautiful qualities. You prefer to be in your own company and spend time on your own, which is a wonderful quality. The world is going to tell you that this is bad and that you should prefer being with people, but this isn't true. Don't let people force on you their ideas about how you should be. Remember, those who are able to be by themselves are strong people. I admire you just the way you are.

When parents haven't worked on their own fantasy movies of parenthood, it's easy to project all their unmet expectations onto their children. These kids intuitively absorb the awareness that they are not stepping up to their parents' standards and are disappointing them. Helping our children find their unique strengths and talents helps them see that they are worthy as they are and don't need to conform to society's expectations of who they should be.

THE REBEL NONCONFORMIST

Do you have a kid who has the will of an ox, one who won't comply with your request until convinced it's something they wish to do, who defies you and argues, who isn't afraid of your authority or influence and resists both? Such a child is bold and confrontational. They don't care to please you one bit. Sound familiar? If yes, you probably have a rebellious, nonconformist kid.

Take it from me, I know how challenging these kids can be. My daughter, Maia, is such a kid. These are the kids who speak their minds at all costs and don't mince words. They express themselves in bold and dramatic ways, with little concern for how what they express may land with others. These children are loyal to themselves and have little fear of going against the tide. They are born leaders and game changers. They don't follow the crowd or desire to belong. However, because of their natural confidence, crowds often follow them. These kids don't fear adults or their authority. They see the world as an even playing field and feel empowered to participate. People-pleasing is not their strong suit. As a result of their iconoclastic inner power, these kids are difficult to parent—or rather, they are difficult to control or influence. As a result, it's easy to shame these children for being "bad" and to demean them for their rigidity and stubbornness.

These children don't take criticism lightly or passively. If they feel they aren't being treated with the respect they are entitled to, they are quick to disconnect and won't give a damn. To connect with such children, a parent has to work hard at earning their trust and respect. The way to do so is by trusting and respecting them first.

Such kids are naturally self-directed and self-governing. They cannot be treated in a cookie-cutter fashion and told to blindly follow authority. They need to feel respected for their inner empowerment. Once they experience this respect from you, they will return the favor. However, the moment they feel disrespected, they will rebel, fight, and flee. These kids keep their parents on their toes and force them to elevate their game. Such children take no prisoners in their pursuit of self-expression and self-ownership. You are either going to join the ride or be left behind.

As intransigent and challenging as these kids are, they are worthy of admiration. Their strong sense of self and their fearlessness in expressing this are truly worthy of respect. Once parents overcome their own loss of influence and control, it's likely they will find many amazing qualities in their children, as I did. Once I released my ideas about who Maia should be and surrendered to who she was—an assertive and empowered being—I could step back and let her take charge of her life.

These kids come into the world with an undeniable self-possession and inner power. They are simply not going to be led passively through their lives. They are going to take the reins and direct the wagon where they want it to go. They won't even care that they are creating disapproval in others. Following their own internal compass matters more than validation or praise from strangers. Sure, such children can rub their parents the wrong way and be off-putting, especially to those who desire servility and compliance—but these kids' strength and courage need to be celebrated.

I encourage the parents of these children to release control and judgment. Honoring the individuality and strength of such children is what's most important. Parents can do so by saying something like this:

> *You are one of the strongest humans I know. Your trust in your inner knowing is impressive. I wish I could have such a strong inner willpower and sense of worth. I admire your ability to follow your own inner voice and not be influenced by trends or the opinions of the popular crowd. You are capable of standing up for yourself and by yourself. You will likely make others uncomfortable with your bold expressions and your disregard for their opinions. Don't lose your inner confidence because of what others say. Don't fight rules simply for the sake of fighting or you will burn yourself out. However, don't stop fighting for good causes. Know the difference between the two. Keep on shining.*

When parents can release these children into their own destinies, they are able to take flight. They are advanced beyond their years and capable of manifesting their dreams far beyond their parents' ability to help them. These children arrived on earth to fully embody their authenticity. They are not going to let any human stand in their way. Parents are advised to fall back and let go. This is the only way to survive the ride of a rebellious, nonconformist child.

THE EASY-BREEZY, HAPPY-GO-LUCKY!

Do you have a child who is a little Buddha, one who always laughs and is in a good mood? The one who is everyone's favorite person? Well, you may have the easy-breezy kid! This kid is always sweet, kind, and loving. They never lose their cool and can always change the mood to a positive one. If you have a kid like this, you are in for an easy parenting ride!

These kids are just easy to be around. They are not fussy, demanding, or bossy. Their temperaments are fun and joyful. Their only downside is that they can be too relaxed sometimes and therefore tend to be unmotivated and to procrastinate. This kind of kid can be a nightmare for Type-A parents, who simply cannot flow with these kids and instead will try to convert them into hyperambitious beings.

Such kids don't run, they amble. They saunter along, coasting through life. They don't stress about exams or deadlines and often wait till the very last minute to get things done. While they know how to enjoy life and smell the roses, their essence could be demeaned as passive and lazy by parents who just don't understand them. Also, their pleasant nature may come across as passive, letting them be taken advantage of by more aggressive kids. It's hard to get these kids to worry—which is a good thing. Because they are so relaxed and chill, they might send their parents into a nervous tizzy. If their parents are unconscious, they could perceive their children as deficient and shame them into feeling unworthy and lesser-than. Doing so could result in a disconnected and dysfunctional communication between parent and child.

As these kids tend to live in the moment, it's hard to plan things for the future. They tend to resist any sort of commitments. They also have a hard time taking things seriously when they "should." On one hand, difficulties wash off their back like water, leading to low anxiety. But on the other hand, it's hard for things to stick. Much to the chagrin of their parents, these kids often don't push themselves to their fullest potential. Parents need to be aware that these children won't readily assert themselves and will need to be consciously drawn out of their comfort zones.

These kids have an admirable, "Zen" presence and deserve to be celebrated for their inner beauty and approach to the world. Their gentle, easygoing nature should be honored and respected for the goodness it spreads to others. They always add joy to situations and never burden others with their woes. Contaminating their flow would truly be an egregious transgression. Here are a few things parents can say to these kids to help them feel valued:

> *You are one who naturally lives in flow and grace, like nature. You are rare and different. Your nature is unlike others because you bring calm and peace into every situation. You are a treasure and need to be treated as such. However, in this crazy world you will be told you are not good enough and need to be more this or more that. This isn't true, and you should resist these pressures. Don't succumb to the stressors of others. They dance to a different beat. Preserve your own beat, because it's a lost rhythm that the rest of us need to adopt.*

These children have jewels to offer this world; they just need permission to be who they are.

Do you now see what it means to be attuned to your children's essence? It means to honor the beauty of that essence—without judgment, comparison, or shame. When we understand our children at this foundational level, we realize that a large part of their behavior comes from this nature. Because they came wired this way, much of their behavior cannot be helped.

To attune means to ask these crucial soul-searching questions of ourselves on a moment-to-moment basis:

Who is my child truly?

Can I understand who my child is without making judgments?

Can I align my expectations with who my child truly is, as
     opposed to who I want them to be?
Can I find the strengths in my child's essence and celebrate these?

Once we are willing to turn inward, we can begin to check on our
own ideas and fantasies. We need to hold these under the spotlight
of our awareness, always asking ourselves these questions:

Where are my expectations coming from?
Are they coming from my past or from the present?
Are they coming from fear and lack or from abundance and joy?

A vigilant awareness of our own projections is vital, so that we can
step back and give our children the space to be in their own power.
Before opening our mouths to bark orders, we can ask ourselves:

Can I simply observe my child right now?
Can I understand where my child is coming from right now?
Can I meet my child where they are right now?
What do I need to let go of within myself to do this?

Once we allow our children to be who they are and we're able to
see value in who they are, they will naturally blossom. Just as we
don't have to direct flowers toward the sun, our kids are naturally
inclined toward self-empowerment and worth; they just need the
right conditions in order to thrive. They have all the ingredients for
their own self-worth until we interfere with their natural ways.

Our job as conscious parents is to attune to our kids' basic wiring and mold our parenting according to their basic infrastructures.
When we do, we flow with a child's nature instead of resisting it. So
many of us were transplanted into gardens not of our own choosing
and forced to bloom in habitats that were a gross mismatch for who
we truly were. As a result, we had to wear one ego mask after another to survive. If only we had been allowed to just be ourselves and
find our own paths, we wouldn't have squandered years and years
chasing dreams that were not authentically ours.

Just as mangoes grow in the right season and under the right conditions, so it is with our own essence and our children's essence. When you force a mango to grow out of its natural habitat, it dies. So it is with our souls. They die when we are forced to be someone we are not. We are stressed and anxious, and we endure physical hardships as well. The cracks and fissures appear in all sorts of places as our lives begin to crack because of the fragility of our impostor selves. The ego-self is always tenuous and brittle, you see? It's only when we are rooted at the depths of our essence that we can touch our limitless power and become unbreakable. For this reason, allowing our children to remain in their own essence as much as possible is the goal of conscious parenting.

Helping our children stay planted and aligned in their essence is a far more important task for a conscious parent than helping them become skiers or chess players. The former task is about being, the latter about doing. If our work on the more important task is rickety, our other efforts will totter as well. As humans, it is only when our own "doing" state is predicated on an alignment with our inner essence that we can enter a lasting sense of inner durability. As parents, when we arrive at this powerful internal alignment—first within ourselves and then with our kids—our approach to our children fundamentally transforms. Instead of bringing them to our ways, we empower them to manifest their own.

In today's world of social media addiction, tuning in to our children's essence is extremely hard to do because of all the noise and distraction in our lives. And even if we do manage to attune to them in their early childhood, they will soon be thrust into a world of insane social comparison and pressure. It will take a lot of inner power on the child's part to not give in to this kind of pressure. In fact, it's more than likely that they won't be able to resist. For this reason, American teenagers (and perhaps teenagers all over the world) are more anxious than they have ever been and are apt to crack under pressure. One of the highly plausible reasons for this anxiety is that, because of social media, they are more exposed and vulnerable to rejection than ever before. Whereas a child might once have occasionally faced rejection from one or two children at school, now their exposure to possible rejection is on steroids. And exposure is not restricted to their friend group, but is now at a global level. Their scales of comparison are, therefore, all the more unrelenting and unrealistic. While the data are still inconclusive, it's likely that the rise of teen suicide in the past decade is highly impacted by the addictive use of social media. Of course, economic downturns, climate change, gun violence, and the devastating global impact of the COVID-19 pandemic have and will continue to have a lasting psychological impact.

Why is this invasion of social media especially relevant for us parents to grasp? Well, it means that our ability to connect to and influence our children's lives is in grave jeopardy. It may have been hard to compete with technology for our children's attention back in the day, but it is now significantly more challenging. Our kids are being influenced by algorithms and mass-marketing strategies that are out of our league. What does this mean for us parents? It means we need to work three times as hard to ensure that we are present and attuned to our kids. We need to pay extra attention to their cues and feelings. We cannot have our heads in the technological sand, so to speak, if we hope to hold on to our children. They need us to shield them from these predatory influences, especially until they are well into their teens. Sadly, parents are not doing so in most homes, and children as young as three or four are on the internet without supervision. More and more, parents are using technology as a surrogate caretaker. Children have fewer social interactions with other kids their age or with their parents and are spending less time out in nature—vital ingredients for their well-being. These deficits have severe implications for the future, and they cannot be minimized or neglected.

If being a parent has always been hard, today it is excruciatingly challenging because of the technological vortex in which we are living. Screens are devouring our children's souls and robbing them of their right to a childhood. The innocence of childhood is being lost amid video games and virtual reality. The fresh aliveness of play, the outdoors, and real-time social connections is fading into a forgotten era. We cannot allow this to happen. We need to help our children reclaim the power of their childhoods. They are trusting us to do so.

PUTTING IT INTO PRACTICE

Attunement is an art and a daily practice. It's not just a pretty concept, but an active way of being in the world. It encompasses an attitude of extreme awareness toward our own and the other's state of being. Many parents want to know the "how" of attunement. What does it actually involve? How do you express it?

To help answer these questions, I use the acronym **WARM**: *witnessing, allowance, reciprocal, mirror*. Using these ways and more, we can lean into our children's psychologies and pay attention to their essences. This "tuning in" is one of the most powerful tools of conscious parenting, as it permits us to adjust and design our parenting according to the kid before us. We tailor and fine-tune our energies to best match what our children need from us. This is a priceless gift we can offer them.

Witnessing

When we are trying to cultivate attunement to our kids, we first need to learn to witness them. We need to observe how they stand and sit, how their voices quiver or jaws clench, how they tense their shoulders or bite their lips, and so much more. On a deeper level, witnessing means we need to slow down, step back, pause, and pay attention to how they verbally and physically express anger, fatigue, or unworthiness. What are their verbal and nonverbal cues? What are their emotional and physical signs of distress and anxiety?

Our children are always expressing how they feel to us. We just need to know how to pay attention to their cues. We think we need to ask them questions, to probe and pry. Not at all. The data are right there; we just need to get free of our own mental distractions in order to notice. For example, if we could just observe something as simple as how our children get off the school bus and enter the house, we could collect so much data about what they need from us, without needing to ask a single question. Are their shoulders slumped, and do they drag themselves in the door? Or do they arrive with a skip and a song? Paying attention gives us clear signs about how we need to be with them. By actually seeing your child each day, you can begin to notice patterns of behavior. I only have to see my daughter, Maia, interact with her dog to know what mood she's in. You can get loads of information from your kids' day-to-day behaviors. Are they singing in the shower? Are they generally joyful and playful, or do they want to isolate? Witnessing without hounding them with questions or commands is a crucial first step in attuning ourselves to them.

When we are observant witnessers of our children's ways of being, we don't need to probe with endless questions. And let's be honest: most kids detest being asked lots of questions. Instead, we learn to see our kids for who they actually are and where they are emotionally at any given time. This is a powerful and necessary way to connect with our children at a deeper level.

Allowance

An attitude of allowance means that we let life and our children flow rather than constantly feeling that we need to adjust, manage, fix, and control everything. It's an attitude of "Let's wait a bit and see how this unfolds" rather than "This is going to go badly. I need to micromanage it."

Allowance requires a key ingredient that most of us don't have: patience. I certainly didn't have it as a young mother. Most of us parents are highly impatient, as we want things done our way, right away. What we don't realize is that children don't work at our pace. They have an entirely different pace—a much slower pace. If we override their pace with our pace, we force them to bypass coming to terms with their own life experience and instead adapt to an artificial way: ours. Jumping in and controlling things for our kids is not healthy for them. It makes them second-guess themselves and robs them of their own natural processing of their experience.

The next key element in a spirit of allowance is the creation of a safe space. What this means is that we "allow" our children the safety of practicing all sorts of behavior—yes, even acting-out behavior. They can practice yelling and screaming or being defiant and oppositional. They can see how it feels and get it all out of their system. Giving our children space lets them find their voices and better understand themselves. This idea may sound radical to many traditional parents: "What!? I should just allow my kid to act out?" Let me reassure you that I am not suggesting that we teach our children negative, acting-out behaviors. Giving our children space means permitting them to express themselves in their raw states, in a safe manner, without being punished. Once they have released and calmed down, we can discuss things with them.

You may wonder why such an approach is important. Here is the reason: When our kids suppress their natural expressions, it's going to show up in another part of their behavioral repertoire. Instead of harming themselves in some indirect way, it is much more therapeutic for our kids to express themselves in a safe container with us so that all their "crap" can be released. If not, this stuff will show up somewhere else. Again, I'm not suggesting that we let our kids walk all over us—not at all. Allowance just means that we don't need to be in a state of panic and damage control 24-7, leading us to jump in and unconsciously silence our kids' expressions and processing. Instead, we allow their chaos, imperfection, ordinariness, and chronic slowness, because this is the nature of childhood. Accept it.

Reciprocal

To engage in a reciprocal relationship with our children means that it is not just about *us-to-them* but very much about *them-to-us*. Reciprocity is the highest form of respect we can give another being. We truly treat them how we want them to treat us. Parents are so often focused on being our children's teachers that we completely forget that *they* are more our teachers than we can ever be theirs. Respect for the reciprocal nature of this powerful relationship is a key ingredient in preserving our children's sense of inner worth.

Although they don't yet know how to cut checks, budget payroll, or pay taxes, we should never underestimate our children's wisdom about their own state of being, no matter how old or how young they are. It's never too early to show reciprocal trust and respect toward our kids. So if they say,

> **"I am tired, I need more time," we need to respect them as we would ourselves.**
>
> **"I don't like my ballet teacher," we need to respect them as we would ourselves.**
>
> **"I am mad right now," we need to respect them as we would ourselves.**

Whether our children's expressions are about their preferences, opinions, or feelings—and no matter how different these are from our own—we need to respect them, just as we would want our children to respect our own preferences, opinions, and feelings.

I can hear you protesting, "Kids are clueless about things! They don't know anything!" And here is my response: "Sure, they don't know everything we adults do, but they do know how they feel in the moment." So, while we don't need to jump at their every feeling—as their feelings do pass quickly—we can certainly honor them and pay attention if the feelings persist. If they continue, they have some valid foundation that we need to honor and respect.

The moment I talk about respecting our children, parents start challenging me: "Should we just give in to their whims and fancies?" They envision children who stay up all night eating ice cream and cookies or who are alcoholics by the age of ten. The reason parents freak out when I talk about respect and reciprocity is that it scares them to relinquish control. They see this kind of mutual reciprocity as threatening their sense of dominance. For this reason, they equate it with negligence and anarchy.

Here is the truth: Conscious parenting isn't about negligence. It is just the opposite. It is about understanding that these little beings we call our children are thirsty for significance, worth, and control—just as we are. When we approach our children with this understanding, we empower them to actively participate in their world instead of having them passively hand over their power batons to us. This approach is not about *giving in* to their whims and fancies; it's about understanding that our children have a right to them. They have a voice—no matter how whimsical and fanciful. It is respect for this right that I am talking about here, not indulging or acquiescing to our children's every whim.

When we give our children the reciprocity and respect they deserve, they feel that reciprocity. They absorb the feeling that they are part of a *two-way* relationship, not just a *top-down* one. They soak in the feeling that they matter, because we treat them as people who matter.

Our children feel us listening and caring about their needs, likes, and wants. They notice how we pay attention and honor them. All of this sinks in and allows them to feel worthy. They begin to grow into themselves and evolve as active participants in their own lives. Once we acknowledge their experiences more fully, the relationship between parent and child is transformed.

Whereas traditional parenting is all about hierarchy and dominance, conscious parenting is all about reciprocity and circularity. Do you see how toxic the former paradigm was for us when we were growing up? This is why we need to shift to a reciprocal relationship with our children: so they feel seen and heard, just as we long to feel.

Mirror

The main energy around attunement is to mirror others in their "is-ness." Let me explain. If we come home from work with the expectation that our kids have completed their homework, walked the dog, and baked a cake, only to find them sprawled on the bed reading comics, our instinct is to pounce on them. We might shout out, "I cannot believe you are being so lazy! You need to be doing your homework. Get up right now!" Imagine how hearing that would land for them—not too well, I imagine.

Here is what it would mean to mirror their energy and attune to them: "I see that you are relaxing. That is wonderful. Are you feeling more rested? Do you think it's time to start doing your homework? Maybe if you started now, we could have dinner soon."

See the difference? The first approach is a shout, a bark, an order. The second approach is more respectful and honoring of where the child is at the moment. This respect doesn't negate the fact that your child needs to do their homework. All the approach does is to cause you to "enter the room" with a different kind of energy. Can you feel how different these approaches are? You see, the first one presumes judgment and blame. It enters the dynamic with an air of superiority and condemnation. No one truly responds well to that kind of approach, which shows distrust toward our children. The second approach is warm, inviting, curious, and respectful. It honors the emotional state of our children and displays trust in their ability to do what is required of them.

Do you see what it means to mirror our children's energetic state? We modulate our tone and our entire approach to match where they are at. We show them that we are joining them and meeting them where they are, rather than damning, resisting, and controlling them. We can become aware of our own moods and adjust them rather than blindly trying to control our kids' moods.

In all these ways and more, we can lean into our children's psychologies and pay attention to their essence. This tuning in is one of the most powerful tools of conscious parenting, as it allows us to adjust and design our entire parenting according to the kid before us. We tailor the nuances of our energies to best match what our children need from us. This is one of the most priceless gifts we can offer our kids.

Step Thirteen:
Spot Your Kid's Ego

My child,
I see the many masks you wear.
I see your eyes glaze behind them
And your face sadden.
They choke and suffocate you
But you see no other way.
It is the only choice you feel you have
To survive out in the cold.
It's my ego, you know, that did this to you,
That snuffed out the warmth of your spirit
And left us both bare inside the icy caves of inauthenticity.
I am now working on shedding my masks
So that I can see your essence more clearly
And honor who it is you are
So you can feel safe to be yourself again.

Every single one of us yearns to be honored for who we are. None of us—and I mean not a single one of us—*wants* to wear a mask. None of us *wants* to lie, cheat, steal, kill, or be rebellious and break rules. We only arrive at these desperate places out of a *perceived lack of choice.* Either we don't know another way to do things, or we may know another way, but don't feel empowered to manifest it.

Take the example of a thief. Do you honestly believe that they *want* to be a thief? Or are they conditioned by a lifetime of desperation? Consider parents who verbally beat up their kids in ruthless ways. Do you think they *want* to? I know that a possible jaded and cynical answer is "They always have a choice. Some people are just evil." This isn't a wise or helpful approach to apply across the board, since it judges without truly understanding anyone's inner motivation and story.

True transformation can come only by understanding the contextual backstory. For this reason, therapy is a powerful vehicle for change. It helps us to understand the power of our backstories in terms of how they led us to the places we find ourselves in now. In this way, we don't get mired in shame or blame. Instead, we begin to understand the *why* and the *how.* This is what this section is about— understanding our children's backstories. *Why and how* did your dynamic with your child come to be the way it is? What are the causes and effects that led to your child acting this way? What mix of complex factors led your child to arrive at this stage?

Trust me on this: your kid doesn't just wake up one day deciding to be a rebel or be disobedient. Many causes and effects had to occur in both your lives before this happened. Understanding the endless cause-and-effect chain is the key to grasping the backstory of our children's lives. This has the power to create compassion and empathy. It allows us to create a bridge to our children's experiences where before there had been an abyss.

Just as our ego masks were created in part through our relationship with our children, our kids' masks are created through their relationship with us. This is natural, isn't it? When they sense our masks, they automatically don theirs. Remember what I said earlier about our children's coping strategies? Their masks are their ways of coping with the force and fury of our own egos. Being aware of how our kids cope lets us step back and understand them with greater compassion. Otherwise we react blindly, which only solidifies their egos and sets up a vicious cycle of reaction between their egos and ours.

Let's try to see how our ego patterns set up our kids' ego patterns and discover how we can use our Third *I* to break the dysfunctional loop between us.

THE FIGHTER KID

While any kid can wear the mask of a Fighter, typically the child who wears this mask is an Anxious Exploder, a Hyperactive Explorer, or a Rebel Nonconformist. When such kids experience rejection or feel demeaned by a parent, they feel defensive and fight back. When our kids become Fighters, our own protective instincts kick in, and it's extremely hard to remain compassionate and gentle with our children. But if we understand that they are wearing masks, we can tap in to their essence and lovingly bring them back to their hearts by saying things like this:

> *I see that I have frustrated you. I understand that I can be maddening at times. I have upset you, and I am sorry. I see that I have hurt you and that you feel invalidated and demeaned. I am so very sorry to have caused you pain. You don't need to fight with me to be understood. I understand you. You can relax now.*

When kids are very young, you can use an abbreviated version, such as one of the following:

Mommy upset you?
Daddy scared you?

> **I see that you are feeling really mad at me. I am sorry I made**
> **you upset. You can tell me all about how upset I made you**
> **in a few moments.**

When we observe our children in their Fighter mode and don't resist them but flow with them, we allow them to feel validated being just the way they are. We don't yell and scream in anger and frustration, which is really the least productive thing to do when our kids are already in Fighter mode. Instead, we own our part in the cocreation of their mask. We understand that they wear their mask to protect themselves from us. Instead of getting upset with them for that response, we take responsibility for our role in it.

Just as our own ego masks developed out of pain, so does the mask of the Fighter within our children. When we understand this process, we can try to tap into their inner pain. This gentle and compassionate approach is the only way to help our children move away from their ego and back into their essence.

THE FIXER KID

It's really hard for a parent to not love a Fixer kid. These are the kids whose ego masks actually work for us. Our egos love this ego mask in our kids! Remember Aneika? She was a classic example of a sweet and pleasing girl who donned the mask of the Fixer to make her parents even happier with her. Wearing that mask eventually burned her out, but she made her parents' egos extremely happy while she wore it.

As we can learn from Aneika's case, this is the trap to watch out for: if we don't pay attention to the impostor nature of this mask, we will use and abuse our children to get our own needs met. The result can be that children disrespect their own boundaries to gain our approval and then become easy prey for others later in life. For this reason, we especially need to watch out for our Fixer kids and resist the ego temptation to abuse them for our own gratification.

The ones who typically trend toward this mask are the Over-pleaser kids and the Easy-Breezy kids. These kids are wired to be agreeable, so it's easy for us as parents to walk all over them and contort them with our own dictates. We justify our actions by saying, "Well, they said yes," or "They wanted to follow our opinions," which allows us not to confront our own shadow.

When we are attuned to the inherent temperaments of our children—specifically, our pleaser-type children—we are better able to see the masks they may take on under pressure. This understanding can keep them from having to wear any masks. We can assure these hyperanxious children that they are fine just the way they are by saying something like this:

> I can see that you are feeling anxious right now, and you want to fix it by going into overdrive. You want to take care of us, but that is not your job. Maybe you are afraid we won't love you just as you are. But we do. You don't need to do anything more than what you're already doing. You are perfectly complete as you are. I want you to remember that.

When we help our children notice their impostor masks in a gentle way without reacting, we allow them to ease into their inner feelings without feeling judged or scolded. Again, we can only do so with them when we are coming from our own place of abundance and worth. If we aren't, it's likely we will use and abuse their egos to serve ourselves, which in turn solidifies their egos. Knowing our kids at this deep level helps us attune to them and meet them where they are.

THE FEIGNER KID

The Feigner ego mask is worn because of a child's desperate need for praise and approval. An Overpleaser can subconsciously become addicted to being a superstar to gain attention and accolades. This mask can also be worn by Dreamer-Recluse kids, who switch to this mode in order to avoid feeling isolated or ostracized. These kids may bend over backward to be noticed and feel a sense of belonging because they've been shamed and ridiculed for their reclusive ways. The Rebel Nonconformist kid may also move in this direction, seeking attention by being a rule-breaker.

This mask can look like those worn by the proverbial class clown, the comic, the drama queen or king, or the "bad" rebellious kid. This is a mask that seeks attention at all costs and will try all sorts of ways to get it. If we could hear the Feigner's inner scream, we'd hear it clamoring for attention—"Do you notice me? Do you like me? Do you care?" When we are attuned to this mask, we can gently and compassionately help our children release it by saying things such as this:

> *I see you right now and always. I notice how amazing you really are. You don't need to carry the burden of trying to get my attention anymore. I have neglected your true needs, and I'm going to change my ways to better meet your needs. You are my most important priority, and I'm going to make sure you feel this from me.*

Attention-seeking masks are worn out of a subconscious desperation to be noticed. As parents, we can own our part in this by asking ourselves questions like these:

What am I doing that contributes to my kid being so desperate for attention?

Am I so distracted in my own life that I'm not paying attention to my child's needs?

How can I better show up for my child with presence?

Feigner children carry the pain of not feeling validated or recognized for who they are. As a result, they feel the need to wear this mask to get what they are missing from their parents. Attuning to their pain will help these kids take off their impostor masks so they can feel free to be who they truly are.

THE FREEZER AND FLEER KIDS

Almost every child can become a Freezer or a Fleer to some degree. It all depends on the level of trauma they are going through. While a Dreamer-Recluse is more likely to trend toward withdrawal, these two impostor masks are less connected to the child's nature than to the nature of the trauma that's involved. The more a parent is unconscious and aggressively abusive toward a child or neglectful of their needs, the more that child will freeze, dissociate, and escape their reality.

The cues that kids are Freezers or Fleers lie in their behavior toward their parents. Do they remove themselves? Do they isolate in their rooms and hide from you? These are signs of feeling traumatized and wanting to separate. These kids wear thick walls of armor around their emotions to protect themselves from the wrath of a parent's unconscious ways. When we are conscious of these masks, through compassion we can gently help our children emerge from under their armor, saying things such as this:

I understand why you are acting this way with me. I have hurt you a lot in the past, and now you don't trust our relationship. You feel as if you are unlovable and unworthy. I have contributed to this feeling. I want to make a change. Will you allow me to show you that I was wrong and that you deserve better treatment? I was unconscious in my ways, and I want to repair and renew our relationship because you matter a great deal to me.

This ego mask hides tremendous pain within a child. When we are able to look beneath the armor to the quivering, fearful inner child, perhaps we can connect in the way the child needs. These children are like abused puppies, afraid of more rejection and trauma. They need tremendous patience and care from the parent to bring them out of their shadows into the light of love and joy.

PUTTING IT INTO PRACTICE

We return now to the idea of paying attention to your children and your reactions to them. This is the most critical practice for spotting your kids' impostor masks. Noticing the nuances in their behaviors and paying attention to their unspoken feelings, all while not allowing your own ego to be activated—this is key. It is one thing to know that our children are in mask mode, but keeping our own masks off is the tricky part.

Staying in touch with your feelings throughout the day will help you to not be activated by your children's masks. Self-care practices such as exercise, meditation, rest, and relaxation help us stay grounded when our children act out. The following are some concrete affirmations that have helped me stay grounded when my child's ego is activating me. Each addresses a different part of the dynamic.

What is going on in my child?
   My child has a lot of feelings that they cannot express.
   My child is afraid and is wearing a mask for protection.
   My child is feeling out of control, and this behavior is the only way to gain back a sense of control.

What is going on in me?
   I am afraid to lose control.
   I am afraid I am a bad parent.
   I am afraid my child doesn't respect me.

Affirmations to heal my inner child:
   You are worthy as you are. You don't need an ego in order to feel worth.
   You are in charge of your own emotions. No one else is.
   Your child's behavior doesn't reflect on your parenting.
   Your worth doesn't depend on your child's state of being.

What does my child need from me now?
   My child needs me to stay present and grounded.
   My child needs me to be the adult in the room.

My child needs me to stay free of judgment.

My child needs me to understand that they are struggling.

Staying in touch with our own feelings is of pivotal importance if we are to create a stronger relationship with our kids, because it reinforces an awareness that our children experience inner pain just as we do. This understanding is key if we are to be healing forces in their lives. Seeing their pain and humanity through lenses similar to those we use to see our own allows us to come closer to our children, feel more aligned with them, and become more connected. This is the power of a shared commonality: it forges union. What could be a more powerful way to achieve this commonality than by seeing our children's pain as an echo of our own?

Step Fourteen:
Master KidSpeak

Your behaviors are a smoke screen.
They distract, detour, and deflect
From the real pain inside you,
From the true root beneath it all.
This is where my eyes need to search
And my heart needs to feel.
I need to focus on your hurts and fears,
And this is where I need to help you heal.

Kids speak in their own language and don't always communicate in direct or articulate ways. For that matter, neither do adults. If most adults struggle to express their inner feelings effectively, imagine what that effort is like for children. If only we had all learned to recognize and express our feelings in childhood, we wouldn't be in the messes we are in now. We miss our own cues and then sloppily dump our feelings onto the external world, or ourselves, in all sorts of unhealthy ways. Sometimes we do so through anger or tantrums, and sometimes through withdrawal or anxiety. It takes our conscious and willing intention to learn how to decode feelings and turn them into clear communication.

One of the main disconnects between a child's ways and an adult's ways is the language of play. Children play, but adults don't. Right here is a huge disconnect between how children process their worlds and how we do so. Most adults don't like playing with children; they find it a waste of time. Sure, many adults will play a sport with their children, or a structured board game, but just play? Nope. Too boring and unproductive. But here is the thing: unstructured, imaginative play is a child's primary language. So if we parents cannot engage with them in their first language, imagine the disconnect.

Children play before they speak, analyze, educate themselves, or work. Their primary language is play. The reason is that the faculty of critical and real-life thinking has not yet developed in them. Their brains are still developing and are in a dreamlike state of existence, at least until around the age of seven. They interpret their world through symbols, images, and metaphors. They don't have words, labels, or critical analysis for their experiences. They live through direct experience.

Their early years are pivotal, because they are the time when children are the most vulnerable and absorbent of the energies around them. As their own faculties for analytical thinking are not yet in place, they are defenseless prey to external influences. The more garbage thrown their way, the more their mindsets are polluted. The less we dump in there, the freer they are to foster a deep connection to their own inner knowing. The years before the age of seven are the most crucial to psychological well-being, as it is during those years that a child's emotional foundation is set.

We force children to abandon their primary language before they are ready and to enter our worlds of structured and competitive games, rules, grades, and instructed learning. Right here our children are already at a disadvantage, having to abandon their natural tongue, so to speak, and learn a foreign language—that of an adult. Playing with children means entering their worlds of imagination and possibility. It means crouching on the floor like a puppy or slithering across the carpet like a snake. Sure, playing with children can be annoying, but this is what it means to enter our children's world instead of transplanting them into ours.

You see, most of us don't understand how children speak, think, or act. We interpret their behaviors through the eyes of an adult and through the lens of our own egos. As a result, we are completely at cross-purposes with our children. If we only understood them better, we could connect with them better. That's what this step is meant to teach you: how to interpret your children's actions and behaviors so that you can forge a deep bond with them.

I cannot tell you how many parents come to me disturbed about their children's crying. Often these children are under the age of seven. What parents do not understand is that this is how children communicate distress—through crying. They don't have words yet to speak about their struggles or fears, so they cry. Parents misinterpret this as unnatural or abnormal.

So many of us parents are triggered and feel bad when our kids talk to us in what we perceive as a rude or uncaring way. I remember when Maia, at around the age of twelve, said "I can't stand you!" because she was upset about something. Oh, how I glommed onto that sentence. My victim mode went into full blast.

"How dare you say that! How could you be so cruel, when I do so much for you?" I went on and on, trying to make her feel bad.

She finally said, "Mom, I was upset. I didn't mean it. What I meant is that I can't stand it, not you! Why do you take everything so personally?"

That moment rocked my world and revolutionized my approach. I'd blown her statement up to such a catastrophic proportion that I felt totally sorry for myself, unappreciated and unloved. My inner child had been fully activated. When I heard her interpretation of what she had said, my thoughts shifted immediately: "Oh, she didn't mean it the way I was taking it. She didn't mean it to be a personal attack. I just did not understand how she uses words when she's upset. I need to decode her language differently." Now when Maia says something that feels personal—even "I hate you!"—I interpret it to mean "I hate *it*, Mom!"

There is a saying that floats around pop-psychology circles, "Kids just know how to push our buttons." What this statement implies is that our children know what our buttons are, and it is their devious mission to do things that push those buttons. This is a complete lie—a harmful one at that, because it makes parents feel on guard around their so-called evil children, who are "out to get them"! Do you see what a setup for disconnection this kind of thinking is?

The truth is that our children do not know what our buttons are, nor do they care. They are not "out to get us." They are more interested in just being themselves and figuring out how to have the most fun in life. Understanding this fact is key to distancing ourselves from the notion that our kids are purposely manipulative and plotting against us. Can children be clever at finding ways to get their needs met? Of course! But this doesn't mean they are intentionally deceitful or evil. And if they do choose to use manipulation against us, the onus is on us to ask ourselves, "How have I contributed to my child's feeling the need to manipulate me in this way instead of asking me directly for what they want?"

One of the most common triggers for parents is set off when their kids lie to them. Eli was such a parent. He was furious with his son, Noah, for lying about his grades in college. Noah had given his dad the impression that his grades were fine and that everything was under control. When Eli discovered later that Noah had been lying and that, in fact, he had barely been passing his exams, Eli lost his mind. He came for therapy with Noah and expressed his anger: "I have raised you to be an honest person, and here you are—the biggest liar in the world. You have shamed and disgraced yourself. I don't think I can ever trust you!"

As he said these words, Noah hung his head low. It was clear that his father's anger was hitting him hard. I had to intervene. I asked, "Eli, can you understand why your son lied? Or why humans lie in general? Don't you think he lied because he was scared to tell you the truth? You would lose your mind. Your son lied because he cared about what you thought about him. Lying looks like a negative thing on the surface, but if we probe more deeply we can see that it is also a positive symbol of the person's desire not to disappoint the other or face their wrath."

When I said these words, Eli was quiet and subdued. Then he said, "You know, the funny thing is, I lied to my dad during high school. He used to drop me off at my violin instructor's house. I hated playing the violin, but it was so important for my dad that I played along with the game of it. But half the time he used to drop me off, I'd never even go. I'd just sit in the park or play ball or talk to my friends on the phone. I covered my tracks for a few months, but eventually my instructor told my dad that I had not been attending. And my dad lost his mind. He did not speak to me for a few months. I cannot even express how ashamed I was. I wanted to scream at my dad and tell him that I was not a liar but that I was afraid of his anger, but the words never came out. My relationship with my dad was never the same after that. And now, look, I am acting exactly the same way with my own child. Isn't that funny?"

I was relieved that it did not take Eli long to empathize with his son and relate to his experience. I find myself repeatedly telling parents I work with, "If your children do not feel safe with you and you overcontrol them, it is natural for them to lie to you. They do so to emotionally survive your disappointment and wrath. They lie because they care about your reactions. If they did not, they wouldn't put in the effort to lie to you." It is hard for parents to wrap their minds around this concept, as we have been conditioned to believe that all lies should be punished. This is a simplistic approach that doesn't get to the heart of the matter. The truth is that lying, like many behaviors, is a symptom and clue that there is something deeper at play. If we focus only on surface behaviors, we lose sight of what is really going on. Lying is the perfect example. On the surface this behavior appears very negative. But when we go within and ask ourselves "What is this behavior hiding from view?" we can be surprised by what we find.

All of your own and your children's egoic and misaligned behavior is a SIGN: *something inside gone negative*. If we can remember this simple truth, then we can pause and go inward to the real need beneath the behavior. The outer words and actions simply need to be decoded so we can figure out what the feelings are within. Feelings direct and underpin our outer behavior—always. If we can begin to use outer behavior as a way to figure out our SIGN, we can begin to arrive at the contextual causes and effects. This allows for compassion, understanding, and connection instead of neglect, rejection, or shame.

Here are some questions we can ask ourselves to help us decode our children's behavior and get to the real feelings within:

What is this behavior trying to communicate to me?
What is the SIGN, why is it there, and how can I help transform it?
What is the intensity level of my child's pain right now?
What resources do I need to activate?

All behaviors are not equal. Some are SIGNs of a level-one inner pain, others a level-five inner pain. Figuring out which is which takes time and careful attunement.

In the illustration on the next page, we can see how a child's words can trigger the parent to react with ego unless the parent goes within to figure out what is going on with the child. Here the child is saying distressing and triggering things to the parent, but as you can see, the child is feeling all sorts of feelings that they cannot express. Understanding the latent meaning is what's key.

The first level we can refer to as a wave; the child's behavior is a sign letting the parent know that something is a bit off, but the child feels secure that eventually their needs will be met. The second is kind of a flag alert: the child is more resistant but is still hopeful and optimistic that their inner needs will be met. The third level is like a flame, with the child more volatile and frustrated about their needs being ignored. The temperature is rising, and we need to pay attention to our child's inner pain and feelings. The fourth level is more like a ticking time bomb, where the child is oppositional and detached to a large degree. The child feels as if the only way for them to manage their inner pain is to erect a huge barrier between themselves and their parent. They shun their parents and thwart any symbols of affection or connection. Their pain is so high that they cannot imagine tolerating even the slightest rejection.

The fifth level is an even higher-risk alarm, at the siren level of danger. Here all the alarm bells need to be sounded, as a child is in severe distress and at the point of harming themselves or others. The child's inner state is devoid of any connection to self or other. The child doesn't feel as if their existence matters. When things get to this level, I encourage parents to seek outside resources and support.

Taking your own and your child's emotional temperature is vital for understanding how to approach your child with connection rather than conflict. All of our children's behaviors communicate about their inner emotional worlds. Figuring this out is the key to connection.

Once we fully understand that our children's behaviors are just a mask or a symbol of something deeper—a SIGN—our entire approach can change. Instead of reacting to their surface behaviors, whether lying or disrespect, we can put on our conscious parenting X-ray vision lenses and look beneath those behaviors to ask, "What is really going on here with my child? What are their true emotional needs, and how can I meet these needs?"

Just as we learned to do for our own inner conflicts, we need to activate our insightful self —the Third *I*—here to help our children feel understood and heard. Just as we did for ourselves in Stage Two, we now need to show up for our children's inner pain in a way that feels compassionate and connected. The following sections suggest what we might say to ourselves to help us stay grounded when our children show us one of the five *F*'s. I am using the same prototype in the parenting examples that follow to demonstrate how each of the different impostor masks of our children can be soothed and validated.

FIGHTER KIDS

Fighter kids attack their parents in some way to regain a sense of control when they've been triggered by a sense of unworthiness. For instance, they might say, "I hate you!" Parents who are conscious and not activated by their own inner child can tune in to their children's emotional temperature and try to understand them from a deeper perspective. When parents do so, they let the words of attack fall away without paying attention to them. These parents are able to tell themselves:

> *My child is using words to explain inner chaos and loss of control. The outer anger and frustrations are a mirror to an inner schism and void. If I react to the words by losing control of my own senses, I will create more chaos. My task as a parent is to understand my child's pain and help assuage this internal distress.*

FIXER KIDS

Fixer kids express their inner anxiety and loss of control in a "fixing" way when triggered by a sense of unworthiness. They capitulate before the power of the parent and try to comply with the parent's wishes. These children hope that by bending to the parent's will, they can assuage their fears around their own unworthiness and gain approval and validation. Instead of simply reacting to this ego mask and "using" their children's desire for their own gain, parents need to realize that their children are experiencing some pain. Parents who can see through their child's mask remind themselves:

> *My child is feeling some internal sense of rejection or unworthiness, and this is why they are acting in such a pleasing and compliant way. This is not their true self. My task as a parent is to understand their pain and help assuage the internal distress by reassuring them that they are worthy as they are and do not need to bend to my ways to feel this worth.*

FEIGNER KIDS

Feigner kids are hungry for attention, seeking and demanding praise and validation when triggered by fears of their own unworthiness.

They start acting out or overdoing their antics. Instead of being triggered by this ego mask, conscious parents understand that their child is missing something from within, such as a sense of worth, belonging, and significance. When the parent is able to go within to find the child's real needs, the parent can connect to the child's inner fear that they don't belong and assure them that they are worthy just as they are. Such parents are able to remind themselves:

> *My child is trying to seek my attention and focus. How can I give this to them so they don't have to resort to extreme behaviors? My task as a parent is to understand my child's pain and help assuage this internal distress.*

FREEZER KIDS

Freezer kids withdraw and become paralyzed when triggered. When parents are able to go within, they can connect to their children's inner fears. Children panic because they feel unlovable and unworthy. Instead of being upset with children's freezer reaction, parents can have compassion and respond in a more conscious and humane way. They are able to remember:

> *My child is shutting down because they feel unsafe and unseen. They are feeling a loss of significance and power, and as a result they feel comfortable only by shutting down. My task as a parent is to understand their pain and help assuage this internal distress. I need to find a way to create safety for my child so that they can slowly come out of their withdrawal and trust me again.*

FLEER KIDS

The Fleer kid dissociates, ejects, and escapes when triggered by a sense of unworthiness. Of course, such a child often comes from a home where there is much trauma and abuse, which is the reason the child has adopted such a severe mask. When parents can go within to find the child's real need, they can connect to the child's inner fears of being worthless and useless. These parents can remind themselves of this key fact:

> *My child is in an extreme state of distress because of the trauma in their childhood. I am directly or indirectly part of this trauma. I need to heal my own dysfunctional patterns so that I can heal my child's trauma. My task as a parent is to understand my child's pain and help assuage this internal distress. I need to undo past patterns and begin to rebuild trust and safety from the ground up.*

Do you see how powerful it is to not activate your own ego and instead connect to your children at a deeper emotional place? When we are aware that our children's surface behaviors all reflect an internal state of affairs, we are able to bond and connect more deeply with our children. Instead of making it all about ourselves and our own reactions, we offer our children the gift of our compassion, presence, and attunement. Once our own emotional "stuff" is out of the way, we can truly understand our children's emotional temperature and use their behaviors as clues to help us arrive at a deeper connection.

PUTTING IT INTO PRACTICE

Let's put what we have learned into practice. If you have young children, try to play with them for short spurts during the day. If you have older children, try to engage with them through games or other fun activities. These bonding moments will go a long way toward deepening your connection.

Asking ourselves what's going on beneath our children's behavior is key to connecting to their feelings and meeting them at their emotional level. Asking yourself these questions will help you enter an awareness of your own and your children's emotional SIGN: "What is the emotional temperature today? Am I or are they stressed? Unhappy? Anxious? Hopeful? Excited?" These underlying emotions all have the power to impact our own and our children's behaviors. Add in stressors such as work or exams and peer pressures, and you have a potential emotional powder keg.

Taking our emotional temperature is vital for staying in touch with where we and our children are internally. Stop throughout the day to tune in to your own and your children's emotional temperature—first thing in the morning, at lunch, or just before you see your kid after school. What are you feeling, and what are they feeling? What can you do to take care of your inner world or their inner world in that moment? Keeping your X-ray "feeling vision" on throughout the day will allow you to stay in touch with what is going on beneath the surface and be attuned to both your own feeling state and your children's.

I often remind myself of the following to keep from getting sucked into my own child's behaviors:

I don't like this behavior, but it is trying to tell me something. What is it?

This behavior is showing me how my kid feels inside. What are they feeling?

My child is acting this way toward me because of feeling this way about themselves. How can I help them?

My child's behaviors are not personal attacks on me but are personal mirrors of my child's inner world. How can I reach them?

Do you see how these questions create curiosity and a compassionate desire to help our children? Maybe you can develop your own list of questions to help you keep your ego in check during triggering moments with your children.

Step Fifteen:
Instead of Punishment, Do This

Why do I believe I have the right to punish you,
Or the right to shame, yell, scream, and degrade,
Or the right to own and dominate you,
Or the right to harm or violate your sovereign body?
Why do I believe that you only learn through fear,
Or that you must obey my word or suffer my wrath,
Or that unless I break your spirit, you will break mine?
Why do I believe such toxic things
That cause me to battle you instead of connect,
That cause me to view you as my enemy instead of my ally?
These beliefs must be discarded, burned, torched, and buried
So that I can start again—in a new way,
Where it is no longer about me versus you,

But about our mutual kinship and reciprocal connection.
This is no longer about my power over you,
But instead about our journey through life together,
Where we walk together, side by side
As two, but in one direction,
Toward our union as teacher and student.

There is a huge shadow of parenting that needs to be exposed, and it's the shadow around the whole idea of discipline. I have written an entire book about discipline, *Out of Control*, that I advise you to read if you want to delve deeper into this topic. But for our purposes now, I'll get straight to the point. The current paradigm around parental discipline is extremely toxic, unconscious, and, dare I say, criminal at times. It's heavily predicated on an attitude of punishment, and the use of this approach absolutely needs to stop. Conscious parenting is not about punishing anyone, least of all our children. It's not about using fear, control, and manipulation to coerce our children into compliance. There is another way. We can teach our children in a manner that has nothing to do with domination.

Before I break it all down, be aware that this section may bring up painful memories because most of us were raised with a traditional approach to discipline, a.k.a. punishment. Most of us were yelled at, shamed, spanked, grounded, or punished in some other way. I want you to become aware of your beliefs around punishment, because your past will strongly influence how you absorb this next section.

One of the first things I would like to address is how prevalent and ubiquitous this notion of punishment is. What is particularly disturbing about the entire "industry" of parental discipline is that it is an unchecked paradigm. We go about employing punishment as if it were universally endorsed and even divinely ordained. I am here to tell you that parental discipline, the way we have been executing it through the use of punishment, is one of the most ego-centered elements of our humanity—one that affects not just our children, but all aspects of our lives.

Traditional parental discipline is basically fearmongering and bullying. It's cruel, lazy, and ego-dominated. By bullying children into shame and fear, parents teach their children that such dominance and violence are acceptable and endorsed. These children then grow into the next generation of bullies, who see no harm in dominating others or the earth itself. At the core of the current destruction of our earth is the toxic paradigm of parental discipline. And it all starts in our childhood.

Traditional parental discipline is centered on the core principle that parents have unchecked and unregulated rights to "correct" their children's behaviors in whatever ways the parents deem fit. They can punish their children at will, and the punishment is glorified as "education." All parents get this right to do as they please to their kids. Think about it: *all* parents have this right, no matter what their level of consciousness is or whether they are healed from their own past traumatic "discipline." It's like putting a nuclear warhead in the hands of an emotionally unstable person. Not wise, is it? Well, this is what we have done. We have given parents unrestrained access to their children's bodies and minds, with no consequences. Put this power into the wrong hands, and you have unmitigated abuse. And sadly, there is no one around to protect our kids from us.

Let's make a list of the things parents believe they have the right to do to their kids:

Publicly or privately shame them
Spank, slap, and beat them
Scream at them
Ground them, lock them up
Throw things at them
Withdraw love
Neglect them
Take away their possessions

No one questions a parent's judgment or resists a parent's authority except in extreme cases of abuse—which mostly remain hidden from public view. Punishment is just the way that parents have corrected their children's behavior for eons, and it will continue to be unless and until there is a different way for us to parent our kids.

As parents we have been given the power to invade our children's lives and dominate them in any way, shape, or form that we desire. No one really dares to stop us; after all, our children belong to us and therefore are our possessions. People are scared to tell parents that their ways are wrong or toxic, for fear of retaliation. Most parents wouldn't dare behave with other adults the way they do with their children. We wouldn't dare "punish" other adults in our lives. Do you know why? The other adults could retaliate in one of these ways:

End the relationship
Fight back
Report the abuse to the authorities

It's because our children are helpless that we give ourselves the right to do with them as we please. This is a highly dangerous power to hand over, and for that precise reason, being conscious of this power dynamic is essential. Here is where conscious parenting comes in. It teaches us that the old ways of discipline are not only archaic, but toxic and dysfunctional. They create stress and strain for the child and erode the parent-child connection in so many ways. The conscious parent understands that such techniques emerge from the ego and corrode the child's sense of worth.

The old paradigm of parental discipline is based on control, fear, guilt, and shame. We haven't known any other way. Some of us may opt out of physically spanking our kids, but we continue to beat them up emotionally. No matter the exact technique used, the main point is that this kind of discipline is based on the parent's ego. So long as that ego goes unchecked, it will keep eroding our children's sense of worth, safety, and self-respect.

Control, fear, guilt, and shame are techniques that don't truly teach our children in the way we hope they will. True teaching doesn't emerge from force or manipulation, but from an organic unfolding of one's inner knowing. These are artificial techniques used to manipulate and oppress another into acquiescence. Sure, they will give the parent a temporary and false sense of dominion and power, but this will not last for long. What parents don't realize is that along with their temporary sense of monarchy comes a host of other problems, all connected to their child's mental unraveling. Dictators use these techniques to brainwash their citizenry to robotically follow their dictates. Is this what you wish for your children—for them to be brainwashed into servility and obedience? Or would you rather arrive at an understanding that emerges from deep within them, as opposed to a reaction that they are forced into by fear?

Children raised with oppression eventually do one of two things as adults: they continue the oppression of the self by becoming their own oppressors, or they seek others to oppress and subjugate. This is not learning or education. This is toxic aggression toward the self and others.

Discipline by the traditional paradigm is often heralded as education or as being in the child's "best interests." This is a completely delusional idea and needs to be called out for its insanity. Traditional discipline is one thing: abuse. Only when we arrive at this conclusion do we become willing to change our own patterns.

Are you willing to embrace a new set of ideals and a new way of being? Can you imagine never having to use force or violence with our children—never needing to ground, slap, or spank them? Can you envision this new reality as a parent? Yes, it's possible—but it requires the parent to undergo a groundbreaking transformation.

One of the first steps I took in my own journey toward conscious parenting was to remove the option of physical or emotional violence toward my child. It simply wasn't an option. Once I got that out of the way, I began to eliminate all language or behavior that suggested an attempt at physical or emotional violence. While I wasn't perfect at doing so—admittedly, I did lose my temper and yell at my kid—I endeavored to diminish these toxic ways of being as swiftly as I could. I didn't do so through self-shame or blame, but through working on my own inner wounds, as I have shown you how to do throughout this book. As time went by and my consciousness expanded, I became better and better at avoiding these toxic techniques—and my connection with my child grew and grew.

So how can we raise our children without using control, domination, and shame? There is a way: the conscious parenting way. The main tenet of conscious parenting is connection, before all else. I often give clients this powerful reminder: *connect before you correct*.

Connection before correction: this is a foundational principle of conscious parenting. We have been putting together the blocks that make up this foundation all through this book. When we ask ourselves, "How can I connect with what my child is feeling right now?" our entire energy shifts, from domination to partnership. Holding this focus is the key to deepening the connection with our children. To break this down further and put it into practice, I use the acronym NBC: *negotiation, boundaries, consequences*. When we follow these three pillars of conscious parenting, not only do we educate our children in a beautiful way, but we also preserve our connection with them. Most important, we preserve their connection to their own worth and inner power. Let's take a deeper look at each of these pillars.

Negotiation

When I talk about negotiating with kids, parents often balk. Why? It is too much work, too much back-and-forth. And guess what? They are right. It's harder to negotiate with our kids than to command them. But negotiation is a far healthier strategy than blindly dictating to our kids, because it allows our children to feel empowered and validated. All humans thrive best when they perceive that they have control over their own lives. Even if they don't have actual control, it's important for them to perceive that they do.

Our children yearn for the perception of control over their own lives. When we blindly give them a barrage of orders and expect them to comply, we abduct their inner authority and teach them to be disconnected from their own inner knowing. But engaging in a dialogue of negotiation, instead, allows them to feel respected and worthy. We communicate to our children that they are important enough for us to consider their opinions and absorb their perspective about things. Instead of mowing down their opinions, we demonstrate that our children are important enough for us to slow down and engage in a dialogue that considers their well-being and nurtures their points of view. We would behave that way with our best friends—so why not with our kids as well?

Here is how negotiation might look: If your teenager wants to have a party in the house when you are not in town, and you are in disagreement about it, how do you handle it? Do you say, "Are you crazy? No way!"? Or do you pause and consider their request, just as you would for a peer? Maybe you can say, "I know you want to have a party, but I don't think it is safe for you to when I am not in the house. How can we come up with an agreement that allows both of us to get our needs met—you get to have a party, and I get to provide safety for you and your friends?" Maybe your child agrees to have the party when you are in town, but you agree to give your child privacy by staying in another part of the house. Or maybe you arrive at another arrangement altogether. Regardless of the outcome, it is the *process* of negotiation between parent and child that is key here. It helps the child feel respected and connected to, as opposed to being blindly controlled and dictated to.

When our children see that we are open to negotiating a new path with them, they feel heard and honored. It's a win-win. Our openness to negotiation allows them to put down their own defenses and open themselves to a mutually beneficial agreement. They understand that this is not a battle and that we as parents are on their team. Instead of fighting with us, they open themselves up to working alongside us. This is a wonderful way to build connection and nurture the bond we share.

When you use the approach of negotiation, it's not so much about who gives in or who wins but about something far more profound— the attitude we have toward the entire situation. Do we come with an attitude of care for each person's point of view, or is it all about one person only? An approach of negotiation shows our children that their voices are equally valid. This approach gives them an awareness of how to use their voices and the understanding that they matter.

Circumstances can get heated and complicated, and sometimes it's hard to come to an agreement. That's okay. The point isn't to arrive at an easy destination. Instead, the point is to communicate to our kids that we are willing to enter into dialogues with them that respect their points of view. In short, an approach of negotiation demonstrates to our children that they are worthy of being heard and treated as autonomous beings, no matter their age.

I can just hear your protests: "But we cannot negotiate everything with them. Some things are nonnegotiable." And you are right. There *are* some nonnegotiables, and knowing what these are is extremely important. We will discuss this topic further in the following sections on setting boundaries. But before you get excited about creating a list of nonnegotiables, let me warn you that only a few things in life can fall into this category. When we say that something is nonnegotiable, that means it's beyond dialogue—it's law and order. Do we want to raise our children in a home run by law and order? Or do we want them to feel that they live in a home where everything is up for discussion and open dialogue? In which kind of home would you rather live?

When it comes down to nonnegotiables, it's important to understand that having too many of them creates rigidity and suppression. Life is simply too complex, with too many intricate cause-and-effect situations, to have unlimited nonnegotiables. We would be living in a dictatorship if we engaged in life this way. We would lose sight of the forest for the trees.

Declaring something nonnegotiable means that we as parents pull the plug, press the red button, and call the shots. It means that we pull rank and don't ask for anyone else's opinion. This approach can only be for hard-line situations. But as we know, life cannot be lived with flow and ease if we have too many rigid rules. For example, if we create nonnegotiables around meal or sleep times, then we run the risk of coming up against these on a daily basis. Making these times nonnegotiable is a recipe for disaster, given that children are in constant flux. Do we want to engage in battles day in and day out? Or is it better to have agreements that are loosely defined and created out of negotiation with our kids? In this way, we don't set ourselves up for constant conflict. We stay open to what shows up, day by day, moment by moment, without putting undue pressure on ourselves.

Honestly, the only nonnegotiables I have come up with are around safety. If there are safety issues, such as harming self or others, there need to be hard lines. I call these "red flag" behaviors—substance abuse, for example, or self-harming behavior such as cutting, or suicidal thoughts or impulses. For the rest of life, I keep an open mind and a fluid approach so I can consider all the complexities before backing myself and my child into a rigid corner.

When you approach life through the lens of growth and fluidity, you see it as a constant series of negotiations—a barter and exchange, if you will. In this approach of reciprocity and mutuality, there is no boss-minion dynamic, nor is there a "my way or the highway" mentality. We see ourselves as part of a flux wherein each link in the causal chain of cause and effect has to be considered and honored.

Viewing parenting as a series of negotiations is really about the attitude with which we approach our relationship with our children. The actual execution of these negotiations takes place at the next level—the boundaries level. That's where we actually put things in place. But first we need to get the attitude right. Approaching our parenting struggles through the lens of partnership, rather than battle, makes all the difference. A partnership approach lets our children work with us in a mutual agreement rather than feeling as if they are at war with us. The outcome is joy and connection rather than stress and strife.

Boundaries

How we execute our boundaries with ourselves and others deeply influences how we show up in our relationships. Without an awareness of our boundaries, we will be washed ashore in our relationships, with little idea of how we got there. This awareness is especially important in our parenting, as our children constantly come up with situations that seem to test our boundaries. If we don't have a clear awareness of how to sort through these situations, we'll botch things up and confuse our kids. Let's break down how we can think about boundaries in a conscious way.

There has been much talk about boundaries in modern psychology. It seems as if the answer to many of our relationship troubles is the erection of boundaries. While this may be true on some level, we need to be careful, because there is a trap here. If we are not conscious, our boundaries quickly turn into walls that we use to protect ourselves from feeling pain from the outer world. As such, they are built out of fear and control from our egos. These boundaries should be called "walls," as they are designed to keep others out of our lives so they cannot cause us any more pain. Rather than deconstructing the pain and healing it, we wall off the other. In doing so, we avoid carrying out the real work needed to understand ourselves on a deeper level.

True boundaries are not always a reaction to the external world, although sometimes they can be. Rather than being established by a knee-jerk reaction of fear and control, true boundaries are created through growth and awareness. They are not erected out of panic and dread, but out of self-love and self-worth. If someone hurts us, we don't create a wall to keep them away. Instead, we create new boundaries around what is acceptable to us and what isn't, based on our own self-love and self-worth. We allow in those who match our ever-growing self-respect, and we keep out those who don't. In this way, it isn't about person X or Y, but about our internal sense of who we are and the standards we wish to create for how others interact with us. Do you see the subtle but profound difference?

Now let's bring this same insight to parenting. We all want to create healthy and flexible boundaries with our kids without walling them off in fear or control. How do we create such boundaries? Well, the first step is always an internal one: We need to sit with ourselves and be really honest. We need to become conscious of the nature of the boundaries we wish to create. Remember, instead of inadvertently creating walls between ourselves and our kids, we need to embody life principles that naturally show up as boundaries but that have less to do with our kids' behavior per se and more to do with our own ways of living and being.

For example, we don't take the chocolate chip cookies away from our kids because they are eating too many and gaining weight. Since we realize they are not healthy for anyone in our home, we limit buying them, period. We don't take away screen time from just one kid who's doing badly at school; instead, we restrict screen time for the entire household, because too much screen time creates disconnection. So we have a screen curfew for everyone, and none of us can look at screens in our bedrooms. Do you see the difference? The former way creates boundaries out of reaction to someone's behavior. The latter creates them out of a life philosophy that is more lasting and applicable to everyone in the home.

When we create boundaries in reaction to another, we tend to maintain the boundaries in a wishy-washy and confusing way. They are neither well thought out nor integrated into any basic philosophy. But boundaries created after conscious and thoughtful contemplation of their deeper relationship to ourselves tend to be clearer and more long-lasting. To contemplate a conscious awareness of our boundaries, we need to ask the following four key questions.

1. *Who is this boundary really for?* Is my boundary based on my own ego's needs or my child's needs? This is a key question to ask

ourselves, one that many parents don't ask because they just assume they are operating in the best interests of their child. But as we now know, this assumption is not true at all much of the time. I'll go so far as to say that our boundaries emerge mostly from our own expectations and desires, and rarely from our children's.

For instance, if we have a boundary concerning how long our kid should practice the piano, we need to ask ourselves whether we want them to play the piano for us or truly for themselves. If it is for them, shouldn't they be practicing willingly? Does our child even enjoy playing the piano? If so, why are we having daily struggles about practice time? Are we being dogmatic instead of being flexible and asking what our child believes is best for themselves?

Or take the issue of bedtime. Did we set the time based on our kid's true needs for rest and their unique sleep cycles, or because we wanted to watch our favorite show on Netflix? Most of our boundaries come from wanting to fulfill our own agendas, and as such these are *ego-enhancing* boundaries. They emerge from our own fantasies, agendas, and expectations and often don't take our kid's needs and desires into account.

This leads us to the next question:

2. *Is my boundary ego-enhancing or life-enhancing?* What does this mean? With an ego-enhancing boundary, like the one I just described, the parent initiates the boundary because it works for their agenda or expectations. A life-enhancing boundary is different. It is a boundary that is truly in the best interest of the child and stands the test of time all over the world (for the most part). What are examples of life-enhancing boundaries? They involve such things as practicing good hygiene, getting an education, staying healthy, not harming self or others, and staying connected to community. Do you see how these are different from playing the piano or learning basketball? Life-enhancing boundaries are vital for our children's sense of self and well-being in the world, without which they will truly struggle. Ego-enhancing boundaries, on the other hand, are about

curated and idiosyncratic desires of the parent that the child doesn't necessarily need to fulfill in order to survive or thrive in the world. In all honesty, I have never played basketball in my life, and I think I am just fine. Nor was I a fabulous piano player. Do you see what I mean?

You might say to me, "All right, Dr. Shefali, but what if my kid wants to do nothing but play video games, and if I agree, then that's all my kid will do?" Here is a key point that needs to be stressed: giving in to our children's desires is not life-affirming if those desires are life-destructive. Do you see how playing video games ad nauseam would be life-destructive for them? This would be my reply: "Wanting to be disconnected for hours on a screen comes from ego needs and desires that are not ultimately life-affirming. It's okay for you to step in and negotiate boundaries, since such boundaries will preserve your child's connection to life." Life-affirming boundaries preserve our children's connections to themselves and to us. Such boundaries take into account our children's temperaments and needs in a wholesome, integrated manner. When we focus on whether or not something is life-affirming for our children, we set our intentions on their well-being and create pathways forward based on those intentions.

To create a boundary concerning our children's desire to play video games, we might say something like this: "Your emotional well-being is my top priority. Playing video games so much is not good for your emotional well-being. It isolates you in your bedroom so you don't interact with family or friends. You don't go outside and play or exercise. I want to honor your desire to play video games, but you need to be able to honor yourself as well. How can we negotiate a way for you to do both things—play video games but also take care of your emotional well-being?"

When we are firm about the message that playing video games to excess is not affirming for their well-being, our children may not like this boundary, but they will understand where we are coming from. When they see that we are operating with their best interests at heart, they are more likely to be amenable to coming up with new solutions.

The third question we need to ask is this:

3. **What is my boundary made of?** What are the ingredients of my boundary? Is it made of stones or of sand? We need to decide how rigid or flexible our boundaries should be. We need to ask:

What are my stone boundaries?
And why do I have them?
Can I adhere to them?

When I first entered parenthood, I was naive and full of arrogance. I had the audacity to have stone boundaries concerning most things. I thought that was what good parents did—they had fixed schedules and plans, as well as consistent and clear ones. So I set out to create such stone boundaries for my daughter, thinking that if I stuck to them, they would eventually become routine.

For example, I had an entire timetable of things that needed to happen after dinner—7:00 p.m. for cleanup, 7:15 p.m. for shower, 7:30 p.m. for story time, 7:45 p.m. for bedtime, and all done by 8:00 p.m. Inevitably, things happened, and the schedule got delayed. When I saw time ticking away, I felt pressure to beat the clock. This made me irritable and frustrated when I saw my daughter dawdle at dinner or take too long in the shower. Then one day I stopped in my tracks and asked myself, "Why are you acting as if bedtime is carved in stone? Who said it needs to be 7:45 p.m. on the dot? Why can't it be whatever it will be, as long as the intention is for it to be between 8 and 9 p.m.? Why am I creating such rigid expectations, which only a robot could meet?" Once I realized that no gun was being held to my head, I exhaled a huge sigh of relief and immediately felt the pressure release. I made a commitment right then that I would no longer set artificial deadlines and expectations for myself, as they directly impacted my daughter's sense of joy and spontaneity.

If your child is having a particularly joyful time in the bathtub, you can bend and ease into the laughter and giggles. There is no need for a stone boundary, is there? Release your pressure valve, and take in the present moment for its abundance and fun. If your children are particularly fussy at bedtime and can't settle down, lean into their emotions and give them space to find their centers. In both cases, you can choose equanimity and release rather than stress and control. Do you see how this new approach of "playing it by ear"— which involves having boundaries of sand instead of stone—allows for so much more freedom and play? The approach of strict time-tables can create an internal volcano of pressure that eventually has no alternative but to erupt.

A huge part of traditional parenting is about consistent bound-aries. While such boundaries are 100 percent the ideal, this goal is not realistic; it is simply not possible to be consistent all the time. On some days we can adhere to the "no TV rule," but if Mommy is ill, no babysitter is available, and the kids cannot be left to their own devices, then maybe on this day TV is okay. Do you see what I mean? When we set rigid parameters, we stick ourselves into tight corners and then feel like failures when we cannot meet these impossible standards.

When we approach our boundaries with the awareness that they are made of sand, we become more lighthearted and relaxed. Having a boundary made of sand doesn't mean we don't draw the line; we simply draw it in the sand, ready to shift and change as the wind moves the grains of sand one way or the other. We have an open and flexible attitude in the present moment. We can have a general con-tainer for our ways of living—for example, a boundary for bedtime at around 8 p.m., or, as they say in India, "8-ish." The "ish" lends an atmosphere of lightness, humor, and ease that encourages us to lean into the messiness of life without stringency and perfectionism. An-other example of a sand boundary is to tell your child something like this: "I can see you really want to go on a sleepover [or it could be about buying a smartphone]. I understand your need. I am saying it is not possible right now, but let's revisit this in a few months [or a few years depending on the issue at hand]." Do you see how we lean into the child's desires but do so with an awareness of what is best for them on an emotional level?

Many parents have a hard time with this approach, viewing it as wishy-washy and confusing. I understand this resistance. I offer a different awareness and understanding of the approach as flexible, not wishy-washy. When we are clear about the overarching framework of creating boundaries that come from a life philosophy rather than from reaction to a particular person or situation, we can afford to have flexibility within this larger framework.

If our life philosophy includes healthy nutrition, occasional flexibility about ice cream night or cookies at a birthday party allows for fun and spontaneity. This flexibility isn't about being wishy-washy as much as it's about being flexible and playful in the moment. If we are settled in our thinking that 95 percent of our lifestyle is healthy, we can be more playful about our boundaries in the present moment.

Finally, the last question we can ask is this one:

4. *How will I communicate my boundaries?* Will I use control or soul? This is another key question we need to ask in creating loving and conscious boundaries. Is our tone and energy loving and caring, or is it controlling and dominating? Do we come at our children with a tone of commander in chief, or with a tone of ally and partner? Do we bark out commands? Or do we engage and invite our children into the partnership?

Barking commands sounds like this:

Clean your room right now!
Finish your homework right this minute!

Creating partnership sounds more like this:

Hey buddy, I know you are tired right now, but can we talk about cleaning your room in five minutes, please?
Hey love, I know you are enjoying your movie, but it's getting late, and we need to eat dinner soon. When are you planning on finishing your homework?

Do you see the difference? Which would you prefer in your own relationships? Would you prefer that someone bark out orders to you or that they lovingly bring you into the agreement you had with them? Our kids want to be treated with respect and honor, just as we do.

Similarly, even when we are asking our children to do something we think of as loving—maybe drink a green smoothie, meditate before bedtime, or donate clothes to charity—if we do so with an attitude of control, we'll end up with the same result as if we'd barked out an order. It isn't so much about the content of what we say as it is about the tone and energy. I remember teaching my daughter meditation when she was young. Even though this was a loving and conscious thing to teach her, I knew that if I approached it with a heavy-handed energy, I would ruin it all. I couldn't bark at her, "Breathe, one–two–three, out-breath, one–two–three, in-breath!" That would have been insane, and I would have been going against the very principles of meditation.

Everything depends on our tone and energy, because these represent our internal awareness of and respect for our partnership with our kids. Are they our partners on this journey of life, or are they our slaves? Do you see how keeping these questions in mind allows us to create conscious boundaries that enhance our flow and connection with our kids? Instead of creating barriers between us, we can build bridges, so that our children feel as if they are on the same team with us, rather than against us. When we remember that connection with our kids is the primary goal, we are able to become effective at creating and holding our boundaries.

Consequences

Let's talk about consequences and what they mean in conscious parenting. Our children are here to ultimately live their own lives. Doing so means they will have to bear their own life consequences. If they are perfectionists, they will have to suffer the consequences of that stress. If they are underperformers, that tendency will come with its own consequences. If they are procrastinators or are overly competitive, those behaviors will have consequences, too. Every way of being is going to have its own consequences. We cannot control these for our children.

Do you know the biggest payoff of allowing our children to deal with their own life consequences, or what we often call "natural consequences"? They grow best when they learn through the direct causes and effects of their own actions. The deepest learning comes from direct experience. We all know this truth intellectually, but when it comes to parenting, we tend to forget. We hold the delusional belief that our children belong to us, and it's our responsibility to control their choices and whatever consequences these bear. What a tremendous burden this is for us!

Guess what? It isn't your job or responsibility to control your child's choices and their consequences, especially after a certain age—say, thirteen or fourteen. At some point we need to release the reins we have on our children and allow them to face their own music. We don't do so because we are cruel, but because we know from our own life experiences that this is the only way to learn and grow. When we have the approach that children learn best through their own experiences, we can step back and allow the consequences to be the teacher. Instead of believing that we need to teach them a lesson and punish them, we allow the consequences to do the work.

For example, if our sixteen-year-old kid fails to complete their homework on time, we don't have to step in and threaten punishment. Why erode the connection? The teacher will mete out the consequences, and the child will have to deal with how that feels. You might say, "But what if they won't care?" My answer is, "You cannot make them care. Your punishment won't make them care, either. It will just breed resentment and disconnection from you."

Natural consequences are life's best teachers, far more profound and effective than any carrot or stick you can hold out to your kids. When they feel the natural reward or punishment, that feeling is the best director for their next steps. But for natural consequences to

happen, you need to step out of the way and let your children's experiences do the teaching. Because of our egos, doing so is hard for us.
We want to have control over our children and their choices, so we
cannot bear to give them the space to figure things out on their own.

When Melissa, a twenty-two-year-old engineering student, decided to change her major midway through college to enter culinary
school, her parents lost their minds. They saw this as a demotion
and were livid with their daughter for not living up to what they
thought of as her potential. Instead of allowing Melissa to figure out
her own likes and dislikes, they wanted to micromanage her choices
to reflect what they wanted for her. They fought and resisted Melissa's choice for six months before coming to see me.

During this time, Melissa developed an eating disorder due to
all the stress her decision was causing in her relationship with her
parents. It was only after they came to see me that things began to
change—slowly at first. It took a long time to help Melissa's parents
understand that she needed to learn from the causes and effects of
her own decisions rather than theirs. They could no longer interfere in how her life unfolded. Those days were past and should really
have ended by the time she'd entered her teens. After much explain-
ing, Melissa's parents finally understood how important it was for
them to release control over her life. They finally realized that Melissa's eating disorder was a direct reaction to their overinvolvement
in her life. It was her way of creating a semblance of control. They
reluctantly eased their control and allowed her to execute her own
choices. Today Melissa is a successful chef at a restaurant, passionate and joyful in her career.

We parents don't know how to let go of our children, and we don't
realize how unhealthy our overinvolvement is. We overparent our
children to an extreme—especially in this modern era. The more
luxurious our lives become, the more we overparent our children.
This is not healthy for them. By the time they reach adolescence,
we need to start cutting the cord and releasing them. By the time
they are in college, we need to have almost completely let go of our

control over them. We need to start allowing them to make their own choices and mistakes without rescuing them. We need to start challenging them to take over their own responsibilities and execute their own plans, more and more, without our help or control.

Conscious parenting includes the awareness that life itself is a huge partner in the parenting journey. With their own egos in check, conscious parents realize that they are not the best teachers for their children. The best teachers for our children are their own experiences. Therefore, conscious parents understand that they can step aside and let life do the talking and teaching. Life is a far more effective teacher than we parents can ever be.

For example, when our kid comes to us and says that they want to learn baseball and basketball, both at the same time, we don't say, "Choose one. That is too much to handle." What do we say? "Sure, go ahead and try. If it's too much, you can drop one later." Or if their schedule is already too demanding or the price tag is beyond our budget, we say something like "If you really want this, let's do one first and then the other. That way you can give each one all your energy." Do you see the subtle but profound difference between these approaches? The first and more dogmatic approach interferes with and manages our children's choices for them. The second trusts that life will show them the right way. The second approach enlists the power of life to be their conscious partner to coparent with them.

Allow your kids to experience the pain and struggle of their own choices. Allow their lives to unfold as naturally as possible. Let there be heartbreak and disappointments. It's okay; they will not fall apart. It's all about how we manage such situations. If we show them that we trust their ability to get through difficult situations, they won't fear them and will actually get through them, albeit sometimes crying and struggling.

I know it is hard for us parents to see our children experience pain, but there is no better teacher. If you want your children to develop true resilience, let them experience their own lives, in whatever shape or form they show up. If your kid is not invited to the birthday party of one of the popular kids, your instinct may be to jump in and fix the situation. Maybe you call the parent of the popular kid and plead with them to invite your kid. The conscious approach does none of this. It views this as a great life experience for your kid to go through to teach them that they cannot expect to be invited to every party and that not everyone can be their friend. Allow their life experience to teach them this lesson. Trust me, it will. Our fear is that such lessons will shatter their hearts, so we jump in to protect them. The irony is that we say we want our kids to build resilience, but then we keep snatching away the life experiences that could teach them precisely this.

When we move away from traditional disciplinary techniques such as spanking, yelling, and punishing our children in other ways, we enter a new paradigm of mutual respect and empowerment with them. In this new model, our children see themselves as worthy of making decisions for themselves within the container of a safe relationship with us. They see us as their allies, not their dictators. As we work in partnership with them, figuring out solutions to life's struggles together, they feel empowered by knowing their voices will be heard and their needs will be considered. The old model of hierarchical dictatorship brings about only disconnection and disempowerment. As we move away from its stale tenets, we refresh and rejuvenate our relationships with our children and create lasting bonds with them.

PUTTING IT INTO PRACTICE

There is a lot to practice, isn't there? Here is a checklist to use every day to remind yourself about key concepts. I encourage you to put it up on your fridge as a constant reminder.

- ✔ No physical domination or violence allowed
- ✔ No name-calling or shaming

✔ No screaming or yelling
✔ No fixing or controlling my child's pain
✔ No micromanaging my child's life decisions
✔ No commanding and dominating my child's schedule

By making a commitment to all of this, we challenge ourselves to do things in a more conscious way. We can post these affirmations, too, to remind us to go about the parenting process in a loving manner:

My child is my partner in this journey called life.
My child's brain is still developing, so they need patience and kindness.
My child is not yet aware of how life operates, so they need care and attention.
My child is a sovereign being who desires respect, just as I do.
My child is not my enemy designed to make my life difficult.
My child's behaviors are not against me personally.
My child doesn't want to be shamed or degraded, just as I don't.

When we remind ourselves of these principles, we can enter a place of loving kindness within ourselves and treat our children with care and compassion, just as we would like to be treated. The old paradigm of discipline—a.k.a. punishment—has no place in the world of conscious parenting. Getting to this place of awareness is a huge step on your journey forward.

Here is a list of things you can do in real time with your new awareness—it is a good idea to post these in a visible place as well:

Trust in your child's life journey—it will teach them what they need to learn.
Listen to your children's feelings and desires—it will make them feel seen.
Be patient with your children's confusions and missteps—they are growing beings.

When you apply the new principles that have been suggested here, you'll make a huge shift in your relationship with your kids and help them to feel more connected not only to you, but also to their own sense of worth and significance. Isn't that an amazing prospect? Wouldn't we live in a much better world if we all felt this sense of resplendence and luminescence? This is what we aspire to through this inner work. We endeavor to replace our cobwebs of shame and loathing with treasures of empowerment and worth. As you evolve, you will connect with your children in ways you could only have dreamed of—ways that will one day help them soar and evolve as never before. This is the inestimable prize of conscious parenting.

Step Sixteen:
Reframe Mistakes This Way

Life is full of curveballs and wild turns.
Sometimes we land at dead ends,
Other times we speed down hairpins.
We break our hearts or our banks,
We get fired or fried,
We lose our way or lose our minds.
This is the nature of life and being human.
Finding the jewels amid the stones is the key.
Digging them out and polishing them is the art.

As consummate fixers and controllers, we parents find it hard to give up these roles—especially when it comes to our children. When our child's life is out of control, we equate this with losing control of our own lives, so we do our best to control the heck out of our children. How do we do this? By forcing them to follow our script as much as we can.

Life is hard to control, isn't it? Imagine adding two or three children to the mix. With each kid added, life spirals more and more out of control. If and when life begins to tailspin in unremitting and unchecked ways, our anxiety goes through the roof. We tighten the reins on our kids by giving them busy schedules with long lists of things for them to do. In this way, we ensure as much predictability as possible. We have the illusion that we know what is about to happen next.

But what happens when our children don't follow their scripts or make mistakes and f— up the plan? We lose our minds. We enter a doomsday mentality and communicate this to our kids. Our kids then feel shame and unworthiness, with a long-term impact on their ability to take risks and entertain new adventures.

Controlling our children with force and dominance is never a positive thing. This approach will eventually erode the integrity of our relationship with them and have devastating effects on our connection with them. It all boils down to our ability to handle life when it doesn't follow our script or ideas around perfection.

The problem we have with our kids is never just their mistakes per se. The real problem is that they messed up *our* script for how things were supposed to be. Going off script leads to our feeling out of control. And this is the real issue. If we are baking cookies and having fun, and then one of us drops a pound of flour on the floor, that may be okay. Why? We are having fun. However, if we are in a rush to get to a meeting and our kid drops a pound of flour on the floor, suddenly we enter into a murderous rage. It is the same pound of flour. The only difference is whether this accident was "allowable," based on our plan for the day. But because we are not willing to own our control issues and say, "Because I have control issues, your mistakes make me feel out of control, and this drives me crazy," we shame our child by saying, "How could you do this? That is so dumb!" Do you see the difference?

It should start with a self-ownership of how we feel inside. The latter comment places blame on our child and makes them feel bad for their error. This is a dysfunctional message to pass on to a child, as they will begin to believe that making mistakes is a bad thing and that they need to be fearful and ashamed. Do you see how toxic it can be to pass on such a message? Because we are unwilling to own up to our obsession with control and perfection and to work on these issues within ourselves, we pass on to our kids the sense that they are "bad" for doing something that is 100 percent human: making a mistake.

Everyone is going to make many mistakes in life, including you and your kids. The reason isn't that we are "bad" or defective, but that we are human. Mistakes are natural and inevitable. Children and adults should never fear mistakes. The only way we can communicate fearlessness around mistakes and failures is by being okay with the idea of losing control and living an imperfect life. Until we are able to confront our own need for control and perfectionism, we will pass these fears and this shame on to our kids.

The reason we parents need this control over our life scripts is that we felt so out of control as children. We, too, were severely reprimanded for our mistakes by parents who had a similar fear of losing control. The cycle continues, you see. So how do we break it? The first step is to honestly reconcile your own relationship to mistakes and failure. Notice how much self-criticism you have in your own mind around mistakes. How much do you blame and judge yourself? This is the birthplace of our projections onto others, isn't it? How we speak to ourselves is how we speak to others. Your own inner voice is harsh, critical, and judgmental. You shame yourself when you are not perfect—and this shame is what you pass on to your kids. When they are not perfect, you judge them as harshly as you judge yourself when you are not perfect. When our children receive our judgments and shame, their connection with us breaks down. They begin to feel bad about themselves, which in turn makes them feel bad about our relationship with them. Because they don't feel positive around us, they begin to avoid us or avoid being their true selves around us. Either way, our connection with them suffers.

Tammy can still remember being scolded by her father for doing badly on her science project when she was around nine years old. "He yelled at me for at least ten minutes, going on and on about how I was not paying attention to details and how I was a sloppy and lazy girl. I know it was just ten minutes because I was about to leave for my swimming class and I was in a hurry, but it felt like a lifetime. I thought I wouldn't make it on time. He made me feel like crap. I literally felt like the worst loser in the world. My dad is a researcher, you know. So he puts great pride in how his kids perform at school. I am not like him at all. I hated science as a kid. I found it boring. I liked the arts more. He could never understand me. He wanted me to be like him—perfectly analytical and academic. But here is the thing: instead of buckling down and studying even harder, I went the opposite route after that yelling. He made me feel so crappy about myself that I literally turned off studying altogether. I was so afraid of failing that I preferred to not even try. I stopped putting in any effort after that. I dropped out of high school, and now I barely talk to my dad. Our relationship kept suffering all through my adolescence."

Tammy's life was marred by a desperate fear of failure. As a result, she is now a virtual recluse. So afraid is she of making mistakes that she would rather not try at all. She is still in therapy with me, where we are working hard to help her release her inner critic. It is hard for her to do so because of her conditioning as a child. Her perfectionistic, overcontrolling father hammered this relentless criticism into her, and now his voice has become her voice. It is a voice she has a hard time letting go of.

Again, it is not our parents' fault per se that they raised us unconsciously. They can act only in the ways they were conditioned to in their own childhoods. If they were raised with self-loathing, it is only natural that they project this onto the world. Their lack of tolerance and compassion toward themselves was placed on us—and then this gets passed down, one generation after another.

Here is the truth: we are human, and this means we are imperfect. And life is imperfect, too. It is unpredictable and out of our control. Kill any shard of an idea that could oppose these realities. The sooner we annihilate the idea of perfection and control, the better we will be able to flow with life when it is neither. The idea that we and our lives need to look a certain way is the whole problem. While we can have visions for our lives, we need to understand the fundamental reality of life—that *it is* ceaselessly unpredictable.

Look at our global experience with COVID-19. Did you ever imagine that you would experience a pandemic in your lifetime? So just because our life script didn't come true and we found ourselves amid a raging pandemic, does that mean that life has made a mistake or has failed us in some way? That life deserves a B grade, or even an F? No, it was just being life, marred with infinite causes and effects. In the same way, our own lives manifest through complex causes and effects. We forget our keys, miss our plane, don't get an A on a test. We are too busy, distracted, or forgetful. This is life as a human. If we harp on our failures and excoriate ourselves, we lose valuable energy and time.

When athletes train, they are taught to let go of obsessing about their last shot or their last race and to focus on the present. If they were to scorn and criticize themselves over every mistake or failure, they'd be devastated, wouldn't they? So it is with our kids. We need to help them let go of that last episode of spilled milk, a forgotten backpack, or a slip-up on a test. How do we do so? We let go through our understanding and acceptance of mistakes as being inevitable and normal.

This normalization of errors takes practice through daily cultivation. When our kid drops things and messes up our walls, we need to train ourselves not to yell but instead to say, "It's okay. It happens! Don't dwell on the mistake. Let's fix what can be fixed and move on." Or when they forget their backpack at school for the fourth time in a month, we say, "It's okay. It happens! Let's create a solution to help you forget it less next time and move on!" With this attitude, we don't passively allow the mistake to occur over and over, but we also don't lose our minds when the mistake does occur. Of course, we can and should help our kids set alarms to remember their backpacks or help them to manage their life better in all sorts of ways, but we can do so with the attitude that their mistakes are normal, instead of reprimanding and shaming them.

When we normalize mistakes and failures, we take the pressure of perfection and control away from our kids. This is liberating indeed. Giving children the safety and permission to be ordinary sounds like setting a low bar, but it is actually a key way to help them live a daring life. Being accepted as worthy and whole in our ordinariness gives us the safety and the space to experiment and dream big. If we have little fear of shame and excoriation, we see the universe as a limitless playing field where we can have adventures and discover new things without fear of repercussions. This perspective creates a powerful impetus to grow and evolve, don't you think?

Finding the jewels in our mistakes doesn't mean that we need to convert those mistakes into something else. Not at all. The jewel is right there in our acceptance of our own imperfections and our potential to do something new. For example, if we open a clothing store and it doesn't do well, it's an opportunity to accept ourselves and try something new. But because of our conditioned response to failure, we tend to shame ourselves and fall apart. Instead of using this as an opportunity to be compassionate with ourselves, we drain our internal resources through our self-blaming and self-shaming. You see, the act of compassion is the growth. The growth is not necessarily in the creation of another project, but in the here and now. Can I show compassion for myself? Can I accept the "is-ness" of this moment with neutrality, let go, and move on? Can I learn from this and make different choices in the future? In this bare and simple honoring of reality—life as it is—lies the actual evolution. Of course, converting the "mistake" into a successful new business in the future is a wonderful possibility, too, but that isn't what's necessary for growth to take place. Growth takes place in the active acceptance of the present moment.

One of our greatest superpowers is our capacity to let go and move on in life through empowered action without weighing ourselves down with derision and loathing. When we are able to do this, we flow like water, moving beyond obstacles without hesitation or paralysis. Water doesn't cling or hold on; it flows around barriers instead of resisting them. When we embody the energy of water, we give ourselves permission to move on and enter new ground. This can only happen when we let go within our minds.

Loathing for ourselves or others is a direct outgrowth of a childhood mired in perfectionism and control. This feeling comes from a subconscious belief that we are not worthy unless we are perfect. Mistakes and failures feel catastrophic and chronic. Because we are often consumed by an unconscious self-loathing, our egos desperately hold on to perfection and control as a way to avoid feeling inner pain.

Our children are capable of feeling whole without being perfect. The two have nothing to do with each other. Wholeness is our inherent right and destiny, without our needing to accomplish a single thing. Just as red is the color of many roses, wholeness is our own intrinsic color, or nature. Our modern culture has conditioned us to believe that only perfection brings about wholeness. This conditioning needs to be dismantled if we are to live in peace and joy.

It is imperative that we reframe the philosophy we've had about mistakes and failures. The more compassion and acceptance we have for ourselves, the more we will be able to project these wonderful qualities onto our kids. Let's raise our children with a self-benevolence and forgiveness for mistakes and failures. Let's teach them that these are normal and inevitable parts of life, and nothing to fall apart about. When we help them absorb this attitude, they will begin to lean into their imperfections with greater ease and alchemize them into growth.

PUTTING IT INTO PRACTICE

Kids are constantly moving targets, and almost every waking moment with them is an opportunity to put into practice the lessons I've just written about. Kids tend to create messes wherever they go and are quick to make errors, because their brains are still developing. Children are simply not yet able to execute life in a thoughtful way; heck, we adults barely can. It is precisely because they cannot control the fact that their brains are still developing that we need to show our kids great compassion and patience. If we stunt their natural progress by shaming them, they will move away from taking bold and fearless steps and instead be filled with a crippling hesitation that will stay with them throughout their lives.

The next time your kid does something "wrong" or "bad," pause and remember these key facts:

Your kid's brain is not yet developed. These mistakes are normal.

Teaching kids that mistakes are normal helps them to be daring in life.

Mistakes are valuable opportunities for embracing self-acceptance.

Mistakes allow us to show compassion and humility.

Mistakes empower us to learn how to move on and let go.

Mistakes teach us how to problem-solve and find ways to recover and rebirth.

When we embrace our kids' mistakes, we show them unconditional love.

Once we approach our children's mistakes with this awareness, we can neutralize any feelings of shame or guilt. And we can use these moments as opportunities to teach our children how to flow with life's ups and downs, to move on, and to enter each new moment with vigor and joy, just as athletes are trained to do.

Here is another practice to help you reframe mistakes. I call this exercise "What If This Was You?" The next time you are triggered by your child's mistake, try to pause and reflect: "What if this was me?" I can guarantee that you've made (or almost made) some version of every mistake your child has made. The potential for error is in every human. When we lash out at our children, we are acting from a place of great egoic amnesia and naivete, because we are presuming that we could never make such a mistake. It is this narcissistic delusion that blinds us with indignant superiority and allows us to degrade our children.

A powerful way to remember that we are as flawed as the next person, especially our beautiful children, is to post the words "I am flawed" or "I make mistakes every day" or "I desire people to forgive my mistakes" on the fridge. This is a way to help us remember to give our children grace when they make errors or mess up in any way. The fact is, human nature is incredibly flawed. Understanding this truth lets us embrace one another with humane compassion. Instead of fighting our flaws, we expand our bandwidth to tolerate them as they arise. In this way, we create a few internal ripples when mistakes occur, not huge tremors.

Tolerating and reframing our imperfections is an art, one that helps us become more empathic and compassionate toward ourselves and one another. Practicing the art of being "Zen" with imperfections lets us flow with life in a beautiful manner.

Step Seventeen:
Drop to the Heart

When you say X, I think you mean Y.

When you say Y, I think you mean Z.

You speak in a code that is hard for me,

But that is because I am trying to be right

Or trying to be logical

Or trying to win the war.

When I drop into my heart and let go the need to be right

And simply focus on understanding you better, everything changes.

Suddenly you express yourself lucidly,

And I fully see who you are,

And all is well in our world.

It all starts with my letting go of my need to be right.

This stage in the conscious parenting journey is meant to drive home one main point in different ways: children need us to connect to them. This is the basis of their emotional well-being. To truly connect to them, we need to understand how they think, act, and feel. We need to figure out *their* style, *their* patterns, and *their* needs.

As kids, we also needed our parents to tune in to us and understand what we were desperately trying to communicate to them. But most of us didn't have attuned or conscious parents. If we didn't receive this connection from our parents, we are now at a loss as to how to give it to our own kids. That's why this approach is so valuable. It helps us learn strategies, step-by-step, for deeply connecting with our kids.

To help us communicate with our children more deeply, I have created a powerful approach that I call VENT: *validate, empathize, normalize and neutralize, transform*. Learning to VENT is a powerful method of managing our children's emotional worlds in a way that lets them be seen and valued for their authentic selves.

VALIDATE

What does it mean to validate another human being? It means meeting them exactly where they are. We respect *their* experience of their reality. It doesn't have to gel with our own experience or expectation, or how we would go about things. All that matters is where the other person is in their own experience.

If your kid comes home really upset and crying over something a friend said, you have the chance to either validate or invalidate that experience. Validating your child could sound like this: "You seem really upset by what your friend said. It really hurt your feelings, didn't it? You are upset with her. I see you. I hear you. Tell me more." Invalidating your child might sound like this: "Oh, stop overreacting. I don't think she meant to hurt you at all. Let's stop this nonsense, and go play!"

Do you see the difference? Which message would feel better to receive from your loved ones? All of us would prefer the first reaction, because it honors and accepts who we are. When we validate another human being, especially our child, we communicate this to them: "You are aware of your feelings. You have every right to them. No one can tell you how to feel. This is your right." This way, we send the message to our kids that they are not wrong for feeling the way they do. We communicate trust in them. We realize that their feelings are real. We show respect by listening and paying attention.

The biggest obstacles to validating our children's feelings are our own ideas and expectations. If we don't believe in what our kids are saying because we have a different set of ideas, then we won't be able to validate them. Rather than honoring their ideas, we honor our own. When we are unable to drop our own beliefs about how our children should respond, we are communicating that what they say is not important. Remember WARM and the importance of empowering a child to think and act without being stepped on. This is critical.

I see parents make this mistake over and over, albeit subconsciously. In fact, many do it out of a sense of protection or fear for their kids' emotional well-being. They don't realize that they are paying attention to their own worries rather than validating the child's state of being. These are some of the ways we subconsciously invalidate our children's emotional experiences:

In my opinion, you shouldn't feel this way.
Stop overthinking this.
Don't be sad—why are you getting so upset?
I don't think this is really something to be upset about.
You always overreact to things.
You are misunderstanding me. I didn't mean it that way.
I was only kidding! Why do you take everything so seriously?
You are so sensitive and blow things out of proportion.
I disagree with you—that's not how I see things.
You need to be more flexible.
You are being irrational.

You don't know what you are talking about.
If I were you, I would . . .
I wouldn't have done that.
You need to be strong.
That exact same thing happened to me, and this is what I did . . .
Why do you always take everything so personally?

I could give you a hundred more examples of invalidation, but you get the gist. Don't you bristle when others react to you with such sentences? Don't you feel as if they just don't get you, or they don't care enough to get you? Doesn't it frustrate you?

We all have a person or two in our lives who consistently steals our thunder and makes it all about them. They want to tell you about their similar experience, how they would react, or how you should feel. We often confuse validating another with giving them our opinion or lecturing them, when these are completely opposite to validating someone. Giving our opinion or lecturing our kids is almost never going to work. In fact, it will result in disconnection.

When we give our opinion without being asked or before listening fully to someone's experience, we inadvertently communicate that their response is wrong. This message robs them of their voice and their right to their own authentic experience. It is unfortunate, but true, that when we send this message to our children, we negate their sense of inner knowing and shortchange their ability to grow and discover their own solutions. Validating someone's experience is a way for us to communicate respect, trust, and care. Validation means to walk beside someone rather than behind them or in front of them. Our children don't need us to prop them up or overtake them. They just need us to walk alongside them and hold their hand. As we do so, step-by-step, we awaken their strength to discover their own answers. Here are some ways we can validate our children and awaken them to their own power:

That sounds rough. I totally get your pain.
This sounds really challenging for you. I hear you.

I may not fully understand, as we have different experiences,
  but I want to.
You are struggling right now. I want you to know that I am
  with you.
You are hurting right now. I get it. It makes total sense to me.
You can cry as much as you need. Tears are healthy. I am right
  here with you.

Do you see the power behind these words? They honor the other person while never judging, shaming, or altering their reality. Such words not only allow the other to feel validated in how they feel, but also give them the space to process those feelings in safety.

When we communicate this way, we teach our children not to be afraid of their big feelings. We acknowledge their responses and empower their feelings as valid. We also give them confidence in their ability to figure out a solution. We aren't stepping in and pushing our beliefs but rather listening, validating, and discussing. There is no fighting, fixing, or fleeing from the situation. There is only a focus on attunement and compassionate support.

Validating our children is the first step in helping them navigate their emotional world. As noted, for many parents this is hard. We want to scream at our kids, fix their pain, solve their problems, or run away. Simply validating them feels too passive. But once we realize the curative powers in validating children's experiences for what they are, we will want to do so more and more. Trust me—it is magic. As we validate them more, our children will open up to us in beautiful ways. And even more important, they will open up to themselves.

EMPATHIZE

Now we arrive at one of the most profoundly healing yet challenging communication techniques: empathy. Many of us are confused about what empathy really is or how we can communicate it in our relationships, so I am going to break it down here.

Let's start with what empathy is *not*:

Enmeshment and fusion—You do not need to have gone through the exact same experience as someone else, nor do you need to feel their exact same feelings, to be empathic.

Enabling and fixing—You do not need to solve anyone's problems or be a caretaker for the person with whom you are empathizing.

Controlling and lecturing—You do not need to micromanage anyone's life situation, create insight, or help the other person come to a new awareness of their own reality.

Judging and shaming—You do not need to make the other feel bad for having the feelings they do.

Empathy is about connecting to how your child is feeling. It means paying attention to their feelings rather than their thoughts. So if your child says "I hate school and my teachers!" an empathic response could sound like this: "I hear you. It sounds like you are having a hard time liking your teachers and school. It must be so hard to get up each day to go there. I can understand and appreciate what you are feeling."

Empathy takes validation to the next level of connection, where we try to feel the other person's feelings. We enter into their experience with them. With validation, we met them where they were; now, with empathy, we join them *as if* we were there ourselves. Simply put, empathy refers to a deep sense of openheartedness to the other's emotional response to a situation. For example, if your child is nervous about an exam the next day, you might say this: "Wow, that sounds really difficult and painful. I see that you are anxious and nervous. I can appreciate your experience and even understand elements of it. I am not you, but I can relate to your feelings. I can see you are experiencing all sorts of emotions right now. Tell me more."

The unconscious approach, on the other hand, might be this: "Stop overthinking it. You are going to do just fine. Believe in yourself, and everything will be okay. You always do better than you think. Grades don't matter to me. I just want you to feel good about yourself."

The second response sounds positive, doesn't it? The parent is saying all the right things. But the response lacks empathy. Why? It takes care of the parent's feelings but doesn't connect to the child's feelings. What matters when we are being empathic is how the *other* feels—no matter how we think they should feel.

Being empathic is extremely hard to pull off when your kids are mad at you or hold you responsible for their pain. When this happens, empathy gets thrown out the window, and we enter a state of defensiveness. Consider this example. Your kid comes home and says, "It's all your fault that I never did better at math. You always yelled at me when I tried to study and made me feel like crap. If you had been patient and encouraging, I would have done so much better. It's all your fault!"

That is hard to stomach. We are faced with a choice. We can respond with empathy, or we can negate and dismiss our kid. Let's see what an empathic response might sound like. Remember, I am showing many ways to show empathy. You don't have to say all of these things at once:

Oh my! I see that you are hurting right now. I understand your frustration. I get how terrible that feels. I see what you mean about my role. I totally understand your anger at me. I can see it from your point of view. I own my part in this. You are 100 percent correct—I was unconscious and impatient. I acted in such a hurtful way. I respect that you are angry. I would be mad at me, too. I need to look at why I did what I did and go deeper into my own self. I need to work on myself. I am so sorry for what I did. I really acted in a thoughtless and hurtful way. I can understand why you feel this way. I am here to help you going forward. I want to change my impatient ways. Please give me a chance?

This is so hard to do, trust me—especially if you are saying to yourself, "What the hell? Why is this darn kid blaming me? What the hell did I do wrong? I was only helping her. Dammit!" If you feel that way, you are likely to react in a way that will set off another tsunami. You are probably going to put on an indignant tone and say, "What are you talking about? Don't blame me for your crappy grades. I was so helpful, so patient, so loving. Don't you remember? I sat up for hours helping you, and you kept being distracted. Please own your own bad grades and stop blaming me. You are so ungrateful. I cannot even believe it!"

I laugh as I write these words, because I cannot tell you how many times I have gone the unconscious route with my own kid. It is so hard to stay calm when we feel attacked by our kids. Our defenses kick in big-time. We forget about how they feel and instead make it all about protecting our own self-image. I don't blame parents. It is so hard to focus on our children, especially when we disagree with them or feel falsely accused. Most of us try so hard. When we hear that our children hold us responsible for pain in their life, we cannot bear the feeling of being attacked, and we lash out at them. Being empathic at such a time feels virtually impossible.

To empathize is a highly evolved art. To help us "do" empathy right, I have created the acronym DREAM to help you go through the key steps of building empathy. If you hit each of these, you will be fine. Let's go through them together:

Detach and depersonalize. Without this crucial step, you won't be able to empathize with your children. Empathy requires that you don't take things personally and don't make their feelings about you, even if they feel accusatory. Chant to yourself, "This isn't about me; this isn't about me."

Recognize and respect. Recognize your children's feelings and respect their point of view, even if you don't agree with them. Here is where you acknowledge their feelings and express that acknowledgment to them in a direct way.

Extinguish your ego. Resist entering a reactive state in which you wear your ego mask. Instead of hiding behind one of your ego masks, try to see the other's point of view. Watch for your ego's reactivity, and try to tame it as much as possible.

Apologize and be accountable. Express true remorse for the pain you have caused your children. Remorse isn't an empty collection of words. It needs to be a deeply felt response to how they have experienced your ego. Owning how your ego may have triggered and upset your children is extremely important for empathic communication. Even if you may not agree with them, it is important to honor what *they* feel about you and your actions.

Mend and make new. Create a plan of action going forward that not only accepts accountability for the pain you have caused but also includes steps for transformation and reparation.

Now let's take another look at the empathic response I used in the example earlier and see whether it hits all these markers of empathy. I'm going to analyze my response sentence by sentence to demonstrate how it meets the standards of empathy.

How did this show detachment? "I see that you are hurting right now. I understand your frustration. I get how terrible that feels." These words make your response about their experience and not about you. Detachment and depersonalization are important for letting our children feel heard and validated for *their* experiences, instead of making things all about *you*.

Compare the empathic response with the second approach in the example: "What are you talking about? Don't blame me for your crappy grades. I was so helpful, so patient, so loving. Don't you remember? I sat up for hours helping you, and you kept being distracted. Please own your own bad grades and stop blaming me. You are so ungrateful, I cannot even believe it!" The second response doesn't even get past the ego taking it personally. It's all about the ego. Do you see the difference?

How did this show recognition and respect? "I see what you mean about my role. I totally understand your anger at me. I can see it from your point of view." Here we recognize and respect our children's feelings without minimizing or altering their own points of view or experiences of reality. We honor their anger instead of calling it an overreaction or something judgmental with comments such as, "You are always angry at this or that. I am tired of your anger. Can you stop being so angry all the time?" Even if this statement is accurate, telling our children that they shouldn't be angry when they are angry is one of the most dismissive things we can do. Instead, keeping our opinions to ourselves until a more appropriate time is always wiser and more loving.

How did this show an effort to extinguish the ego? "I own my part in this. You are 100 percent correct—I was so unconscious and impatient. I acted in such a hurtful way. I respect that you are angry. I would be mad at me, too. I need to look at why I did what I did and go deeper into my own self. I need to work on myself." Here is where we own our ego. This is the hardest part of the empathy process, especially if we haven't yet healed from within. If we are still broken ourselves, seeking validation from the external world, ownership of our ego will feel like a defeat. We might inadvertently say something like this: "You are wrong! I am tired of your reactions to me! I try so hard and you just don't appreciate me!" Do you see how an egoic reaction might sound? It is hard to step away from that reaction, isn't it? Yet this is exactly what we need to do to help our children with their difficult emotional experiences.

How did this express an apology and accountability? "I am so sorry for what I did. I really acted in a thoughtless and hurtful way. I can understand why you feel this way." Of course, the ideal way to express an apology is with your heart and soul, so that it isn't just empty words and lip service. Your children should really "feel" your apology. They may not receive it as heartfelt, but you need to at least try your best to express as much feeling as possible. Sometimes we think we are apologizing when we are actually not. Many times we pretend to say we're sorry, but in effect we are covertly blaming the other. An insincere apology might sound like this: "I am so sorry you feel this way. You were yelling at me so much that I finally broke down and started yelling, too. Next time, please don't yell. I am really sorry that you are now hurt by me."

Do you see the difference in the two apologies? One says, "I am sorry that *I* . . ."; the other says, "I am sorry that *you* . . ." The first takes accountability for our role in the dynamic. The second blames the other. Awareness allows us to see the difference between the two.

How did this mend and make new? "I am here to help you going forward. I want to change my impatient ways. Please give me a chance?" We mend and make new by creating an action plan for a do-over of sorts. An apology on its own isn't enough. Our children deserve to see actual transformation. That way, they can truly feel that we care beyond just our words. When we fail to make changes, our words will fall on deaf ears.

Our children don't want us to simply apologize; they want us to transform our behaviors. We owe them this transformation. By reading these pages, you are already displaying a tremendous willingness to gift them with the treasure of your own growth.

NORMALIZE AND NEUTRALIZE

No human wants to be told that their ways of experiencing the world are "weird" or "out there." We all want to feel that we are "normal" and that others would behave just like us if they were in our shoes. So it is with our children. They, too, long to feel normal in their responses to and experiences of life—and we can play a large part in helping them feel that way.

When kids experience their big feelings, it's important for us to normalize these experiences for them. The best way to do this is to say something like "I totally get why you are acting like this. I understand. Most people would feel the same way." With a younger child, we can just say something like "It's okay to feel this way."

The next significant way we can help our children is by neutralizing the effects of their experiences. We can do so by not reacting to situations with our own emotional energy, staying neutral instead. For example, if our child is screaming with fear over seeing a spider, we can normalize and neutralize their experience in this way: "I understand that you are scared of the spider. Many people are. I was terrified when I was a kid, too. But look, the spider is not even paying attention—it's busy doing its own thing." By not allowing our own energies to get involved, we neutralize the power of the spider over our emotions and help our children understand that what they are afraid of is actually neutral in nature.

One day at the amusement park, my daughter was scared to go down a tall water slide. Maia kept saying, "I am scared, Mom." I said, "So am I. This is how I feel, too. But instead of running away from the fear, I make friends with it. I can teach you how." Within moments I created a song out of both of our fears. We shivered in fear all the way to the top of the water slide, chanting, "I am filled with fears. I am shedding a hundred tears. This is how I feel. It's no big deal!" When it was our turn, we took deep breaths, giggled, and kept singing our little tune all the way down. I told Maia, "Fears and tears are normal. We all feel them. We don't have to hide from them. They are just how we feel. No big deal."

When we approach life in its *as-is* form without attaching labels and judgments, it begins to lose its power over us. We embrace our experiences without judgment or shame and let them inform us in the moment. Being afraid, upset, or anxious—these are all integrated into our life experience and serve as teachers. In this way, we grow with life instead of shrinking from it.

TRANSFORM

What does it mean to help our children transform their emotional states? As you can see, it certainly doesn't mean to simply change these states. To change something means to alter it from the outside. Transformation, on the other hand, is about growing and evolving from the inside.

As a parent, this means that we notice and observe our children's and our own capacity to grow from an experience. If our children are losing their minds over an exam, after we first validate, empathize, and normalize their emotional state of being, we can help them transform their experience into growth. By highlighting their strengths, we can help them reframe their current anxiety and channel it into courage. This is what we might say:

> *I see you struggling to maintain focus and stay calm. I respect what you are going through. It feels hard for you right now. I want to point out that while you are still struggling, you are handling the situation completely differently from last time. The last time you couldn't even go for the exam. This time, you are planning on going tomorrow. Do you see the huge difference? This means you have learned to cope with your stress better. All that matters is that you are doing better than last time. You are growing, and I am so proud of you. The actual exam doesn't matter—what matters is how you are handling it all. I know this is hard for you, so we can just be together while you go through this experience.*

If we were focused on just changing a child's emotional experience, we would instead say something like this: "Let me study with you or get you a tutor so that you do well on your exam. Come on, let's sit up and focus. You need to get good grades tomorrow, and I am going to make sure you do."

Can you see the difference between transformation and change? Transformation focuses on the emotional experience and the internal growth that takes place. Change focuses on the external task at hand. With our kids, we want to focus on transformation, not change. There is no one to change, nor is there any situation to change. The only real change is internal, and because it is internal, it is transformational.

Transformation teaches our children that the matrix of "success" is on the inside. It's all about inner growth. Children who are raised with this focus approach themselves with compassion and acceptance. So in the previous example, even if the child showed no difference in their ability to cope between this time and the last, the parent could say something like this:

> Each time you go through this, you are becoming stronger within. You just don't realize it. I trust that you are learning how to be better friends with your feelings. It just takes time, and there is no timeline for success. Just allow yourself to take your time with this, and it will slowly become easier. I am with you all the way.

Do you see how calming and reassuring this approach is for our children? By placing the focus on accepting the as-is, we calm them and let them be themselves. Doing so directly impacts their self-worth, which in turn affects their level of anxiety and stress. Those raised with the "change" approach feel pressure to live life differently. As a result, they feel shame and reproach themselves when they do not succeed.

Conscious parenting is all about inner transformation. When we focus on this, we don't become our children's police officers or judges. We become their allies and partners on this challenging and often maddening journey we call life.

PUTTING IT INTO PRACTICE

We get to practice VENT at every meltdown moment with our kids, which means we will have plenty of opportunities to do so. Validate. Empathize. Normalize and neutralize. Transform. These are the key steps we can take to consciously connect with our children in any situation. When they are upset or angry, we can activate our inner awareness to ask ourselves: "How can I use the principles of VENT right now and allow my child to feel seen, heard, and validated?" When we keep practicing these four vital connection strategies, our children are bound to feel worthy and secure from within, which in turn will help them face life with resilience.

Once you have a conceptual understanding of these steps, it is important to become consciously aware of implementing them, one by one. Try each step separately. Put the steps into your daily routine. Get a feel for how the dynamic shifts with your child. Build your awareness muscles. Soon these key tools will be accessible when you need them most. I assure you that using them will make a profound difference in how your kid responds during a challenging situation—and, perhaps more important, how you respond.

Step Eighteen:
Find the YES!

My child, you live in a world of infinite possibility
With complete trust and expansion—
Unlike me, who lives in relentless lack and scarcity.
My instinct in life is to say no—
To restrict, curtail, and impede
So that I can feel comfortable and safe.
What I don't realize is that in doing so
I shrink your world and bubble-wrap your dreams,
I fill your balloon with lead and bricks,
All because I am so scared that you will fly away
And leave me behind in my desolation.

Children come into the world with a gigantic "YES" in their souls.
They don't see lack or unworthiness around them. Instead, they see
the world through the eyes of abundance and expanse. Everything

has the potential to cause them wonder and awe—from the spaghetti noodles they slurp, to the clouds floating in the sky, to the ants in the grass. Their natural state is one of openness, trust, and abandon.

This is not the natural state of adults, is it? No. On the contrary, we adults tend to primarily occupy the opposite state—great anxiety, lack, and unworthiness. Given that this is our tendency, you can imagine how we energetically clash with our children's natural states of being. This clash of energies has the potential to lead to disconnection and conflict in our relationships with them—for no other reason than that we occupy different energetic states of being in this world.

I can still clearly remember an argument I had with my daughter when she was around the age of seven. She wanted to play outside at around five thirty in the evening. I did not; I was tired and wanted to be done for the day. She was still full of energy and zest. She wanted to go to the garden near our house and play among the flowers. I said to her, "Maia, this is not the time for play. This is the time for rest. We cannot go outside now." My energy was low, and I was shut down to her. Before I knew it, she was in tears. "But only for a few minutes, Mommy! Just a few minutes!" I immediately felt my hackles rise. "You are being difficult, Maia. I said no, and that's all there is to it!" Maia stormed off to her room and proceeded to have a massive meltdown.

Thankfully, my mother was visiting us at the time. She was sensitive to both our moods and gently said to me, "Shefali, you are exhausted. It is not a big deal for me to take her to the garden. It is still a summer night, and Maia doesn't have school tomorrow. Let me take her." Maia heard and ran to hug her. I agreed to the plan—not because I had changed my mind but because I just wanted to be left alone. Off they went. They were back in no less than twenty-five minutes, and the Maia who returned home was a different Maia from the one who had left. She had collected a bag of gifts for me: stones, sticks, and a few trodden flowers. She was delighted. But more important, she was tired herself now and said to me, "That was so fun! But I am tired now and I want to go to sleep!" She was asleep in ten minutes.

Upon reflection, I realized an important lesson: Maia was not being "difficult," as I had judged her to be. Not at all. She was being curious, playful, energetic, and enthusiastic—in other words, she was being herself, an adventurous seven-year-old. If I had been in another mood, I would have taken her with joy, as my mother had. The only difference between me and my mother was my fatigue and resistance in the present moment. I wanted my way and didn't want to give in to my child's natural way. I was focused on the "what if": What if she didn't sleep? Or what if I was too exhausted later? Instead, had I just focused on the "what is" and joined her, I would have saved a huge meltdown and potential disconnection between us.

I reflected deeply on that moment. I asked myself, "What would it have meant for me to find a way to connect to her desire instead of rudely shutting it down as I had? Would it have been a big deal if I had flowed with her state and her desire to connect to me and taken her for a few minutes?" I realized then that I had completely missed the moment. Moreover, I had judged my child harshly for what she wanted to do.

To approach her differently, I could have said, "That is a great idea, Maia! I am tired right now, but I really want to honor your request. Can we make a deal? I will take you, but we have to return soon. Do you agree?" Had I said that, I am pretty sure Maia would have negotiated wisely and we would have averted a potential major meltdown (which, thanks to my mother, we did anyway). Instead, I entered a state of lack and fear. I was afraid that she'd stay there forever and burn me out. I was afraid that I would be too exhausted to cook dinner later. I was afraid of all things that "might" happen. As a result, I completely missed an opportunity to connect to my child in the present moment.

We parents and our children clash in three very consistent and fundamental ways. All of these ways are variations of a core difference between children and adults. Children say yes to the present moment—even if that means saying yes to tears. And adults? We primarily are in resistance to the present moment. This difference shows up in these more subtle ways all through our relationship with our children:

- ✔ Children primarily live in the present, whereas we adults live in the past and the future. They live in the "what is" and we live riddled in a fearful world of "what if." We hold on to past regrets and grudges, or we live in anxiety about what lies ahead.

- ✔ Children primarily live in abundance and joy, whereas we live in lack, fatigue, and anxiety.

- ✔ Children live primarily in a "being" state whereas we live in a doing state. Even their doing comes from being—being playful, explorative, curious, adventurous. A child has no real agenda other than being in the moment and flowing with what shows up in the moment. We adults primarily are in a "doing" state. This doesn't come from a deeply connected sense of being, typically. No, it is mostly from ego. We do because we want to save, or win, or succeed. It is not a process-oriented being state like that of children, but instead a goal-oriented doing state predicated on external validation and cultural indicators.

Because we live in such vastly different energetic states, we clash. But it is not our children's job to match our states; it is our job to match theirs. Because their state is so vastly different from ours, it can feel like a threat to us—so we try to shut them down. We judge, shame, and punish them. We engage in a dysfunctional loop with them and breed disconnection.

When I tell parents that they should try to "Find the Yes" in parenting, they take that phrase to mean that I am encouraging indulgence and entitlement. This is a highly triggering idea for us parents. We default to panic mode, thinking that we are "giving in" to our children's demands—and that they will grow up to be spoiled brats. But giving in is not what this approach is about. To "Find the Yes" means to align with your children's desires, but it doesn't mean that you need to give in to them or indulge them. It means that you find common ground where you can say *yes* to them so they feel understood and validated. The "yes" can be conceptual:

Yes, I totally understand your desire.

Yes, I would want that, too.

Yes, I feel the same way about that.

Yes, I get your craving for that.

Yes, I want to do that, too.

Yes, I was the same when I was your age.

Yes, you totally want the same things I do.

Or the "yes" can be practical:

Yes, I want you to get that, so let's make a plan.

Yes, I will get that for you, and I will do so at the right time.

Yes, I want you to go there, and we can talk about it after your exams.

Yes, I will help you achieve your wish after you have finished your chores.

In both cases, the intention isn't to physically or materially cave in and indulge a child's sense of entitlement, but instead to emit the energy that their desires are understandable and valid. All the while, be acutely aware that your child's wishes might not be practical at this point in time.

Remember this crucial fact: our children are overwhelmed by a world of distractions, gimmicks, and shiny objects. It's natural that they want to possess everything they can. That desire doesn't make them bad children or even greedy. It makes them natural and normal. When we keep saying no to this and no to that, we actually perpetuate their cravings and sense of lack. They want what they can't have. It is the classic case of desiring the forbidden fruit. This in turn fuels their obsession with wanting to possess more and more. Moreover, our children begin to feel ashamed for wanting things and to feel a sense of scarcity because they are always being told no.

Now, you as a parent might have a legitimate concern: "What if I genuinely cannot afford the shiny object, even in the future? Aren't I setting them up for more disappointment in the long run?" My answer to you is this: Saying yes in the moment is all about saying yes to the desire. It doesn't mean you need to give in to that desire or fulfill it. Once you validate children in terms of their desires, you can create a plan for the object they want. They may not get it tomorrow or even next week; they may have to wait until next year. The point is not in the execution but in keeping the fire of desire alive for as long as it needs to be. It's up to the child to keep that fire alive, not the parent. But we cannot be the ones who constantly extinguish it. Most of the time our kids lose their passion for the particular thing they wanted and let go of their desire on their own.

Children have a hundred desires every week. Most of them fade away due to distractions and the passage of time. Only the ones that stay for more than a few weeks need to be addressed. For these unremitting desires, we can help our children understand—with compassion and patience—why they may not be in alignment with the family's financial situation or logistic concerns. The child feels seen and heard and doesn't feel that their desires are being unmet or unheard. The more we just say no, the greater the sense of lack and the stronger the demand that the child's desires be met.

For example, what if your kid comes to you at around the age of twelve and says, "I'm not going to college after high school. I'm going to get an ice cream truck and sell ice cream. I'm going to own the biggest ice cream truck company in the world!" As a parent, you now have a choice of going with a mindset of scarcity or one of abundance. What do you think you will say? A scarcity mindset will feel the pressure to be "practical," and you will let the kid know how ridiculous the idea is. You'll say something like "That's ridiculous!

College is essential for you, and you have to go to college after high school. Ice cream trucks don't make a good living. That's not a good idea."

What do you think the kid will feel? Your child had a dream in the moment that was fueled by an age-appropriate passion and naivete. Who are we to shoot down this desire of the heart? The reason we do is that we immediately go into a state of lack and fear. The possibility that our kids might be conjuring all sorts of ideas about their future scares us. We think of the future and see a bleak horizon. All these emotions get stirred up in us, and we project them onto our children. Instead of encouraging them to dream outside of the box, we shove them right back into it.

Here is what an abundance-based mindset might sound like. "Wow! That is a super-cool idea. I love ice cream, and I will be your best customer. You are going to have so many more ideas by the time you are older. Make sure you write them down so you don't forget them. Then one day we can see which one comes true!"

Do you see how simple it is to say yes to our children's innate desires and longings? You flow with where they are rather than reacting and resisting out of your own projections. In this way, we allow them to feel okay in their dreams and encourage them to keep thinking outside the box without curtailing this freedom. To give them this encouragement, though, we ourselves need to come from a place of inner bounty and adventure.

We immediately panic that our kids are going to struggle and fail, and then what will we do? We see ourselves carrying the burden of their care into the future, and this prospect doesn't feel appealing. Do you see how this thinking is all about lack? We then feel an imaginary pressure to make their dreams come true. Because we don't know how, we feel upset. What we don't realize is that the burden of making our children's dreams come true doesn't fall on us; it falls on our kids. It's up to them to manifest their dreams, not us. All we need to do is support them with a plan.

When my client Belinda communicated to me her major frustration with her daughter Zoe for wanting to drop out of college and open a spa, I understood where she was coming from. All Belinda saw ahead was doom. She couldn't understand how Zoe could throw away a perfectly good college education for something as whimsical as a spa business. So she fought Zoe tooth and nail. She was angry with her. Moreover, she was resentful because all the time and money that had been spent on college seemingly was going to be wasted.

Belinda was stuck. It was only when I gently encouraged her to see things from Zoe's point of view that she began to budge. All Zoe wanted was support, such as a good friend would give. She didn't need Belinda to rescue her or to pay for this new enterprise. "Just help her figure out *how* to make it happen," I advised, "but you don't need to actually make it happen for her."

That was the moment it all clicked for Belinda. She had been resisting because she thought she needed to fund the entire show. She immediately relaxed when I said that all she needed to do was show up as a good ally and guide. "You don't need to pay for a thing, but you cannot resist what she wants. If she wants to pay for it and go into debt and take the risk, it's her life, not yours. All you need to do is help her figure it out. When our kids are this age, we are not responsible for the consequences of their choices. This is something they need to bear, not us. But fighting our kids' choices demoralizes them and makes them feel scared to fail."

Belinda finally got it. She shifted from within and began to help Zoe as she would a good friend. Their relationship vastly improved. Zoe, for her part, began to understand that this business endeavor was more than just glamour and fun. She actually chose to stay in college longer, until she could figure it out.

A common challenge that many young parents face today is with children demanding their own cell phones before they are the "right" age. Of course, most young (and older) kids want their own cell phone. Why wouldn't they? After all, they see all the adults around them completely obsessed with their phones. Kids naturally want the same thing for themselves. They probably wonder, "Why is every grown-up looking at their phone all the time?" or "Why would Mom rather be on her phone than pay attention to me?"

So how do we address our kids' desire for a phone without giving in to their demand for one? I'm suggesting three answers to this question. The first lies within us. We need to stop being on our own phones 24-7, especially when our kids are under ten years of age. They need us to be present and focused on them and the relationship we are cultivating with them. The more present we are with them, the less they will want a phone. The second answer is to think about how we can help our kids have a childhood in which they don't feel the need to be on a screen. How can we help them be more interested in real human connection so that being on a screen is not as interesting to them? And the third and final answer is to help your child to understand that once they reach the right age, they will indeed be able to get a phone; let them know that you're willing to meet their demands at the age-appropriate time.

When we get away from our knee-jerk reactions of lack and unworthiness and begin to say yes to our children's innate desire to be part of this world, we dissolve their persistent obsession about "things." That obsession only increases when we don't address their ideas. Our resistance increases their persistence. We think that if we ignore a request or say no, kids will just let their obsessions go. What we don't realize is that by fighting them, we're actually working against ourselves—by making their desires stronger. We perpetuate those desires instead of neutralizing them. Addressing their desires with a yes energy addresses their need to be heard and validated. This is half the magic.

Supporting our kids as we would a friend gives them and their desires the respect they crave. Helping them create plans doesn't mean these need to be executed right now; it just means that we give our kids attention about and show respect for their wants and needs. When we help our children create plans for achieving their desires, no matter how far in the future, we lend them a sense of empowerment. Even if they never meet a particular desire, making a plan validates that having what they desire is possible and that they can work on it if they choose. Who is to say that they won't be able to fulfill this desire after ten years? Why should we be their buzzkills?

My daughter, Maia, had wanted to have a dog since she was three years old. My life situation did not allow me to give her a puppy at that time. Also, I wasn't sure whether her desire was a mere whim of the moment. I wanted to be sure that she was deeply in love with dogs before I took on another responsibility. I needed to honor myself as well as her, because I knew the burden of care would fall on me. My truth was that I wasn't prepared to make this investment of time and energy at that moment. So now I had two choices as a parent. I could either squash her desire completely, or I could let her see it as a future possibility.

As life is unknown, many things are possible that may not appear to be so at present. Do we close all our options, or do we keep them open? Our choice depends on our mindset, doesn't it?

Parents may fear that they will be leading their children on by giving them something to hold on to. But this is not what we are doing when we say yes to their desires. What we are doing is helping our children understand a vital life philosophy: life has infinite possibilities. Life can take us around many wild curves and turns. There is no way to foresee all of them from our present vantage point. If we want something badly enough—and are willing to work for it, and it is within our biological capacity—it could absolutely happen in the future, even if it seems unlikely now. Time and effort can bring about unexpected possibilities. Teaching our children this valuable life philosophy will allow them to embrace their own and life's limitless potential.

I told Maia, "I love that you love dogs. Right now Mommy cannot take care of a dog. One day in the future, when you grow up, we could make a plan for it, okay? You don't have to stop loving dogs just because you cannot own one." I used to take her to pet stores so she could cuddle dogs, and I let her hang out with friends who owned them. I nurtured her love for dogs, all the while holding steady to my own inner knowing that I couldn't get her a dog just yet. You see, just because we cannot indulge our children's desires in the present doesn't mean they aren't able to nurture them for a later manifestation.

Guess what happened with Maia? She kept her passion for dogs alive. She literally commented on dogs on the street every single day. I observed her passion and understood it to be deep and true. When she turned fourteen, my own life circumstances changed enough so that I was now able to see myself caring for a dog—and guess what? Maia got a puppy! What a moment it was for this young woman. It was because she had never stopped loving dogs for more than a decade while I kept working on my own inner comfort level to get her one. I saw how true her love was. Because I kept myself open to the possibility of her passion being manifested one day, her dream came true.

Charlie is now six years old and is the love of our lives. When the right time came, Charlie was able to enter our lives and thrive. Maia held on to her desire for a dog all through her childhood, and she was able to see this passionate dream bear fruit. This process gave her an insight into the power of passion, and the ability we all have to manifest our passions if we are steadfast and patient.

I know many parents who might not have budged. That choice is okay, too. If parents cannot take care of a dog, they shouldn't go against their inner knowing to indulge their children, as doing so would lead to disaster. Instead, parents can help their children understand that they can keep dreaming and will be able to manifest their desires when they are adults. Not every desire can be indulged right away. Some desires may take decades to manifest—and this process can be just as beautiful as having our desires fulfilled immediately.

This approach teaches our children about the power of persistence and resilience—that when we want something, we need to be strategic and fight for it. This is such a valuable lesson. This way of saying yes is the opposite of constantly spoiling a child with everything imaginable. Saying yes as part of the "*Find the Yes*" approach means listening, acknowledging, and helping our children learn the value of their wants and desires. Instead of either saying a blanket no or indulging a desire immediately, we go deeper and challenge our kids to dig deep into themselves. How much do they want this thing, and why? Giving our children the space to dream and go deeper within themselves helps them understand how true their desires really are. If we said no right away, they would start wasting their energy fighting us. If we gave in and indulged them right away, we would squander a valuable opportunity for them to dig deeper and feel what it means to have persistence and passion. Do you see how powerful such a lesson is for the child?

Delayed gratification is a powerful life lesson. It teaches us that there is a right season for everything. Nature is our best teacher for this lesson. There is a right time for mangoes and a right time for snow. Learning to be patient and persistent are key values for our children to learn. Nature says to us, "Yes, you can eat mangoes and be persistent in your passion for them, but not right now. You need to wait for them to ripen."

The reason this approach is so powerful is that it teaches children to be okay with their desires being desires, and that they are just fine without their desires being met in that exact moment. Parents are afraid of their children's desires because they have two subconscious beliefs: (1) If the desire is there, it needs to be met soon. (2) If the desire is not met soon, children will be unhappy—which is a "bad" thing. Both of these beliefs are false. Our children can be unhappy about the desire not being met, and this is actually a good thing for their development. In fact, it's a healthy emotional strength that we can nurture. Children can also become unhappy even if their desires are met—as I am sure all parents have seen.

We all have soul stirrings within us. Some of us dream of having dogs, like Maia, and others dream of opening a spa, like Zoe. Still others dream of living in a foreign country. All plausible dreams can be manifested. Whether their dreams come true just depends on the person's circumstances and how they navigate their reality.

Even if a child says something implausible, like "Mommy, I want to fly to the moon," we don't need to counter with "That is so dumb! You don't have wings, and the moon is too far away." This response misses the point of the child's communication. Instead, we could say, "I would love to fly to the moon with you. So sad that we are not big birds and that the moon isn't closer! Let's imagine what that would feel like." What this communication does for the child is to normalize their desire and allow them to dream and imagine. Later, these dreams become valuable ingredients for a life of passion and possibility. A lot boils down to how we as parents handle our children's soul stirrings.

PUTTING IT INTO PRACTICE

Your children will give you plenty of opportunities to practice saying yes, as they will have desires all day long. Again, do not mix up saying yes and indulging them. So today, how will you respond when your child expresses their desires, such as "I want more cookies/ screen time/shoes/makeup/time at friends' houses/junk food . . . "? You might be inclined to respond, "I am sick of your demands. The answer is no!"

You could find a more conscious response, such as "I also want to eat cookies/watch screens/buy more shoes/buy makeup/hang out with friends/eat junk food. All these things are so addictive and fun. But if we do these things too much, they become unhealthy. There will be plenty of time for this stuff you want to do, but first we need to take care of our responsibilities. So let's make a plan to give you what you want while also taking care of all the other stuff in life. Let's make a plan that helps you manage it all."

Do you see how this approach places the responsibility back on the child? Instead of being the enemy, you align with the child and show them you are on their side. The "enemy" is the long list of chores that need to get done. As long as you both can find a way to do it all, you are fine. In this way, the child cannot fight you, as you are not the one standing in the way. Their own inability to handle it all is the obstacle.

Here are some common examples of how this approach might work:

Screen Time

Child: "I want to watch more screens in bed at night."
Conscious response: "I understand why you would want that. But you need to do these tasks for school tomorrow and you need to get at least eight hours of sleep. So how will you do those things? If you can do it all, I am willing to negotiate with you."

More Junk Food

Child: "I want to eat more junk food."
Conscious response: "I want to eat more junk, too. First you need to eat this healthy food, and then you can eat the junk. So let's make a plan for this together. Will you have your green juice/vegetables/ healthy meals first, and then we can discuss the junk food part?"

More Consumerism

Child: "I want more stuff/shoes/toys!"
Conscious response: "I often find myself craving new things, too. I can relate to you. You get pocket money to spend as you wish. Let's create a budget and a plan for how you can buy these things yourself."

Do you see how this process works? By aligning yourself with your children's desires, you place the onus for their manifestation on them. By taking yourself out of the attack zone, you free up their imaginations to fulfill their needs. You are clearly the "helper," not the "obstructor." In this way, you allow your children to have a direct relationship with their own desires instead of stamping them out because of your own limitations or fears. The focus is on them and their dreams. While you may not be able to directly manifest these dreams in the present moment, you are willing to help them do so for themselves when they are ready, sometime in their future.

Step Nineteen:
Start Right Now

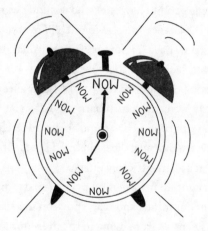

I look at the time gone by
And am filled with regret and remorse.
I am consumed with guilt and shame.
I keep thinking of the damage done
And the moments missed
And wonder how I can retrieve it all
And turn back time.
I want a do-over, a makeover, another chance.
But here is what I forget—
Even if I got all those moments back,
I would still be the same me and you would be the same you,
Because what makes us new right now is all those moments
in between.
What has transformed us to wisdom is exactly all that unwise,
wasted time.

> I could not become this without that,
>   And this is what I fail to see—
> That I was exactly who I needed to be back then
> In order to become who I am right now.
>   Without that there wouldn't be this.
> Therefore I am exactly at the right place, right here.
>   It is called the *now*.

There isn't a single parent I have met who wouldn't want to rewind the clock and have the chance to raise their child over again with all the experience they now have. I know I certainly would. If I could parent my own daughter, Maia, with this consciousness, I would be so much better at parenting. I would be the parent I had always hoped to be. Here is the catch: we cannot turn back time. Do you know why? Because who we are right now has come about precisely because of all our ups and downs, our mistakes and blind spots. There is no "this" without "that." It's all inextricably linked.

We all get caught up in obsession over the past, finding it hard to resolve things in our minds and truly move on in a transformed way. This obsession keeps us from living in the present moment, which is one of the key ingredients to parenting. Our obsessive thoughts take the form of three specific patterns: guilt, blame, and regret. When we engage in these, we cling to what was, mulling over the past again and again. Our minds just cannot let go of what happened in the past. We become obsessed with how things "shouldn't" have been.

Guilt is always *self*-directed and says, "*I* shouldn't have done that!"

Blame is always *other*-directed and says, "*You* shouldn't have done that!"

Regret is *past-life* directed and says, "*It* shouldn't have happened that way!"

In each of these three patterns, we keep ourselves stuck in an unresolved state of misery and shame. We stay in resistance and constant turbulence over how we didn't behave or how life didn't turn out according to the ideals we had. This preoccupation keeps us from entering into the present moment. Our children sense this and feel the disconnect. Let's look at each of these patterns—guilt, blame, and regret—so we can understand how they stop us from living in the present with our kids.

Guilt. Let's start with guilt. When we are stuck in self-blame and guilt, we appear to be remorseful. And our preoccupation with guilt keeps us fixated at the surface level. We may say to ourselves or those we hurt that we "shouldn't" have done whatever it is we did and that we "should" have acted better. This kind of mental repetition gives us and those around us the illusion that we are going to transform our ways. However, here is the thing about internal transformation: it doesn't happen by resisting who we are and what we did. Saying "I shouldn't have" or "I should have" is just the surface layer of the awareness we need. By itself, saying these words creates only an appearance of transformation. If we stay stuck here, we will circle in stagnation.

What is the pathway forward? It's to understand how this kind of "should have" thinking and blaming of the self emerges from a hidden narcissism—one that believes we should have been more emotionally savvy than we are actually capable of being. So when we act in unbecoming ways, we say to ourselves, "I shouldn't have."

However, when we don't have any delusions of grandeur about who we are emotionally and psychologically, we say completely different things to ourselves. We might say, "I behaved exactly as I was meant to. That behavior reflected my internal wounds and lack of healing. Denial about where I truly am stops me from fully embracing the shadows within me." Do you see how guilt is actually hidden narcissism on some level, keeping us from truly doing our inner work to figure out the core of our unconscious reactions?

When we stop making ourselves feel guilty about how we have behaved with our kids in the past, we accept our shadow energy and hold ourselves accountable for our actions in the present. We don't keep swimming in the swirling circles of self-inflicted guilt, but instead use the data we have to transform ourselves from within.

Blame. Now let's look at blame. It operates on the same level of resistance as guilt, but blame is turned toward the other. As long as we see someone else—especially our children—as the cause of our reactivity, we won't go within ourselves to own our own shadows. We will keep our awareness stuck at the surface level, saying to ourselves things such as "I would never have yelled like that if *she* hadn't said that" or "I wouldn't have lost my temper if *he* hadn't done that." These thoughts, like our guilt-based thoughts, emerge from a narcissism of superiority that consoles us by saying, "I would never have behaved in such a way if the *other* hadn't done what they did." Do you see how we use this tactic to prevent ourselves from going deeper within our own selves?

Regret. Let's look at regret. Regret basically says this: "Life shouldn't have happened the way it did." When we resist life itself, we stay stuck in the idea that if our life had been different, we would have been different.

Do you see how these thought patterns keep us stuck in not owning our own internal experience? In these ways, all three reactions of guilt, blame, and regret keep us blocked from deeply owning our emotional and psychological realities and their shadow elements. It's only when we own up to these unresolved and unhealed parts of ourselves that we can release the ways we were unconscious in the past. Then we can enter the present reality with our children with a sense of vigor and transformation.

The moment we justify our internal experience as occurring because of "something"—even if that something is our own lack of perfection—we remain stuck at this level. The brutal truth is that our experience was what it was because that was our internal state of affairs. Anger occurred because there was anger inside, hatred because there was hatred, and love because there was love. The moment you add a "because," you deflect the entire state of being and presume that it was reactionary rather than causative. Our internal experience is what creates the reaction—never the external situation. Once we own this truth, we can begin to transform our entire reality. Reparations in parenting start with a brutal acknowledgment of all the ways we have caused hurt to our kids, without looking for the real reason. There is no reason at the end of the day except for one: our own unresolved wounds. Period. The more wounds, the more lashing back. The fewer wounds, the less lashing back.

Our children evoke and provoke our internal experience by what they do and say. However, they don't create our internal experience. Our internal worlds were already there by the time our kids came along. Owning up to this fact is key to being able to own up to our parenting garbage in the present moment. Becoming aware of how our thought patterns of guilt, blame, and regret have kept us stuck in the past is critical for shifting us into the present. As we move out of these patterns, we create a new awareness of ourselves in the present. We can begin to accept how our past has helped us create the person we have now become. When we truly accept this reality, we can actually appreciate how positive our past unconsciousness has been in terms of influencing our current state of awareness.

It's natural that on some level we wish that we never had any moments of unconsciousness. Again, we must remember that thinking we should always have been so evolved is not only naive, but also delusional. It underestimates the raging power of our egos. Instead of wishing we hadn't been so unconscious, let's celebrate the dark moments of our egos as the precise wake-up calls we needed to disrupt our patterns and set newer, conscious ones in motion. Honoring our unconscious moments helps us make peace with them and learn from them. Instead of resisting, we have gratitude for their role in helping us see our ego. We can look back at these moments and experience a sense of peace and resolve. Each of us can begin to understand those past moments differently:

The time I yelled at my kids helped me realize my ego.
The time I cried from exhaustion helped me realize my ego.
The time I acted just like my own mom helped me realize
   my ego.

The time I called my kids "bad" helped me realize my ego.
The time I ignored my kids helped me realize my ego.
The time my kids said they hated me helped me realize my ego.
The time my kid failed a test helped me realize my ego.
The time I felt I was failing as a parent helped me realize my ego.

Do you see what I mean? Our mistakes are precisely how we can wake ourselves up. If we don't own our failures, how can we see our wounds when we look in the mirror? Sure, being aware of our screwups is never easy. As the saying goes, "Ignorance is bliss." Breaking out of ignorance stings and bites us. It hurts and pokes us. Of course it does—consciousness has bristles. It shatters the shells of our egos. If it is not cracking us, our ego shell isn't breaking.

You see, the entire process of waking up involves an uncomfortable confrontation with the truth of our ego. Transformation comes about only through the emergence of this truth. The two go hand in hand. Therefore, the only moment worthy of consideration is the present moment. What happened before is no longer here. Its only purpose was to bring us to the present moment. Period.

The wisdom that is within you right now came about from your darkest hours. It didn't just pop into your consciousness one day. It evolved over the course of many years. It's quite likely that the darker your hours, the greater your wisdom. I know that in my own life, most of my wisdom has been born directly from the burning embers of my pain. To desire being wise without any struggle is naive and delusional. They go together, hand in hand. For example, an ex-alcoholic who is now sober and wiser became that way after an intensely painful process of withdrawal and the disruption of old patterns. The torture involved in such a process is unimaginable. Now on the other side of the hellhole, this person perhaps feels regret and remorse for what they put others through. While experiencing those feelings is natural, staying stuck there is never wise, because this is simply not the same human anymore. The person who was once an alcoholic simply does not exist anymore.

As we become more and more evolved, old parts of us die and more conscious parts of us are born. Looking back from this new place of conscious awareness to who we used to be is a setup. We act as if it's the same person who is looking back, but this is not true. That old person no longer exists. Understanding this fact is crucial if we are to move on in our lives with vigor and renewal. If we cannot "get" this, we will bury ourselves alive with guilt and shame for all that we failed to be as parents. You can say to yourself:

I am who I am because of who I was. I cannot deny my history or my past. It has made me who I am today, and I am going to stand strong and proud in its face. I will use my struggles to create compassion for myself and others. I will use my pain to create joy for myself and others. I will stop living in regret for all that I wasn't and instead embrace all that I have become right now.

I always remind myself and my clients that the only moment that's relevant is the one we are in right here, right now. In this moment, we can rewrite our narratives and begin anew. This moment, in the now, is a new one, when we can start fresh. The past is no longer here—and even when we remember it, it is contaminated by time and imprecise memories. We will never remember the past exactly the way it happened. For this reason, there is no point in regurgitating the past over and over. The only way the past is relevant is in how it influences our present. So the question to ask ourselves is this: Can my past influence me in a positive way right now? If the answer is yes, the way for it to do so is for us to enter the now with full proclamation, declaration, and reclamation. We need to shout from the rooftops, "I am here, this is now, and I am ready to begin again."

Similarly all our worries about tomorrow are equally detrimental to our state of being. All our "what ifs" prevent us from accepting the is-ness of "what is" happening right here before us. Redirecting our thoughts from the past or future into the present moment is key.

There is so much we can do in this moment if we apply our full presence. No matter whether our kids are grown and have flown off or they are still babies at home, it's never too late to start again, never too late to show love or to apologize. And it is certainly never too late to connect with our kids as they are in this present moment. The present moment is replete with opportunity and invitation—all we need to do is see it this way. We don't need to wait for some perfect time in the future to turn our lives around. We start with one small step, then another, and then another. This is how the present moment becomes the birth canal for a whole new tomorrow.

When the voice of guilt, blame, or regret bubbles to the surface, remember to have compassion for yourself. Teach yourself to release judgment about who you used to be and instead gently usher yourself into who you are right now. See yourself through the kind eyes of forgiveness, understanding that you were a victim of circumstances and that, back then, you simply didn't know what you didn't know. Giving yourself the benefit of the doubt—believing that you would have been more conscious had you been given the right tools—lets you be a bit more forgiving and loving toward yourself.

With this approach to living, you can see the errors of your past unconsciousness as a gold mine rather than a land mine. You can alchemize your ego into essence and your mistakes into jewels. No matter how old you or your kids are, you can start on a new path in the present moment. Whatever was in the past isn't here now, so you can begin again. There is a lot that you can heal and transform by showing up for your kids in a new way in the now. Remember, consciousness is not a destination but a process, one with many twists and turns. The more curves there are, the greater the potential for awakening and transformation. Judging our life journey for having curves is to undermine their value. Instead, let us celebrate these curves, for they have made us who we are today—humans who are far more healed, wise, and compassionate.

The process of evolution involves going through huge swaths of unconsciousness to arrive at consciousness. One cannot arrive at consciousness without pain and effort. The Buddha sat under the Bodhi tree for years at a stretch to achieve what he eventually did.

He fought for his wisdom. There was pain involved. Nothing comes from nothing. Everything comes from something else. So it is with wisdom: it comes from the darkness of our unconsciousness. To ask for there to be no unconsciousness is like asking that there be no heat from the sun or waves in the ocean. It all goes together as one. There is no separation. All is one.

Learning to be in the present moment is the most valuable lesson of parenthood. When you start again, and then again and again, you release all that was and begin to embrace all that is right before you.

Your children don't need your guilt, blame, or regret. They just need you to be a human who is willing to do the work to transform your relationship with them. Your children need you as you are, in the present moment, ordinary, fallible, and authentic. Children don't need "parents" as much as they need humans who are willing to work on healing all that is broken in themselves. When you present your children with the gift of your transformed consciousness, you give them the greatest treasure of all—your own healing. There is no toy or gadget that can rival the gift of your evolving consciousness, for this is what will open the cages of their souls and set them free.

PUTTING IT INTO PRACTICE

Entering the present moment is not just a practice, it is a lifestyle. It is the singular most powerful way to live life. If we don't live in the present, we will swirl interminably in the storms of a bygone yesterday and on the horizon of an unknown tomorrow. When I want to strengthen my practice of the now, I literally set my alarm for hour-long intervals to remind me to "enter the now." The alarm jars me to become present to what is going on in the here and now, springing me back from wherever my mind had wandered to.

This practice has been a game changer for me, especially when it comes to trigger moments with my child. Each time I am triggered,

I can ask myself, "What about the present moment is causing anxiety?" And often, the answer is "Nothing." Try it. Ask yourself, "Why is this moment creating angst?" And for the most part you will find that there is very little reason it should. Do you know why? The reason is either that the "bad" thing has already happened or that we imagine it is going to happen in the future. If we are alive, the present moment is almost always just as it is supposed to be. Our resistance to its as-is nature is the problem. If our kid got a C grade, then we are resistant to the fact that this has already occurred, or our imaginations take us to a scary future. However, in the present moment, nothing has really happened. Do you see what I mean?

Asking ourselves "Is the now really terrible?" is a wonderful way for us to realize that it rarely ever is. When we can see that the now is okay, albeit sometimes challenging, we can enter a state of gratitude and surrender. These two elements make a powerful combination to enable peace and joy. Try asking yourself this question, and you will discover the magic of the now.

Step Twenty:
Embrace a New You

How does it feel?
To have your skin finally shed
And your masks finally crumble?
To have patterns be disrupted
And the ego be tamed?
It must feel strange and foreign,
Lonely and bizarre,
To suddenly be in a new consciousness, mind, and heart.
There are no words to express this joy, are there?
Inner liberation is, after all, indescribable.
It can only be experienced by those who have walked this path, as you have.

You have made it to the last step! You have arrived. Let's take a moment to pause, as this is a significant point. You have come to a new threshold. How are you feeling? Do you feel as if you are a whole new you? If you do, welcome to the new you!

"Waking up" is never a comfortable process. It involves opening your eyes to a new way of seeing yourself and your children. This is especially hard if you have been asleep for many decades. The more asleep you have been, the more uncomfortable the awakening process. Before, you may have readily believed in things; now, you are challenging every single thing that you think, see, or perceive. I am hopeful that you are seeing things as they are for the very first time in your life. This can be a highly disorienting and discombobulating experience.

My most profound moment of awakening as a parent was when I had the epiphany that our modern parenting paradigm was based on ego. That moment of realization was shocking. I had believed that we parented our children out of selflessness. And while parenting itself can be an act of selflessness, the way we parent is far too often rooted in selfishness. Once this awareness hit my consciousness, everything shifted for me. After that moment, the entire cover of parenting was blown apart. I saw not only my own ego in my parenting, but also the ego in every other parent. I wanted to scream from the rooftops, "Do you all see your egos? I do! Here is your ego! And here is yours!" But no one was really paying attention. I felt as though I was talking to the wind.

I then went through an intense period of feeling completely adrift—as if I was floating around with this new consciousness and seeing everyone I knew, even myself, with completely different eyes. Who was I? Who was anyone I once thought I knew? Nobody and nothing looked the same anymore. Everywhere I looked, I saw ego, ego, ego. It was a very strange experience indeed!

I call this place in the journey "no woman's/man's land." It is where you feel as if you have died. You see, in a sense we have died at this point; our egos have died. When we arrive here, absolutely nothing resembles anything from before. It is as though we are aliens living on the strangest planet.

The journey doesn't stop here, though. This awareness expands to everything around us. I not only saw the ego in myself and my loved ones, but also in the institutions and processes all around me: schools, politics, businesses—everything. And of course, the more ego I saw, the more pain I saw as well. This experience was confusing, because on the one hand, the blatant egos repulsed me, and on the other hand, the pain beneath them broke my heart open. As I let go of my anger and disgust at our insatiable egos, I was able to stay focused on the wounds beneath our masks. My compassion for humanity soared exponentially, and so did my desire to act on it. That is the reason I do the work I do and write books such as this one. My great passion now is to help others awaken and shed their own veils of ignorance and unconsciousness.

If you are feeling any of these same feelings, know that you are not alone. While this journey may feel isolating, the truth is that many others are on the journey with you. You just need to find them. As you keep shedding your own ego masks, you will move toward those who are of a similar consciousness, and you will move away from those who are not. There will be those who feel betrayed by your growth, as if you have abandoned them and left them behind. Facing the wrath of those they eclipse is a common experience for those who evolve at a more rapid pace than the people around them. If this happens for you, be reassured that it is not an indication that you should stop evolving. On the contrary, you absolutely must keep moving forward. Your next tribe awaits you. You just need to keep walking toward them.

Conscious parenting is often an extremely lonely journey. As most around you were raised in the traditional, behavioral paradigm of anger, blame, shame, and guilt, your new ways may be scorned and degraded. Such responses from others may feel disheartening, even terrifying. You may second-guess yourself and buckle under pressure from others to be more "tough." I ask you to stay strong and stalwart. Remember: these messages around control and fear come from the old paradigm.

Those around you who espouse these traditional ways are not being evil to you or trying to pressure you. Their way of parenting is all they know based on their pervasive cultural conditioning. Expect resistance—and have compassionate understanding about it. These more conscious approaches to parenting can scare others. They shun what is unfamiliar because they weren't raised in such a compassionate way. Perhaps you remind them of all that was never given to them. Regardless, it is imperative to realize that this resistance is not against you personally. People are not attacking you. They are attacking their own fears about what this new way of parenting brings up for them. Instead of reacting, you might say, "I hear you. I understand where you are coming from. You don't have to agree with my approach, but it is the one I am going to stand by. I don't need to raise my child the way we were raised, based on fear and control. I am going to raise my child in a whole new way. You are welcome to agree or disagree. That is your choice. But I am not going to leave my path."

Many parents ask, "What if my partner or coparent doesn't believe in conscious parenting?"

I always say this in response: "Conscious parenting requires only one parent. While two or many would be wonderful, more than one parent is not required. Just one parent is enough to start creating transformation. You need to become that parent for your child. It is better to have one conscious parent than none."

Many parents are afraid to go "against" their marital partners, because to do so feels like a betrayal of the relationship. I always respond this way: "When it comes to raising your children, you need to place their well-being above and beyond the needs of your marriage. Your focus needs to be on what is the most conscious way to raise your children and not on how to make your spouse happy with you." Accepting that idea is extremely hard for some marital partners. I can understand why, especially for women. We women are raised to be good wives. We gain a sense of identity from being obedient and compliant. Deviating from these qualities to defy our partners carries a lot of emotional charge for us. We are scared to go against the grain. Yet when it comes to our children, we need to get out of our comfort zones and break out of our patterns to show up for our children.

Another dictum that we have falsely believed in is that parents need to have a united front. I always say, "Yes, this is what it mostly is—a front; a facade and a guise. We do not need to be united if our partner is unconscious. Being united in that situation would mean that we are perpetuating unconsciousness." It is understandable that parents struggle when both partners are not on the same parenting page. A lack of unity definitely makes parenting more onerous. But this doesn't mean we get onto our partner's unconscious page just so we can be united. That's not evolution; that's unhealthy enmeshment. Such partnerships are not good for our children's souls. Our kids would do much better as evolving beings if they witnessed their mother standing up to their father's abuse and fighting for what is right rather than joining her husband in abusing them. Sure, in the short term, disagreement between their parents might cause children confusion and anxiety. However, in the long term, they will understand how to fight abuse and unconsciousness instead of passively capitulating to it.

Often, a parent who initially refuses to adopt this approach may, over time, start using the techniques they see being effective with their child. When we do the work, the parent-child relationship blossoms, and the family dynamic is transformed. The odd parent out will likely slowly start to change their approach. You might notice it in a dinner conversation or a ride to school. Every parent yearns for this bond, and the parent who at first refused to start looking inward may suddenly begin doing so more regularly. The important thing to remember is that each of us shifts in our own time and when we are ready. The parent who is ready to embrace conscious parenting needs to begin their journey, no matter where the other parent is at that point.

This path of evolution and conscious growth is often lonely and isolating in the beginning, as you move away from those who no longer match with you anymore, and there is a chance that you might enter a state of despair and fear. Maybe you will embody an attitude of nihilism, feeling that nothing is worth it anymore and that you might as well just give up. I want to caution you that this is the voice of your ego talking. Your ego wants you to stop evolving, you see? As you are growing and transforming, you are listening to your own essence more and more. For you to do so is threatening not just for other people, but also for your own ego. Your ego will try every manipulative shenanigan it can to get you to stop growing. The more you grow, the less you need the ego, you see? Your ego may convince you that you are a betrayer for leaving your old belief systems behind, or that this is all rubbish and you should stop, or that Dr. Shefali is a cult leader who wants to indoctrinate you, or that everything is pointless, so you might as well just give up.

I cannot tell you the number of times women have come to me and said things such as "My husband hates you. He told me not to put on your videos anymore" or "My mother thinks you have possessed me and are hypnotizing me!" I laugh hard at these comments, because I understand where they come from. I can only imagine the fear in these loved ones' hearts as they find themselves taken off their pedestals and banished from the tyrannical control they once had over their family members. Their voices may terrify you, and your ego may try to convince you that you will be abandoned by them all if you continue on this path. Your ego will try all sorts of ways to take you back to an older state of consciousness so that it can maintain its stronghold in your psyche.

My ego still acts up constantly. It whispers to me that I am a bad Indian girl for getting a divorce, a brazen woman for daring to achieve so much, and a selfish person for living life on my own terms. Many times, my ego succeeds in pulling me back to its toxic trenches for a few moments. Thankfully, my meditation practice helps me recognize that such thoughts are coming from ego, and I can snap out of it.

If you are having thoughts like the ones I've described, recognize them as coming from the ego. You can gently say, "Dear Ego: You are free to f— off. You have served an amazing role in my life, but I have now moved past you. I no longer need you to protect me, because I have healed the little child within. My inner child doesn't need protection anymore because it has finally grown up. I am finally whole and healthy. You are now lovingly fired. Please leave your masks at the door, as I am going to burn them."

It is scary as heck to let go of our ego masks. Trust me, I know. In my book *A Radical Awakening*, I describe this process in all its excruciating detail. For me personally, letting go of the mask of Fixer and Savior was hardest, as these roles had been seared in my Indian-female brain for forty-four years. I was finally able to shed that mask and tear it to pieces. The aftermath of that process was fear, for sure, but also a profound sense of liberation.

As you read this, what mask do you think will be the last one you will burn? Which is the hardest to let go of? What are your fears about letting go? One of the main reasons we don't enter the birth canal of transformation is that we are so afraid we will not be loved or approved of on the other side. Although it is true that many people you knew may fall by the wayside, it is also true that you will meet many new, like-minded people on your journey to and on the other side.

I always remind my clients, "Your wish to evolve needs to be greater than your wish to stay the same. When this desire to evolve is greater, you will trust in the unknown and surrender. Staying the same has got to be unbearable. Only then will you endure the shedding of the old and the embracing of the new."

So now I ask you: Is your desire to evolve greater than your desire to maintain the status quo? If the answer is yes, you are well on your way. Take one step forward at a time. There is no rush, no urgency. Just keep taking a step forward. And as you do, stay connected with your inner voice of knowing. Let it guide you where you need to go next. It will tell you exactly what direction to go. Follow it. Onward you go.

PUTTING IT INTO PRACTICE

This is a stage of letting go of the old and letting in the new. An exercise that I often do with clients at this point is to have them create two baskets—one called "Shedding" and the other called "Embracing." And every week they are to throw all the masks they are shedding into the first basket and place the new ways of being that they are embodying into the second basket. After a few weeks, they process everything that has shifted within them. You might try this exercise with a friend so that you can help each other in this process of release and surrender.

Another powerful exercise is writing letters. One that is particularly therapeutic is a letter to your ego. You can thank your ego for all the ways it has protected you but tell it that you are now ready to release it, as you have outgrown it. Equally therapeutic is writing a letter to the new, true you!

You are birthing a new self, and doing so takes courage and wisdom. I applaud you for getting to this point. Your journey has just begun. Your walking steps will turn into a run—and soon you will take flight and soar. As you feel the wind lift you up in an effortless embrace, you will watch your life from above. You will see the world below and remember it fondly. But the freedom of the air at that height will be too intoxicating to leave behind. You cannot go back to the old; that part of you has been released. You are not the same person who began this journey. Let go of who you once were and embrace the new. Your children are ready to be one with you. They always were. They were just waiting for you to return to your true home—yourself.

Welcome to your new world.

Conscious parenting is not just about raising children. It is about raising humanity. When we understand its profound and powerful principles, we heal not only our own past wounds, but those of others around us. Such is the tremendous restorative potential of this work: it has the capacity to transform trauma into health.

Family after family has given testimony to the power of conscious parenting in their lives. This is slowly but surely becoming the new parenting model in the world, and you are now part of the global rising of parental consciousness. Your embrace of these teachings is pivotal in the spread of this work through the globe—one parent and one child at a time. You are an ambassador of this message and an emblem of its healing power.

When you become a conscious parent, you become an advocate and agent of transformation in this world. In this way, all children are your children, and all ego is your ego. You see yourself as one with others, interconnected and interdependent. When you see things this way, you embody consciousness not only for your own children, but also for everyone you encounter. That is the power of this approach: it is a universal panacea for all that we struggle with.

What you have learned in this book will hold true for every struggle in your life. Apply these principles bravely, for they are universal. Return to these pages again and again, as these values take time to embed themselves in us. After all, we must undo generations of conditioning.

By committing to this work, you are now the pattern disrupter in your family lineage. You are where the unconscious buck stops. You are where childhood traumas end. You are the last bearer of the egoic legacies of generations past, the last holder of the shame that may have been coursing through the family from eons past. Finally, you have arrived at the place where shame and pain can be released, for it was never yours to bear. Finally, you have arrived at the threshold of a powerful consciousness, where a new narrative can be written. This is daunting, I know. But follow the scent of consciousness and you will never go awry. Ask yourself at every choice point, "What does consciousness say to me?" And then follow its way. It will never lead you astray. The voices of fear and lack come from ego. Remember to discern the difference.

The pages of your life are now new; the past is now erased. These pages are empty and fresh, awaiting the most glorious reality of all—your own authentic manifestation. They await *you*. It is time to embody your new self. You are more ready than ever to begin. The moment is now.

A Note from Me

What a journey you have been on, my dear parent.
You revealed parts of yourself that were buried from sight
And confronted pieces of your psyche that shocked you.
You read words that seared, pierced, and tore you asunder.
Yet you didn't stop, did you?
You kept turning the pages until you finally arrived here
At the threshold of the death of your old self,
Where the birth of a new you awaits.
You will now take steps you have never taken before
And speak a language whose sounds you have never heard.
You will stumble at first and break some bones.
You will lose some friends and throw some stones.
But ultimately your path will lead you to the edge of the cliff
Where you will look back at how far you have come from your past.
And then you will look forward, at the skies ahead
And with a smile on your lips, you will step off the ledge
To a horizon that is unknown and wild.
Your children will watch as you take flight
And they will rejoice, for they know that this liberation
Is now part of their destiny as well.
Know that your purpose is now complete,
For you have fulfilled your most sacred obligation.
By releasing your children to their own life experiences,
You have become the guardian of their essence.
There is nothing more to be done now
Except to keep moving forward toward a brilliance of your own.

Acknowledgments

Maia, my dearest daughter, is always my muse for my parenting books. It is through mothering her that I have traversed the arduous journey from ego to essence. Without her audacious and authentic presence in my life, none of my parenting wisdom would have been unleashed.

Gideon Weil, my editor at HarperCollins and dear friend, has held a bright torch for this book from the start. He believed in its crucial necessity and allowed it to freely blossom into fruition. It is because of our mutual passion for conscious parenting and living that we are a team made in heaven.

Ferzin Patel and Tina Daroowalla, my two loyal sounding boards, have seen me through the angst of writing this book from start to finish. The best cheerleaders a woman could ask for, they championed me through all my doubts until I got to the other side. So grateful to have these sisters on a mission together.

Jon Hyman, the most stellar parent and human I know, has taught me about life, the matrix, and how to deconstruct it more than anyone ever has. He is the teacher's teacher, for sure. Enough words of gratitude have not been invented yet to express how much his mind and being have elevated my existence and infused every wisdom I teach.

Index